Tourism, Planning, and Community Development

The intersection of community development, tourism and planning is a fascinating one that has occupied the attention of policy makers in both the developed and the developing world. The approaches to community tourism development and planning have typically focused on economic dimensions with decisions about tourism investments, policies and venues driven by these economic considerations. More recently, the conversation has shifted to include other aspects – social and environmental – to better represent sustainable development concepts. Perhaps most importantly is the richer focus on the inclusion of stakeholders.

An inclusionary, participatory approach is an essential ingredient of community development and this brings both fields even closer together. It reflects an approach aimed at building on strengths in communities, and fostering social capacity and capital. In this book, the dimensions of the role tourism plays in community development are explored. A panoply of perspectives are presented, tackling such questions as, can tourism heal? How can tourism development serve as a catalyst to overcome social injustices and cultural divides?

This book was originally published as a special issue of *Community Development*.

Rhonda G. Phillips, Ph.D., AICP, CEcD is a professor, a planner and community economic developer with experience in tourism-based development approaches. Her research and service outreach includes assessing community well-being and quality-of-life outcomes, and fostering balanced approaches to planning and development.

Sherma Roberts is a lecturer in tourism and programme leader for the M.Sc. Tourism programmes, University of the West Indies, Cave Hill Campus. Dr. Roberts recently co-edited *New Perspectives in Caribbean Tourism* and *Marketing Island Destinations*. Her research interests include tourism policy and planning, sustainable tourism, tourism entrepreneurship, and community participation.

Community Development – Current Issues Series
Series Editor: Rhonda Phillips

The Community Development Society (CDS) in conjunction with Routledge/Taylor & Francis is pleased to present this series of volumes on current issues in community development. The series is designed to present books organized around special topics or themes, promoting exploration of timely and relevant issues impacting both community development practice and research. Building on a rich history of over 40 years of publishing the journal, *Community Development,* the series will provide reprints of special issues and collections from the journal. Each volume is updated with the editor's introductory chapter, bringing together current applications around the topical theme.

Founded in 1970, the Community Development Society is a professional association serving both researchers and practitioners. CDS actively promotes the continued advancement of the practice and knowledge base of community development. For additional information about CDS, visit www.comm-dev.org.

Tourism, Planning, and Community Development

Edited by
Rhonda Phillips and Sherma Roberts

Routledge
Taylor & Francis Group

LONDON AND NEW YORK

First published 2013
by Routledge
2 Park Square, Milton Park, Abingdon, Oxon, OX14 4RN

Simultaneously published in the USA and Canada
by Routledge
711 Third Avenue, New York, NY 10017

Routledge is an imprint of the Taylor & Francis Group, an informa business

British Library Cataloguing in Publication Data
A catalogue record for this book is available from the British Library

ISBN13: 978-0-415-52432-2

Typeset in Times New Roman
by Taylor & Francis Books

Publisher's Note
The publisher would like to make readers aware that the chapters in this book may be referred to as articles as they are identical to the articles published in the special issue. The publisher accepts responsibility for any inconsistencies that may have arisen in the course of preparing this volume for print.

Printed and bound in Great Britain by the MPG Books Group

Contents

Introduction

Rhonda Phillips and Sherma Roberts

The intersection of community development and tourism planning is a fascinating one which tourism and other scholars have over time sought to interrogate. Within the context of transformations in governance structures, strident demands from civil society for equity and fairness, the growth of international tourism, and the ubiquity of social media, among other noticeable trends, the need to explore this interplay between tourism development planning and communities become even more urgent. Noticeably, is that this explorative and discursive conversation has now been expanded to include cities or urban spaces rather than the traditional focus on peripheral jurisdictions and developing countries. This collection of nine chapters adds to the conversation by providing unique insights into the role tourism plays in community well-being and development across a range of differently constituted communities as well as demonstrates how community development approaches can enhance the tourism planning process. The tensions involved in what is largely considered to be power-sharing exercise have been also considered by many authors in this volume.

Traditionally regarded as a development strategy by governments in both developed and developing countries, approaches to tourism planning have typically focused on economic dimensions with decisions about tourism investments, policies and venues driven by these economic considerations. More recently, the conversation has shifted to include other aspects—social and environmental—to better reflect sustainable tourism development concepts. Perhaps most importantly is the richer focus on the inclusion of citizens, residents, or "stakeholders." This is an essential ingredient of community development and the inclusionary, participatory approach brings the two fields even closer together. It reflects the ideas of building on strengths in communities, and enhancing social and environmental issues.

The Community Development Context

Community development can be defined as activity with the main objective of improving conditions and quality of life for people within a place-based community by strengthening economic and social progress (Aquino et al., 2012). As Joppe (1996) describes, the community aspect of the definition needs some edification: "community is self-defining in that is based on a sense of shared purpose and common goals... It may be geographical in nature or a community of interest, build on heritage and cultural values shared among community members" (p. 475). Indeed, Joppe's definition of community has resonance in many developing countries where the "sense of shared purpose and common goals" embraces the many diaspora communities of these geographies scattered across the world—who are actively engaged in community advocacy and capacity building action through different media (Roberts, 2010). The idea of sharing, shared value, and community development can then be explained not only as a process centering on building social capital and capacity, but also as outcomes across the dimensions of concerns for communities—social, environmental and economic to name the major types (Phillips and Pittman, 2009). While some focus on community development as an outcome, it should be considered in a wider realm of dimensions, such as improvement in quality of life and increasing capacity across spectrums of community concern (Green and Haines, 2008; Phillips and Pittman, 2009). The notion of capacity is paramount, "it is capacity building that can be seen as the strength of community development, with this collective capacity allowing citizens to participate purposively in the creation, articulation, and maintenance of efforts designed to support and/or change social structures" (Aquino et al., 2012, p. 4). Notwithstanding, the implicit and often explicit barriers to making positive change, we argue that one way to increase capacity is via participation of those impacted by planning and development.

The Importance of Voice

Embedded within the precepts and practice of community development is the notion of citizen or stakeholder participation. Without a "voice" to make known their concerns and desires, development process and outcomes may leave out those for which it is intended. Community development has long included citizen and stakeholder participation in processes as a means to reflect the voices of those most impacted. Having a voice is especially relevant for people living in tourism-dependent areas who may have multiple perspectives on tourism development's impacts and how their quality of life is affected (Budruk and Phillips, 2011; Chase et al., 2012). It becomes clear that one voice may not be enough to represent all affected, and ensuring that stakeholders have a means to express themselves becomes paramount in the tourism planning and community tourism development processes. This is not a new idea; public participation in community tourism planning has been encouraged for a while now, with studies from the 1980s exploring and advocating applications for tourism (Haywood, 1988; Keogh, 1990; Murphy, 1988). The plethora of literature more recently suggests participation is now much more embedded in tourism planning processes, not least because of the industry and academy's embrace of the notion of sustainable tourism development. For example, a self-assessment instrument for communities presented by Reid et al., in 2004 helps with participation as a central focus of a community-centered tourism process. Chase, et al., (2012, pp. 488–489) provide considerations and challenges for planners or developers seeking to engage stakeholders:

1. Identify important stakes
2. Be inclusive
3. Consider using multiple techniques for incorporating stakeholder input
4. Encourage constructive deliberation and understanding
5. Find ways to balance competing interests

Challenges to engaging stakeholders include:

1. Resistance from some stakeholders
2. Ensuring equity and fairness
3. Problematic relationships among institutions
4. Communication issues
5. Lack of time and money
6. Difficulty defining and measuring quality of life

As seen in the list above, there are numerous considerations for engaging stakeholders. Despite the challenges, it is vital that tourism planning and community development processes strive to include the "voices" of those impacted. There is not one right way as the chapters in this volume reveal. The call is therefore for a flexible, placed-based approach to participation that brings the "silent voices" to the centre of the process. The discussions by the authors here reveal that not only will the process be enhanced by participation, but the outcomes will be as well. It should be noted too that while community development focuses on citizen and resident stakeholders, tourism needs to include others as well in the in these processes—the organizations and tourists, for example.

Planning Dimensions

A simple definition of planning is that it provides the opportunity to envision what a community wants, and how to get there. It includes the idea that it will represent what people value in their communities. There are numerous models and approaches for tourism planning, as movement away from only physical dimensions of planning occurs. There is a

> more inclusive perspectives common in recent sustainable development dialogues and debate...tourism planning is moving gradually from the edges of planning proactive toward the center, and with this movement will follow important questions regarding socioeconomic, political, and cultural representation and equity.
>
> (Harrill, 2004, p. 263)

Approaches and models for tourism planning include sustainable development, systems, community, integrated planning, comprehensive planning, flexible, and functional systems (Chhabra and Phillips, 2009). While many integrate related concepts of community development, the community approach centers on several of these:

> Community Approach: This focuses on decentralization and facilitation of coordination between different stakeholders of tourism. This approach stemmed from the increasing emphasis on democratization and gained significance when political power political power shifted from the central government to states, cities, towns, and neighborhoods, thereby giving voice and empowerment to local communities to address their own problems and find appropriate solutions. This approach calls for better participation between the tourism industry and the local residents. It is hoped that the involvement of local residents in decision-making processes will facilitate better working partnerships between the host communities and the travel and tourism industry.
>
> (Chhabra and Phillips, 2009, 238–239)

Community approaches can be enhanced by integrating community development precepts. Mair and Reid (2007, p. 407) note that the "promise of combining the broader goals of community development with less traditional approaches to planning tourism" can hold potential to overcoming existing deficiencies of community-based tourism approaches. We agree that community development holds relevance for tourism planning and can help achieve broader dimensions of community improvement and change. We propose that building social capacity is a means to elicit effective change and transform communities.

Planning processes typically start with an inventory or research phase and cycles to an evaluation or monitoring of outcomes phase, noting that the process is reiterative as conditions and desires change through time. It should also be noted that "planning is a process and a movement; not merely an outcome or product," and can provide ways to enhance community expression and control (Mair and Reid, 2007, p. 407). The following considerations illustrate briefly a planning process that incorporates community development elements such as participation and decision-making (Chhabra and Phillips, 2009, p 241).

1. *What do we have?*

Inventory assets (people; organizations; cultural/heritage; natural, financial and built resources) and contexts (political, economic, social, environmental) of the community. This is the research phase and can include a variety of sources and tools such as surveys, focus groups, asset mapping, etc. It includes considering the social capacity and capital of the community.

2. *What do we want?*

At this point, the all important vision as a guide to seeing what could happen is crafted by stakeholders—those in the community that have an interest in helping achieve a more desirable future. Belief is a powerful tool and can inspire a community to achieve remarkable outcomes. The vision should be bold enough to inspire and realistic enough to attain.

3. *How do we get there?*

This stage is about developing the plan so it is a guide with specifics for achieving the vision and includes goal statements and actions. Most importantly, it selects the strategies or approaches desired. It also identifies which organizations or groups of collaborators will be responsible for the tasks and action items. Collaborative efforts typically work best, but in some cases, it takes a "champion" to start the efforts and others will join in later.

4. *What have we done, and what do we need to do now?*

Monitoring is critical to see if the above steps are working; if not, then adjustments and revisions are needed. Because the nature of this process is continuous, it provides feedback for refining on-going activities as well as starting new initiatives until desirable change is elicited (and adjusted and maintained).

While these are simple questions, they show several of the major aspects important to community development and planning, helping bring together the ability to elicit desirable change at both the micro and macro levels.

Structure of This Volume

This volume presents panoply of perspectives, tackling such questions as, can tourism heal? How can tourism development (and by implication management of, and policies for, tourism) serve as a catalyst to overcome social injustices and cultural divides? Other considerations include the need to capture intangible benefits of tourism. This issue is one that community developers and tourism planners wrestle with continuously —how do we measure and convey the benefits of our actions beyond the tangible aspects? We feel tourism planning and community development are intricately connected; it is our hope that this volume will inspire tackling these and other challenging questions in the quest to foster community well-being.

Chapter 2, "Incorporating social justice in tourism planning: racial reconciliation and sustainable community development in the Deep South" by Alan W. Barton and Sarah J. Leonard provides a close look at the healing potential of tourism. An interpretive approach is used to gain insights about "Reconciliation Tourism," one of four models of tourism for social equity and justice. The other models are "Educational Tourism," "Development Tourism" and "Pilgrimage Tourism." Their investigation focused on monthly meetings of, and personal interviews with, the nine white and nine African-American members of the Emmett Till Memorial Commission (ETMC) in Tallahatchie County, Mississippi. Emmett Till was a black teenager from Chicago who was murdered during a visit to relatives in 1955. A local jury acquitted two white residents accused of the crime and the verdict left "a pall of fear and shame on the county that continues to shape race relations today." ETMC is an organization working to create racial reconciliation through tourism. It is currently engaged in three tourism efforts: the restoration of the Tallahatchie County Courthouse in Sumner; the Emmett Till Interpretive Trail Community Development and the creation of an administrative structure for tourism planning and management in the county. As a result tourism planners are not only developing a story of reconciliation as a tourism narrative, but they are also engaging in a process of reconciliation among their members and in their community. The most significant impediment has been a lack of understanding on the part of county residents as to the value of the story they can market to tourists. This chapter shows the power of narrative and the need for stakeholders to be engaged with, and aware of the "story" of their place as represented to others including tourists.

Chapter 3 by Sherma Roberts provides a look at the role of community participation in tourism development with, "An analysis of factors mediating community participation outcomes in tourism." It is now widely acknowledged in the contemporary tourism literature that community participation is crucial to sustainable tourism development, the latter of which emphasizes local participation in the decision-making process. The rationale for resident involvement is that it helps minimize the negative social impacts of tourism development, it increases the level of buy-in into tourism projects and it creates an environment for the host community to receive optimal benefits from the industry. These assumptions have been challenged based upon the heterogeneous nature of communities and the power differentials in participation which can often undermine expected beneficial outcomes. While acknowledgment of these issues is crucial to any discussion on community participation initiatives and outcomes, this paper argues that there are other factors that mediate the extent to which communities are able to access the benefits of community participation initiatives. These factors have been identified in this study as clear and consensual objectives, sustained interest and institutional support. The study was conducted using interviews and a focus group among residents of a small community on the island of Tobago.

Chapter 4, "Tourism planning and power within micropolitan community development" by William L. Obenour and Nelson Cooper investigates power structures within community planning processes. Their focus is on a micropolitan community (a rural community with an urban cluster of 10–50 thousand and total population of less than 250,000). They found that while a proposed iconic tourist attraction, in this case, a celebrity named performing arts center, produced immediate gains, long-term sustaining symbolic capital development did not occur. Conversely, organic growth of selected recreational assets into tourist attractions was successful because of a collaborative approach with transparency, accountability and public involvement. These elements are considered in high quality planning processes, and ensuring their presence in the tourism planning process can enhance the tourism planning process. However, it is noted that the authors conclude that a typical comprehensive planning model traditionally employed by the micropolitan region cannot easily adapt to iconic and unique tourism attractions that can create more chaotic activity.

Chapter 5, "Community understanding of the impact of temporary visitors on incidental destinations" by Ken Simpson and Phil Bretherton explores the extent to which residents of local communities on the brink of tourism industry development are fully aware of the conventionally accepted ramifications of such a move. Their study was motivated by the observation that such communities are frequently encouraged to enter into such an activity by the promise of high level economic benefit, accompanied by manageable social and environmental change. The authors point out that tourism development literature may be partly to blame when it emphasizes maximizing the cost-benefit equation in contrast to the community development literature which emphasizes the empowerment of communities and their residents. The authors surveyed 782 residents from four reasonably comparable communities reflecting varying stages of tourism intensity development: Buxton (England); Waterford (Ireland); Rockhampton (Australia); and Whangarei (New Zealand). Results confirmed the authors' observations that residents have a generally realistic local awareness of the economic aspects of increased numbers of visitors, but an over-optimistic assessment of environmental impacts, societal impacts, and the ability of local stakeholders to successfully manage tourism industry development. This finding has much relevance for current conversations about the long-term, sustainable impacts of tourism on host communities and shows the need for thoughtful, inclusive planning in the tourism development process.

In Chapter 6, Oksana Grybovych and Delmar Hafermann present "Sustainable practices of community tourism planning: lessons from a remote community." Against the background of the literature about "deliberative democratic planning and decision making" the authors outline how the small remote community of Ucluelet on the west coast of Vancouver Island, British Columbia, Canada help remedy the weaknesses of traditional planning approaches by eliciting greater breadth and quality of community participation. Ucluelet engaged in extensive community dialogue to gauge resident attitudes and opinions towards the future of the community in which tourism would be an integral component in a diverse economy. With help from students from Malaspina University-College who were viewed as a "neutral" third party, an interactive website and the online Wiki mechanism, a broad range of stakeholders successfully negotiated revisions to the Official Community Plan. This plan is the official guide for decisions on planning and land use management recognized by the Government of British Columbia and as such, is a guiding document. Faced with the threat of tourism development "going out of control" Ucluelet used unconventional public engagement methods to design a range of pioneering and innovative design and policy approaches to guide potential developers. The emphasis on deliberately seeking to encourage broader public engagement led to enhanced planning and decision-making.

Following on the theme of community engagement, Chapter 7, "Engaging residents in planning for sustainable rural-nature tourism in post-communist Poland" by Marianna Strzelecka and Bruce E. Wicks introduces community field theory to tourism planning, and applies the concept of social capital to theorize about the process of local interactions. The authors seek to discover how a tourism development project can enhance relationships among local stakeholders and community action in post-communist Polish localities. Tourism planning is explored in the context of Polish governments struggling to build strong capitalist markets and develop democratic political systems because of the belief that economic growth relies heavily on the quality of the democratic regime. Despite this focus, the majority of citizens in rural Poland have avoided participation in the democratic planning process. The authors argue that development projects must first fit into existing agendas for individuals to provide any attention. If this occurs, then stakeholders might engage in other local activities to realize broader social goals. The authors propose that tourism projects can serve that purpose. The chapter reports on a project set out to define priorities for the planning and development of tourism and recreation in the eight communes of the "micro-region" of the Greater Poland National Park by engaging local stakeholders in the decision-making process. A series of meetings and workshops with tourism experts attracted 146 local participants. Although the authors make no conclusions about the specific results of the project, they contend that planning for tourism development has the potential to gain the interest of locals and should be regarded as an opportunity to enhance community action.

Chapter 8 presents, "Participatory modeling as a tool for community development planning: tourism in the Northern Forest" by Lisa Chase, Roelof Boumans and Stephanie Morsec. Focusing on a tool for engaging citizens in decision making, the authors discuss a dynamic computer model (STELLA). Participants in six communities in the Northern Forest region of the north-eastern United States developed a model of the complex relationships associated with recreation and tourism development. In a series of three workshops the university modeler projected the community components and linkages on a large screen for all participants to see as the model was developed. Discussion and exchange of new ideas was the most valued aspect of the first series of the workshops to the participants followed by learning about STELLA. Participants were generally excited about using the model. However, by the third series of workshops the interest shifted from model building to reaching a better understanding of the linkages of recreation and tourism with rural community development and a discussion of quality of life.

Chapter 9, "Golden geese or white elephants? The paradoxes of World Heritage Sites and community-based tourism development in Agra, India," by Surajit Chakravarty and Clara Irazabal examines the relationship between World Heritage Sites (WHSs) and local community development. Two interrelated themes are discussed—the role of planning in developing the tourism potential of the Taj Mahal and other World Heritage sites, and the impact of these on the development of the city. Developmental paradoxes are revealed, with recommendations directed toward the development of pro-poor, community-based heritage tourism with the aim of informing integrated planning for the community and for heritage and tourism resources. Illustrating these development paradoxes and potentials of economic, tourism, and community development, the case of Agra echoes those of other developing localities which host World Heritage Sites around the world. Following an assessment of problems and challenges, a set of recommendations is directed toward the development of pro-poor, community-based heritage tourism with the aim of informing integrated planning for the community and for heritage and tourism resources in the future.

The complexities of tourism planning and community development can be daunting to communities as they engage to develop tourist venues and manage or revitalize existing efforts. From the diverse perspectives presented in this volume, it is clear that there are many considerations, including the need for valid, meaningful participation by stakeholders. Having democratic decision-making incorporated into tourism planning processes relies on the presence of meaningful participation—and achieving desirable community development processes and outcomes mandates it.

References

Aquino, J., Phillips, R., and Sung, H. (2012). Tourism, culture, and the creative industries: reviving distressed neighborhoods with arts-based community tourism. *Tourism Culture and Communications,* forthcoming.

Budruk, M. and Phillips, R. (2011). *Quality-of-Life Community Indicators for Parks, Recreation and Tourism Management*. Dordrecht: Springer.

Chhabra, D. and Phillips, R. (2009). Tourism-based development. In Phillips, R. and Pittman, R. (eds.) *Introduction to Community Development* (pp. 236–248). London: Routledge.

Chase, C., Amsden. B., and Phillips, R.G. (2012). Stakeholder engagement in tourism planning and development. In Uysal, M., Perdue, R., and Sirgy, J.M. (eds) *Handbook of Tourism and Quality-of-Life Research, Enhancing the Lives of Tourists and Residents of Host Communities* (pp. 475–490). Dordrecht: Springer.

Green, G.P., and Haines, A.L. (2008). *Asset Building and Community Development*. Los Angeles, CA: Sage.

Harrill, R. (2004). Residents' attitudes toward tourism development: a literature review with implications for tourism planning. *Journal of Planning Literature* 18:3, DOI 10.1177/088541220326036.

Haywood, K.M. (1988). Responsible and responsive tourism planning in the community. *Tourism Management* 9:2, 105–118.

Joppe, M. (1996). Sustainable community tourism development revisited. *Tourism Management* 17:7, 475–479.

Keogh, B. (1990). Public participation in community tourism planning. *Annals of Tourism Research* 17, 449–465.

Mair, H., and Reid. D.G. (2007). Tourism and community development vs. tourism for community development: conceptualizing planning as power, knowledge, and control. *Leisure* 31:2, 403–425.

Murphy, P.E. (1988). Community driven tourism planning. *Tourism Management* 9:2, 96–104.

Phillips, R. and Pittman, R. (2009). *Introduction to Community Development*. London: Routledge.

Reid, D.G., Mair, H., and George, W. (2004). Community tourism planning, a self-assessment instrument. *Annals of Tourism Research* 31:3, 623–639.

Roberts, S. (2010). *Unearthing new gold: The Potential of the Canadian Diaspora Market for Guyana* paper presented at the Caribbean Studies Association XXXV Annual Conference, The Everyday Occurrence of Violence in the cultural life of the Caribbean. St. Peter, Barbados, 24–28 May 2010.

Incorporating social justice in tourism planning: racial reconciliation and sustainable community development in the Deep South

Alan W. Barton[a] and Sarah J. Leonard[b]

[a]Social Sciences, Delta State University, DSU Box 3264, Cleveland MS 38733, USA;
[b]The College Board, Chicago, USA

Tourism can serve as a vehicle for sustainable community development by contributing to equity and social justice. This happens as tourists learn about marginal groups through educational tourism, engage in development projects with host-area residents, undertake pilgrimages that bring greater meaning and cohesiveness to an ethnic identity, or encounter stories that transform their view of social injustice and spur further action to reduce inequities. Tourism planning can produce a sense of reconciliation when it brings historically divided groups together. An example is found in Tallahatchie County, Mississippi, where a group of white and African American residents are collaborating to develop tourism projects designed around a narrative of reconciliation, while they use the process of tourism planning to work towards racial reconciliation within their community. This case illustrates strategies tourism planners employ and challenges they face when they envision tourism as more than merely a means of economic growth.

The advantages of tourism to rural communities are generally painted as economic: developing a tourism industry brings in "fresh" dollars, provides jobs and offers opportunities for local entrepreneurship (National Agricultural Library, 2008; World Travel & Tourism Council, 2008). When tourism focuses on local heritage, cultural advantages can accrue as well, as local residents learn about, take pride in, and conserve their own stories (Barton, 2005; Howard, 2002; President's Committee on the Arts and the Humanities, 2005). A growing body of literature argues that tourism can also contribute to social equity and justice in rural communities, and that social and cultural factors are important elements in sustainable community development in many rural contexts (Higgins-Desbiolles, 2008; Moore & Jie Wen, 2009; Scheyvens & Momsen, 2008). Recently, the social justice aspects of tourism have received substantial attention in the media as well (see, e.g., Gentleman, 2006; Lancaster, 2007; Markey, 2007; Popescu, 2007; Rao, 2009; Weiner, 2008).

We consider one aspect of social justice, the case of racial reconciliation in the Deep South. The Civil Rights Movement that emerged in the mid-twentieth century in America made substantial progress in the extension of political rights to African Americans, but economic disparities and cultural differences continue to separate black and white residents in much of the region (Andrews, 1997; Austin, 2006; Edelman, 2005; Hill, 2007; US Commission on Civil Rights, 2001). We draw on a case study of a rural county in the Mississippi Delta to examine how tourism might contribute to or detract from equality and social justice in rural communities, and the challenges that community planners face when promoting tourism as a means of addressing ingrained racial disparities.

Sustainable community development

When assessing tourism as a community development strategy, community planners must consider how tourism will contribute in a sustainable way to community well-being (Haywood, 1988; Richards & Hall, 2000). The literature on sustainable development has emphasized three crucial dimensions: economic efficiency, environmental integrity and social equity and justice (Edwards, 2005; Klein-Vielhauer, 2009; World Commission on Environment and Development, 1987). Finding a balance among these factors that is appropriate in a given context increases the chances for sustainability, and distortions arise when one of these elements dominates the others. In the tourism industry, economic considerations frequently drive decisions, while the potential for negative impacts such as environmental deterioration and increased inequity are given less attention.

Sustainable tourism

Tourism has the potential to produce social inequities in a variety of ways. Mass tourism organized along industrial lines is largely a product of modern society (Eadington & Smith, 1992; Malkin, 1999), and like many industries, tourism produces core-periphery inequities (Frank, 1986; Murphy & Andressen, 1988; Sharpley, 2001). When tourists travel from an industrial/post-industrial region to a less industrialized region, they tend to exacerbate the economic differences. Host (tourist-receiving) areas benefit economically, as tourists spend money locally on entrance fees, food, gifts and transportation; locals obtain jobs in tourism-oriented businesses; and tourists often pay special taxes. But tourists also purchase services from providers based in core areas, such as airlines, cruise lines, chain hotels and chain restaurants. As a result, the host region does not benefit fully from its hospitality, and often there is a net transfer of value from host to home (tourist-sending) region. One dimension of inequity, then, is the gap between the host and home regions.

Tourism often leads to greater inequities within a host region as well (Thomas, 2009). Some residents are better positioned to capitalize on entrepreneurial opportunities and capture a larger portion of tourist dollars. Others are relegated to low-paying service jobs, and still others are excluded from the tourism industry entirely. An influx of free-spending tourists may drive up prices of basic commodities like food and increase property values, leaving residents outside the industry in a squeeze. Another dimension of inequity is the increasing differentiation within host communities.

The inequities produced by tourism are not solely economic, however, as tourists extract other intangible, often unquantifiable values as well. Heritage tourists take away knowledge and information from a unique museum; tourists on a pilgrimage to a sacred site feel an increased sense of pride in their culture; and tourists who work on a development project in a poor community experience a transformation in their worldview. Does the extraction of these non-monetary values ultimately benefit or harm the host community? Tourists can create relationships with host-area residents, which could lead to benefits to the peripheral area. Tourists who return year-after-year can create the basis for a sustainable local industry. But these factors are conditional, and difficult to quantify (Robinson, 2000). There is no systematic recipe for how a region can optimize its opportunities to capture intangible benefits or reduce intangible losses from tourism.

A similar dilemma arises with respect to culture. The tourism industry appropriates and packages cultural stories, often eroding their authenticity and cultural value (Robinson, 1999). All cultural stories are produced by winnowing through variation to create a meta-narrative (Hitchcock & King, 2003), but what criteria are used to produce that narrative? And whose interests are represented by the narrative that emerges? In industrial tourism, often the criteria and interests are commercial in nature, and the story that emerges is one that will sell to a mass public, bringing money to tourism providers (Cohen, 1988; Kirtsoglou & Theodossopoulos, 2004; Silver, 1993). A third form of inequity, then, is produced by how the tourism narratives are framed, benefiting cultural identities framed as mainstream, and sidelining or excluding others.

By increasing opportunities for local coordination and organization, tourism can build skills and capacities that can be applied in other areas. Organizational systems are a critical part of community development (Fischer, 1989; Flora and Flora, 2008). Tourism builds relationships, and under the right conditions, relationships can grow into institutions, which create the stability necessary for sustainability. Stable relationships and institutions are facilitated under circumstances of relative equality and justice.

Narratives in a tourism industry

The product that tourism providers and officials market is a narrative about the host community; this is the commodity that generates economic growth, as well as social and cultural meaning. The production of this narrative is a complex process of social construction, involving many voices (Edson, 2004). Inequities arise in the construction of the narrative, as some voices are better represented than others, and some may be excluded entirely (Porter & Salazar, 2005). As noted it is often the tourism industry that produces the dominant narrative for public consumption, driven by commercial interests. The narrative, as a result, is often a sanitary version of a much larger, more complex and possibly more uncomfortable story (Kelner, 2001; Kirtsoglou & Theodossopoulos, 2004; Silver, 1993). The distortions that arise from this process marginalize groups whose voices are ignored or underrepresented.

While the processes through which groups are marginalized are complex and context specific, the general process is one in which cultural identity is eroded. This may occur through homogenization into a broader commercial identity, loss of identification with a particular group, or a transformation of identity into something different (Brown, 2003; Edson, 2004).[1] Under some conditions, this refined story may take on new and empowering meaning to peripheral communities; under other conditions, it erodes cultural identity (Cohen, 1988).

Creating narratives of justice through tourism

Tourism contributes to equity and justice by increasing the wealth, power and/or prestige of marginalized groups, by raising awareness among privileged groups, and in some cases by challenging their sense of privilege and entitlement. Several models of tourism for justice have emerged. All are forms of alternative tourism, that is, tourism with a mission that is more than finding sun, sand and sea (Eadington & Smith, 1992).

One model is *Educational Tourism*, in which members of privileged core communities visit less privileged peripheral communities to learn about their reality. Tourists in peripheral regions often see poverty, but educational tourists intentionally visit impoverished areas with the specific goal of learning about them, and the impoverished people are organized to benefit from the tourists. Educational tourism allows marginal groups to tell stories from their own perspective, awakens awareness among members of core communities, clarifies misperceptions that privileged tourists may hold, and channels some money into marginal communities. One example of educational tourism is eco-lodges that take visitors to view the hospitals, schools and community centers that are sustained by their visits (Pearce, 1992). Another is visits to slum areas that have been organized to show visitors both the good and bad in their environment; the money they generate is then used for community development. This sort of tourism, dubbed "poorism," has been controversial, as some see it as exploitative (Lancaster, 2007; Weiner, 2008). Distinguishing community development from exploitation may be difficult, but generally depends on how much of the value created by tourism is controlled by the marginal community and how members of the marginal community view the overall enterprise. In the realm of civil rights, monuments to African American heroes are being erected around the southern US, to right historical wrongs and to take advantage of a growing interest in civil rights tourism (Parker, 2001). Monuments and historic sites provide tourists with opportunities to learn more about the South's civil rights stories. However, learning by itself does not lead to reconciliation nor even necessitate reflection.

A second model is *Development Tourism* in which privileged tourists visit less privileged groups to carry out community development projects together (Raymond & Hall, 2008). As they collaborate, they construct a narrative through interaction and working together, and become more equal as they partner for a common goal. While educational tourism is observational, development tourism involves more direct interaction, and as a result the narrative is not simply received by tourists, rather, the tourist participates in its construction (McIntosh & Zahra, 2007). One example of development tourism involves young people who participate in programs such as alternative spring breaks or "gap year" travel.[2] Another version is volunteers who travel to assist on a research project during their vacation (Clifton & Benson, 2006; Ellis, 2003). Despite its positive intentions, development tourism also generates controversy. Community development is a long-term enterprise, requiring extended commitment and a resiliency to failure. Idealistic youth may have good intentions, but lack the knowledge and skills necessary to accomplish something meaningful in a short time. Well-organized development tourism may generate personal and community benefits. But it may create a false sense of accomplishment among tourists, while members of the host community understand little will change when the tourist leaves. Development tourism may serve relief efforts well, however. Following Hurricane Katrina, a steady stream of volunteers traveled to the Gulf

Coast for short periods to assist in clean-up and recovery. Indeed, their labor made a significant difference in many people's lives.

A third model is *Pilgrimage Tourism*, in which members of defined groups travel to study and connect with their own story and heritage (Collins-Kreiner, 2006; Gatewood & Cameron, 2004; Hasty, 2002; Kelner, 2001). People engage in pilgrimages to experience first-hand places with sacred meaning, or because they feel a personal connection to a leader or story. Pilgrimage tourists are generally associated with religious groups (Povoledo, 2008), but non-religious pilgrims travel as well (Carrier, 2004). For example, African Americans carry out pilgrimages to visit their ancestors' homelands in Africa (Hasty, 2002; Pierre, 2009) and to visit meaningful sites in North America, including iconic sites in the Civil Rights Movement (Allman-Baldwin, 2006; Dewan, 2004; Grant, 2005). Cities with substantial African American populations, including Washington DC, Philadelphia PA and Atlanta GA have created African-American themed heritage trails, museums and other amenities to attract African American tourists (Carrier, 2004; Cobb, 2008; Grant, 2005). This approach to tourism can empower group members by extending a central narrative throughout a community, creating shared meaning even across large spaces, and by instilling a sense of transformation as group members connect to their roots in a deeper way.

A fourth model is *Reconciliation Tourism*, which involves using tourism as a means of reducing conflicts and constructing linkages between groups (Hemming, 1993; Higgins-Desbiolles, 2003, 2008). Conflict produced through stratification calls for reconciliation to ease differences and enable groups to construct a narrative that represents a wider range of voices. As such, reconciliation tourism frequently aims at providing transformational experiences to tourists (Hasty, 2002). For example, the United States Holocaust Memorial Museum in Washington, DC tells a tragic story "like it is," challenging visitors to think and act rather than sanitizing a narrative to make them more comfortable.[3] Examples from the American Civil Rights Movement include the National Civil Rights Museum in Memphis, TN (http://www.civilrightsmuseum.org/home.htm), and the Martin Luther King, Jr. National Historic Site in Atlanta, GA (http://www.nps.gov/malu/index.htm). Building tourism enterprises can also lead to reconciliation among those organized to provide the tourism services. For instance, Lang (2004) chronicles how the construction of the Gateway Arch in St. Louis, MO, led to a new social movement among African Americans who were displaced from their homes and excluded from the project's higher-paying jobs.

Method

This study began with informal discussions about racial reconciliation and its role in tourism development, which led us to conduct a formal literature review on the topic. A serendipitous series of events then connected us to the Emmett Till Memorial Commission (ETMC) in Tallahatchie County, Mississippi, an organization working to create racial reconciliation through tourism. Our observation began with a visit to one of the Commission's monthly meetings in early 2008, followed by a series of exchanges with ETMC leaders, and an invitation by one of the Commission's chairs to observe the next monthly meeting. At this meeting, we were introduced to the members of the ETMC, who agreed that we could continue to observe their activities as part of a formal research project.

Research questions

Our initial interest in the subject of racial reconciliation and tourism stemmed from current conditions in the Mississippi Delta. From its settlement, racial disparities have shaped the character of the Delta. Since the late 1970s racial roles have been changing, and opportunities have been opening for African Americans that historically were proscribed (Austin, 2006), particularly in politics and education. At the same time, the region's economy is shifting from agriculture and small industry to services. A substantial push towards tourism has been growing since the early 1990s (Austin & Middleton, 2006). Since 2003 heritage tourism has grown, focusing on the Delta's claim to be "the birthplace of the blues" (Barton, 2007). Efforts to promote other aspects of the Delta's heritage, including the role of Delta residents in the Civil Rights Movement, are in their early stages. In many Delta communities, tourism is still a cottage industry, but a stronger tourism industry is emerging in some of the larger towns, in the region and in the state.

From these circumstances, our initial question in this study was whether tourism could expand opportunities for social mobility among the region's African Americans, and provide a sense of healing in race relations. Our on-going study of the Emmett Till Memorial Commission has led us to question how reconciliation comes about and what reconciliation means, beyond simply healing fractured relationships.

Methodological approach

Our research uses an interpretative approach. Interpretive studies aim for contextual understanding, gaining insights about theoretical and policy issues from close attention to specific cases (Greene, 1990; Yin, 1984). Interpretive researchers generally rely on qualitative data, and follow an inductive path to discovery (Patton, 1990; Ragin, 1994). An interpretive approach is appropriate for case studies as its focus is on context rather than universal application, so data collection is fluid and researchers have flexibility to follow changing circumstances (Babbie, 1986). Interpretive research also allows for more depth of understanding and nuance, as researchers can observe attitude and expression in addition to content.

Interpretive research is useful in community settings, where relationships are more rooted in emotional than instrumental ties. Where science and technology form people's worldviews, quantitative methods may be more appropriate (Berg, 2004). In communities, where people know each other and establish personal bonds, the flexibility inherent in an interpretive approach allows researchers to shape and mold their understanding and account for inconsistencies and changes. The ETMC had been in existence for nearly three years when we began our observations, so we opted for a non-participant approach, and have resisted taking an action research stance so as not to interrupt the progress the Commission has made on its own.

Data collection

We have employed three techniques to gather data: observation of ETMC activities, a review of documents, and open-ended interviews with ETMC members. These are the three most commonly used forms of data collection in qualitative studies (Miles & Huberman, 1994).

Observation

Our observation has focused primarily on the monthly meetings of the ETMC. At least one of the authors has attended all of the Commission's monthly meetings since we initiated the study. We took detailed notes during the meetings and completed field notes following the meeting as a way of filling in details and additional information, including our perceptions.

In addition to the monthly meetings, we also observed other events carried out by ETMC members in Tallahatchie County communities. ETMC members have participated in events organized by our campus as well. For events that we could not observe directly, we have observed artifacts, such as the signs posted for the Emmett Till Trail, discussed below.

Document review

As part of the observation of artifacts, the authors reviewed documents produced by the ETMC and others related to the case. Principal among these were minutes of ETMC meetings that occurred before we began our study, which produced insight into the early days of the Commission. We also reviewed websites produced by the ETMC and by the William Winter Institute for Racial Reconciliation at the University of Mississippi, an ETMC collaborator. Also, we collected newspaper articles and other sources of information in the mass media pertaining to the ETMC, and to the Emmett Till case. Finally, we reviewed the Commission's organizational documents, such as by-laws.

Interviews

When we began our study the ETMC had 18 members, nine white and nine African American. The membership included co-chairpersons, one of each race. Other collaborators occasionally attended the group's meetings, including representatives from the William Winter Institute and an attorney who works with the ETMC.

Our goal was to interview all ETMC members and some collaborators. Commission members were personally contacted at the monthly meetings, and the authors explained the project and extended an invitation to participate in an interview. We completed interviews with fourteen Commission members and one knowledgeable partner. Interviews were conducted between April and September 2008. Two members declined to be interviewed; and two were unavailable during the interview period.

All interviews except one were conducted in person. An open-ended questionnaire was sent by e-mail to one informant who was unable to participate in a face-to-face interview; the informant used this questionnaire to respond in writing. We carried out one additional interview with two members, and later interviewed each individually. Face-to-face interviews typically took place in the respondent's home or office, with a few occurring in public places such as a park or City Hall. Interviews typically lasted about one hour.

Role of the researcher

Given the complicated nature of race and class relations in the Delta, the authors recognized that some interviewees might be less forthcoming than others. We are both white and represented universities at the time of the interviews, and neither of us is from the South. Going in, we recognized that African American informants might feel uncomfortable talking about race relations with white researchers and that white informants might try to demonstrate their open-mindedness; that informants might feel uncomfortable sharing cultural information with outsiders; and some might be hesitant to provide information to people who were university-affiliated. However, we found informants to be candid in their responses, speaking openly and (for the most part) on the record about their feelings, thoughts, and experiences. At the same time, these interviews only provide a snapshot of race relations in the Mississippi Delta. The issue runs much deeper, and a single interview with an individual only scratches the surface of the nuances that are so entrenched in the culture.

Data analysis

We recorded and transcribed all interviews, and independently reviewed each transcript to identify topics and themes in the conversations, then compared our individual results. In our discussions, we further developed the topics and themes, and drew in observational and documentary evidence to triangulate our interview findings. We then went through and coded the interview transcripts. We have extracted quotes that are illustrative of concepts pertaining to racial reconciliation and tourism, and built the description of our case study based on these quotes and themes.

Once we had completed the analysis, we shared the results with our informants and asked for feedback. Specifically, we asked them to assess whether the description of the case study accurately represented their perspective, and whether anything was omitted that should be included. We revised our analysis based on the comments provided by informants.

Case study: the Emmett Till Memorial Commission

Located in the Deep South, Tallahatchie County, Mississippi, has a stark, persistent and entrenched racial divide between the county's black and white residents (Austin, 2006). The pervasive effect of race on social structure and social interaction in the region is hard to overestimate. In 1955, Tallahatchie County gained international attention when a local jury acquitted two white residents accused of murdering a black teenager named Emmett Till, who was visiting relatives in the area from his home in Chicago.[4] The trial verdict left a pall of fear and shame on the county that continues to shape race relations today.

The context

Tallahatchie County is small, rural and remote. The western part of the county lies in Mississippi's "Delta" region, and the eastern portion is in the region known locally as the "Hills" (see Figure 1). These two regions have distinct cultures, and there is substantial competition between them (Adams & Gorton, 2006; Asch, 2008). As they described their community, the informants in this study took pains to distinguish themselves from "the other side." The distinction has immediate ramifications for the ETMC, related to the restoration of the Tallahatchie County Courthouse in Sumner, discussed below.

Countywide, nearly 60% of the population is African American, but in the western part of the county, almost 80% is black (see Table 1). Like most of the Mississippi Delta, Tallahatchie County reached its highest population in the 1920s and 1930s, surpassing 35,000 residents, but the numbers have steadily declined since (US Census Bureau, 2009a). The 2000 census counted 14,903 residents and today the population is estimated at slightly more than 13,000 (US Census Bureau, 2009b).

Politics in Western Tallahatchie County center around the Board of Supervisors, other county offices, and on the municipal governments of the region's four towns: Tutwiler, Sumner, Webb and Glendora. There are two county seats in Tallahatchie County, Charleston in the East (Hills) and Sumner in the West (Delta), each with its own functioning courthouse. The county offers a variety of services, but has

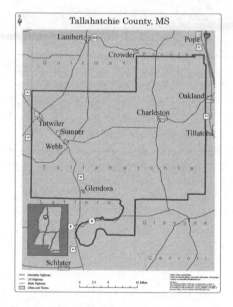

Figure 1.   Tallahatchie County, Mississippi.

Table 1.   Population and race in Tallahatchie County, Mississippi and its towns.

Place	Total population	White	Black
Tallahatchie County	14,903	5867 (39.4%)	8784 (58.9%)
Western Tallahatchie County (Census Tracts 9403 and 9404/Block 3)	5704	1106 (19.4%)	4491 (78.7%)
Eastern Tallahatchie County (Census Tracts 9401, 9402 and 9404/Blocks 1 and 2)	9199	4761 (51.8%)	4293 (46.7%)
Sumner Town	407	236 (58.0%)	158 (38.8%)
Tutwiler Town	1,364	160 (11.7%)	1186 (87.0%)
Webb Town	587	206 (35.1%)	360 (61.3%)
Glendora Town	285	13 (4.6%)	254 (89.1%)
Charlestown Town	2198	852 (38.8%)	1299 (59.1%)

Source: US Census, 2000.

relatively little in the way of public infrastructure. Up until the 1970s, all of the political offices were held by white residents, even though the majority of the population was African American. Beginning in the late 1970s, black residents have occupied more of the town and county offices. Today, the mayors in three of the four towns are African American, and several positions in the county are held by African Americans, including, since 1994, two of the five seats on the County Board of Supervisors.

Outside of agriculture, Western Tallahatchie County has little in the way of commerce. There are a few small businesses in the towns, but residents typically travel to one of the larger towns in adjacent counties to shop. There is no chamber of commerce, but there is a public Industrial Authority organized to attract business to Tallahatchie County. A private prison in the northwest corner of the county provides one of the largest sources of employment for residents, and a state prison in an adjacent county is another source of employment. A public Prison Authority, derived from the Industrial Authority, coordinates the prison. Landownership is a significant indicator of economic power, and in the absence of other institutions, a few churches, the local country club and a service organization function as the seats of economic power.

Social life is largely based on families and churches, and the pace of life is slow and rooted in personal relationships. Like much of the rural South, interaction between black and white residents is generally cordial but strained, and occurs in the context of substantial racial stratification (Schultz, 2007). African Americans often serve as laborers on white-owned farms, or as domestic help, much as they have for generations. Some black and white residents develop genuine friendships, but economic and cultural differences intercede in many cases. A small number of well-to-do African Americans do intermix with the white elite. A Habitat for Humanity chapter founded in 1984 created the county's first interracial board, largely through the efforts of its founder. Since 2005, the ETMC was created, and two of the county's historically white organizations have added African American members.

The Emmett Till Memorial Commission

The initial impulse for the Emmett Till Memorial Commission was to restore the Tallahatchie County Courthouse in Sumner, where the trail of Emmett Till's murderers was held. The County Board of Supervisors decided to create a biracial commission of concerned citizens to take on this task, bringing black and white residents together in a spirit of racial reconciliation. The supervisors and town mayors appoint members, who are diverse in age, gender, income, length of residence in the county and most notably race. One member who has lived in the county for several decades explained that this was the first time white and black residents have sat down to work together as equals. The ETMC has decided that the courthouse restoration should include a museum on the Emmett Till case, and have found other ways to use heritage tourism as a vehicle for racial reconciliation. This case illustrates some of the social justice benefits, as well as the challenges, of heritage tourism.

The ETMC started slowly. Few of the white residents who were appointed got involved in the beginning. Tallahatchie County operates on an informal basis, and some explained that they were not notified that they had been named to the Commission. Participation among black members fluctuated initially as well. After a few months, the ETMC formed a partnership with the William Winter Institute for

Racial Reconciliation at the University of Mississippi. The Winter Institute helped the ETMC develop goals and a working procedure. The ETMC settled on a racially balanced membership, and increased their numbers to nine white and nine black members. Participation stabilized. Staff and students from the Winter Institute brought expertise in reconciliation, as well as experience with other groups in the state who have similar missions. The ETMC was able to draw on the work of these other groups, reviewing by-laws and other documents to help craft their own. The Winter Institute has operated mostly "behind the scenes," however, and has not been directly involved in facilitating meetings.

Reconciliation and tourism projects

The project to restore the courthouse has grown into an effort to develop local tourism opportunities, primarily oriented around the story of Emmett Till and the Civil Rights Movement. This has been driven by an interest among local leaders to honor Emmett Till, by a still-small but growing demand from tourists, and by the growth of the tourism industry in the state. The ETMC is currently engaged in three tourism efforts. The first is the courthouse restoration of the Tallahatchie County Courthouse in Sumner; the second is the Emmett Till Interpretive Trail and driving tour, which was initiated with a Public Proclamation to the Till Family; and the third is the development of a tourism infrastructure in the county, including a tourism specialist housed within a newly created county Department of Recreation, Parks and Tourism.

Courthouse restoration

The Sumner courthouse is picturesque and historic. It was built in 1909 in the Richardsonian Romanesque style and in 1990 it was declared a state landmark by The Mississippi Department of Archives and History (Mississippi Department of Archives and History, 2009). However, the building is structurally deficient and inadequate for current administrative needs. Residents of Sumner are aware that the courthouse supports a legal profession and employs many residents. Residents fear that if the courthouse is shut down, even temporarily, they will lose their legal infrastructure to the courthouse in Charleston, and Sumner might slip into the same doldrums as other impoverished Delta communities. The ETMC has raised money and coordinated the courthouse restoration. Current plans are to configure the courtroom to look like it did during the 1955 trial, and to add a Civil Rights Museum to commemorate Emmett Till. The restoration would accommodate heritage tourists who want to visit the site of one of the most important incidents in the Civil Rights Movement.[5]

Restoring the courthouse is one step toward achieving racial reconciliation. The story of Emmett Till has been told many times, but owing to local residents' reluctance to discuss the topic, their voices have been muted in shaping how America understands this story. The courthouse and museum provide an opportunity to present these voices, crafted by a biracial commission. Thus, the ETMC's activities construct reconciliation tourism by contributing a local perspective on the wider narrative and meaning of the Emmett Till case in American society.

The value of this project toward reconciliation at a local scale is more complex. The project brings black and white ETMC members together to work on a common project, although as one member explained, the motivation of the two groups is probably different:

> In this instance, I think [reconciliation] specifically has to do with the fact that both races are trying to attain the same goal. Now, the motivation on each side might be different. I think for the white part of this Commission, probably the strongest motivation is saving the courthouse. And the black motivation is probably honoring or memorializing the Emmett Till trial.

Although the black and white members have different motivations for involvement in the courthouse restoration, according to some members the process of working together on the project engenders racial reconciliation as a by-product. One lifelong resident of Sumner said working together on the Emmett Till Memorial Commission has "enhanced mutual respect among the races," and this has led to a more positive tone in interracial interactions.

Not all members agree, however. Some believe the African Americans on the Commission are marginalized, and that interactions between black and white members follow the same stratified patterns that have long existed in the county. As one member said:

> The beginning of the Emmett Till Commission—it started out, basically, all African Americans, and there were a few Caucasians on the Board, about three or four and about eight or nine African Americans. The first or second meeting, it was proposed by a Caucasian member that the body should be fifty-fifty. We're talking about racial reconciliation and so forth, and we ought to be nine African Americans and nine Caucasians. And the body voted for that, and that's what took place. But, after that, no more participation by the African American community, as far as being open, and expressing whatever they talked about or wanted to see or was hoping for. Basically because, what happened was, when they changed the Commission, and brought on the additional members, everybody was from the affluent—everybody was the bossman.

This quote suggests that the structure of the Commission affects the level of trust felt by members. Because white residents historically have held virtually all power in Tallahatchie County, and continue to hold substantial economic power today, black members of the ETMC still feel like a minority, even if the membership is racially balanced (Gallardo & Stein, 2007).

Additionally, the emphasis on Emmett Till in local tourism development is not wholly supported by all ETMC members and other residents of the county. Some members believe the county is doing too much to honor Mr. Till, while others are uneasy because they believe their actions exploit a family tragedy (Jubera, 2007).[6] On the other hand, some members believe the name "Emmett Till" has come to transcend the personal tragedy of one 14-year-old boy, and carries an iconic status, particularly among African Americans. Outsiders will come to visit as educational, pilgrimage and reconciliation tourists, and the county should provide for their needs and tell the local version of the story. These contrasting views impose barriers to reconciliation that the ETMC must address.

Emmett Till interpretive trail

This driving tour consists of historical markers located at eight sites in the county, which chronicle events in the death of Emmett Till and the subsequent trial. Members worked with historians to ensure that the locations and the information on the signs were as accurate as possible. A ninth marker, erected by the State of Mississippi, commemorates the trial at the courthouse in Sumner. A brochure that describes the historical background of the Emmett Till murder and trial, with photos and descriptions of each site on the trail, is available on-line.[7] The interpretive trail was inaugurated in October, 2007 with a ceremony that included a public "Statement of Regret," expressing the county's regret to the Till family for the injustice committed fifty years earlier (Jubera, 2007). The text of the Statement of Regret was crafted with assistance from the Winter Institute, and it was signed by all members of the ETMC.[8] Surviving members of Emmett Till's family attended the event. Public statements like this are a common practice in reconciliation efforts. This was a significant step in racial reconciliation, as it broke a long-standing silence regarding the murder and unjust trial in Tallahatchie County.

The historical markers along the interpretive trail have generated interest from tourists, but have also produced controversy in the county. One marker was vandalized in October 2008, and the ETMC is responsible for replacing it (Associated Press, 2008). It is unknown if the vandalism was racially motivated. Another marker has generated a backlash for referring to the Ku Klux Klan; many local residents refute the claim that the KKK was ever active in Tallahatchie County. This is a source of pride for them, and they feel that to have alleged Klan activity publicly displayed on a sign projects an undeserved negative image.

Members of the ETMC feel the interpretive trail and the story it tells are important for a variety of reasons. "It's all trying to understand where we were and where we've come, how far we've come, and have we come very far at all? I really do think we've come a long way," one member commented. Another member explained how some sites on the interpretive trail have the potential to generate a sense of healing:

> It has been my experience [that] whenever we have [visited the site where Till's body was pulled from the river] it was a negative feeling but it was a positive, it was a healing, or it was a connection. And I think that each site is a connection to some part of each individual. Where the body was pulled out is the most negative [site on the trail], but it can be the most positive also, because that's the site that will make you think the most, make you feel the most. So if you're gonna get it, you're gonna get it there. You're gonna feel the loss, you're gonna feel the pain, and maybe that will inspire you—never again, never again.

These comments illustrate the idea that while reconciliation and healing are difficult, often painful processes, acknowledging and confronting that pain may be a way to move past it. While the driving tour is marketed to visitors, the process of discussing the sites and their meaning has brought greater understanding and healing to ETMC members as well.

Tourism planning

A third project, initiated at the beginning of 2009, is the creation of an administrative structure for tourism planning and management in the county. The County Board of Supervisors requested that the ETMC act as an advisory council on tourism development. During 2008, Tallahatchie County developed a parks and recreation program. The initial impetus was to provide after-school activities for the county's youth. The county acquired a building near Sumner as a headquarters and recreation center, named in honor of Emmett Till, and they hired a part-time recreation manager. In early 2009, the supervisors added tourism to the mission of this program. The County Administrator was named interim director of the Parks, Recreation and Tourism Department, and they began developing a means of recording tourist visits. They also began fundraising to hire a tourism professional to run the county office, and guides to take tour groups around the Emmett Till Interpretive Trail. These efforts are in their early stages.

One town in the county has been working to build a local tourism infrastructure as well, in conjunction with Mississippi Valley State University. Glendora has its own Emmett Till Museum, a park named in honor of Emmett Till and a small bed and breakfast, the county's only lodging. Glendora was where one of Emmett Till's murderers resided, and four of the eight markers on the Emmett Till Interpretive Trail are in Glendora. The town also recently inaugurated a marker on the Mississippi Blues Trail to honor Sonny Boy Williamson, a noted harmonica player who grew up on a plantation near Glendora (Barretta, 2009). However, Glendora is a very poor town; over 68% of the families live in poverty (US Census Bureau, 2009c). The shop fronts on its main street are mostly boarded up, and a visit to Glendora would likely appeal only to a select group of tourists.

Tourism as an engine of reconciliation

The Emmett Till Memorial Commission provides an interesting study of the relationship between tourism and reconciliation. The most compelling aspect is that the planners are not only developing a story of reconciliation as a tourism narrative, but as they do so they are also engaging in a process of reconciliation among their members and in their community. One example is the Statement of Regret the ETMC prepared and read in public. The statement itself opened a door for reconciliation between black and white Americans, as the Emmett Till story has national significance. But the process of crafting the statement also required ETMC members to confront various issues, think about definitions, and express their sentiments about Emmett Till and the trial. Certainly, this process did not resolve the issues that make race such a significant divide in Tallahatchie County, but black and white members did sit down and discuss the issues, something that was inconceivable not long ago in this context.

In many places in the US today, different racial groups working together may seem mundane, but in Tallahatchie County, with its long history of strict racial segregation and exclusion, residents consider it remarkable that black and white residents can hold equal positions on a public commission, and can sit down and work together in a climate of equality. The personal stories of some members illustrate this. Two of the African American members grew up on plantations owned by two of the white members. From subservient child to equal partner, this is truly a transition for these individuals and for this community. On the ETMC, black elected officials sit beside the landed white gentry, and all have an opportunity to shape how the county creates its story, to decide how it builds its tourism industry, and to engage in the processes by which reconciliation may occur.

During our interviews, some members expressed the positive repercussions the ETMC's work could have on reconciliation not only within the membership, but within the greater community.

> I think that by restoring the Sumner Courthouse to its condition in 1955, creating the Emmett Till Interpretive Trail, and hopefully also creating a visitors center for potential tourists is a great step in the process of healing race relations in Tallahatchie County. For too long, the story of Emmett Till has been suppressed and neglected by the general population of Tallahatchie County. It is as if the people here have remained in denial about what happened, hoping that if it was ignored and not spoken of it would somehow disappear. The formation of the Emmett Till Memorial Commission has no doubt shown the people of Tallahatchie County that the murder of Emmett Till, and especially the injustice that followed, is not to be ignored. The Commission sends the message that not only is it time to accept this black spot on our county's history, but it's time to memorialize the name of Emmett Till to give him the respect he deserves.

As this member explains, telling the story of Emmett Till through heritage tourism has the potential for tourists and residents alike to experience reconciliation. Heritage tourism allows residents to tell their own story, and to share their experiences with others. Through this process, acknowledgement, acceptance, and healing can occur.

Challenges to reconciliation

While the ETMC has made some strides toward racial reconciliation, they still face several challenges. As previously noted, some members of the ETMC question the notion that the Commission operates on an equal playing field. The ETMC has tried to create a sense of racial equality on the Commission by maintaining a balance in the number of black and white members. However, this does not take into account the historically produced perceptions of the relative power held by each member. Several of the white members come from the elite ranks of Tallahatchie County, including families that have owned plantations for generations. Several of the black members hold important political offices, but all of them have risen to these positions relatively recently, as these positions were unavailable to African Americans in the past. Residents have become accustomed to particular codes of conduct that subtly and perhaps unintentionally enforce racial stratification in the county, and these rules do not fully disappear when the county supervisors create a commission. The statuses that have existed for generations outside the Commission continue to shape how people interact at ETMC meetings.

Other members have highlighted cultural preferences that impede reconciliation. One expression of cultural differences is in ideas about what reconciliation means. To some, reconciliation is produced through black and white members interacting with each other. Under this view, the racial divide was created because blacks and whites were raised differently, and thus have different cultures. The solution is to find ways to get to know each other and appreciate each other's cultures. As one member stated, "If I can't be around you, I can't get to know you." To other members, reconciliation is a by-product of working together toward common goals. Those who expressed this view believe that ETMC members need not focus explicitly on their differences, on building friendships or respect, or on openly discussing cultural differences. Rather, they need to take on common tasks and work together, and through these activities they will build common values and respect for each other. To illustrate this point, one member said, "I think the reconciliation is starting out with the [ETMC] board and I think that we're working together to get things done and I think we're going to get things done because of that working together."

For the most part, these distinct approaches represent cultural differences in the black and white communities. African American members of the ETMC are more likely to see reconciliation as happening through interaction and discussing racial issues openly, while the white members tend to see reconciliation as stemming from common work. These differences are also represented in other preferences expressed by ETMC members. For example, one topic raised in interviews was how their monthly meetings should be run. The African American members are comfortable with an informal meeting structure, in which everyone can talk and which covers a wide range of topics. One gets the sense that the product the black members wish to produce is as much a sense of community as specific outputs. The white members, on the other hand, demonstrate a clear preference for a business-like meeting, following procedures such as Roberts Rules of Order. Privately, some white members have expressed dismay at how the meetings ramble and stray off-topic, and during the meetings the white members are much more likely to enforce established procedures. It is white members, for example, who typically make motions to vote on matters, and who require that new business be formally submitted one month before it may be officially considered. Before there was a strong white presence on the ETMC, the black members ran the meetings in a much more fluid manner, admitting non-members to participate and even vote, and not taking into account set procedures to resolve issues.

In addition to differences in preferred and observed behavior, there are underlying tensions within the group regarding racial issues. Some white members of the Commission stated that they felt unfairly blamed, both at the time of Emmett Till's murder and subsequent trial, and now during the reconciliation process. They recounted how Tallahatchie County, though not the site of the kidnapping or murder, became known as a hotbed of racial tension, the site of a brutal murder where the Civil Rights Movement began. One member explained, "What we don't like is the fact that it was committed by two [men] who were citizens of Leflore County and [Emmett Till] was kidnapped in Leflore County, and Tallahatchie County got blamed for it." This idea of the community being blamed for such a gruesome act is in contrast with how some Commission members described Sumner, which may be why they feel the focus on their town paints it in an undeserved negative light. As one member commented, "Sumner is a wonderful, wonderful place. We have virtually no crime. It's just, you know, a pretty free place to raise children. [In the past] it was just Mayberry. I mean, the policeman really didn't have any bullets. He kept one in his glove compartment." Another Commission member explained what the community was like around the time of the trial, saying, "It was a very prosperous farming community with lots of people, lots of young people, lots of families, vigorous economy, and a lot of educated people. Sumner's always had a high percentage of people who were well-educated. That's always helped it."

So why was this seemingly idyllic community selected as the site for the murder trial? As one member explained the situation, Emmett Till's body was pulled from the Tallahatchie County side of the Tallahatchie River. When neighboring Leflore County, site of the kidnapping, refused to indict the suspects, authorities in Tallahatchie County stepped in. This member went on to explain that Tallahatchie County did not deserve the reputation is has acquired. "At least we indicted them. We didn't convict them, of course, but at least we indicted them and there was a trial, which we should get some credit for."

With regard to feelings of blame, some white members of the Commission also made attempts to remove themselves from any responsibility for wrongdoing. "As far as I know, nobody from Tallahatchie County was in any way remotely involved in that murder. Yet we inherited the stigma of being the place where it happened because the trial was held here," one member explained. Another commented that the trial, "absolutely tore this community apart. The white people felt like they were—I didn't live here then, but I've heard stories—the white people felt like they were unfairly blamed and the press was horrible and negative." The interruption about not living in Tallahatchie County at that time indicates that this member may feel separate from any repercussions that have resulted from the trial in the ensuing years as the community has struggled to redefine itself. Maintaining removal from the problem may make it difficult for this member to be part of reconciliation efforts.

Another member expressed the concept of blame in relation to the Statement of Regret that Tallahatchie County extended to the Till Family in October, 2007:

> I had problems with the first statement and then we had to kind of regroup. [A member of the Commission] took the statement and reworded it and then we discussed it in the meeting and really kind of picked it apart and changed some things and came up with the Statement of Regret. The first one was a Statement of Apology and all of the white people said, 'We're not going to apologize for something we did not do.' We regret very much that it happened, but I'm not going to say that I'm sorry for what happened. I wasn't even living here at the time.

Again, there is the idea of distance from the actual events removing all blame, when in reality there are systems and cultural norms embedded in Tallahatchie County and the Delta region that perpetuate racism to this day. An individual may not have directly been responsible for an act, but at the same time can benefit from and participate in systems that are racist and oppressive. This is why the focus on reconciliation through the ETMC becomes so important. If Tallahatchie County is to truly move beyond these horrible events and find some sense of peace and healing between the races, community members must recognize and transcend these systems that perpetuate oppression and segregation.

Conflicting goals and objectives among members is another challenge to the reconciliation process. Early on in the life of the ETMC, members determined a list of priority activities, which included restoring the courthouse, tourism initiatives, and creating a community center, among others. It became clear through these interviews, however, that many members are divided over what their priorities are or should be.

These conflicts seem to be divided primarily along racial lines. "I think that we both think we have different agendas and it's probably true," one member commented. White members showed a preference toward restoring the courthouse to ensure economic viability. "There's a lot of fear on some of the people that if we lose the courthouse we really will lose [our community]," one member explained. This member went on to add, "There's always something going on, it employs a lot of people, and it's sort of a symbol for the town. We want to have the courthouse redone and we want it to be a viable, working courthouse." Another echoed this sentiment, saying, "[I think] the reason the white people signed on is because of the restoration of the courthouse. And we see this Till thing as a way to get the funds to restore the courthouse, which it needs."

While recognizing the importance of restoring the courthouse, African American members tended to favor a commemorative focus through projects such as the interpretive trail, museum, or reconciliation activities. "Most things is about the restoration of the courthouse, but for me it's more about the museum and the community and the youth. It might even be further than that as far as relationships," explained one member. Another added, "At first they were just in terms of talking about the courthouse, but now we're working on civil rights, education, recreation, and everything that we can add in to help promote this county other than just the courthouse." Someone else suggested that telling the story as accurately as possible might be the most profitable outcome in terms of understanding. "I think Emmett Till, his life story, would be something good to help people see how important it is to value people and that type of thing. My priority is that we learn from history."

Recommendations for community planners

In part stemming from the publicity generated by the historical markers and driving trail, interest in tourism to Tallahatchie County has grown. While the number of visits remains relatively small, the supervisors and others have fielded telephone calls from groups interested in touring the Emmett Till Interpretive Trail and other landmarks. Members of the ETMC and other town residents lead the tours on an informal basis. Tallahatchie County stands on the cusp of taking tourism from a cottage industry to a diversified and professionalized enterprise. But getting to the next level requires planning.

Building tourism, building reconciliation

The most significant impediment to building a tourism industry, to date, has been a lack of understanding on the part of county residents as to the value of the story they can market to tourists. The Emmett Till story provides an opportunity for Tallahatchie County to create a sustainable tourism industry, based on its status as "ground zero in the Civil Rights Movement," if residents are willing to overcome the legacies of the past and take ownership of the story. The starting point is an honest accounting of the county's role in the Emmett Till case and the extent of injustice manifested by the verdict. The ETMC has started this process with the public Statement of Regret, but there remains a "culture of silence" in the county regarding the case, and reluctance, particularly among white residents, to acknowledge the iconic status that Emmett Till has in the struggle for civil rights in the US. The county's leaders and the ETMC have taken an appropriate step in linking tourism to reconciliation. In this case, though, reconciliation is not just the nature of the story the county is marketing, it is also necessary for the county to undergo a process of reconciliation before they can truly create a sustainable tourism industry.

Mississippi has recently undergone a similar story in relation to the blues. For a long time, the blues was viewed by many Mississippi residents, both black and white, as "the devil's music," and blues culture was seen as an embarrassment. Recently, however, Mississippi has created the Mississippi Blues Trail and has established a series of historical markers around the state, which have been widely supported by local residents as well as tourists. Today, many Mississippians, even if they are not blues fans, recognize this music's significance in American popular culture, and are proud to see its practitioners recognized. Many other Mississippians appreciate the markers because they attract tourism and build economic development at the local level. The story of Emmett Till could provide similar benefits to Tallahatchie County if the residents could come together and agree to honor Emmett Till and the Civil Rights Movement though open, honest dialogue about race. This could truly become a means of community development. The central need is for people to eradicate racial divisions and co-exist respectfully and appreciatively. Reconciling the pain and injustice is essential for this community and others like it to move beyond the past and embrace a collective future.

The ETMC probably missed an opportunity early in its existence to build a form of reconciliation in relationships on the Commission itself, for example, by sitting members down and having facilitated discussions that drew out the diverse perspectives in the room. Members likely would have benefited from taking time to understand each other, and particularly the various notions that members have about how to put reconciliation into practice. Instead, the Commission forged ahead with its projects, and by default, adopted one version of reconciliation, which is that it will emerge as a by-product of working together. This limits the potential for reconciliation, because it channels the activities of the ETMC away from visions of reconciliation that focus on healing through interaction and understanding, instead expressing a vision favored by white members of the Commission, reinforcing the existing power structure. An initial attempt at creating new relationships may have been strained in this context, however, since many of the members already knew each other well and had long-established patterns of interaction. One member thought an initial exercise was probably unnecessary, and said he was pleasantly surprised at how amicably the members were able to work together on the Commission. But without skillful facilitation and thoughtful reflection, efforts like the ETMC run the risk of simply reinforcing entrenched patterns of discrimination, and can deny a voice to the full range of perceptions and positions. In effect, this could delay or even impede reconciliation.

Of course, to truly benefit from this tourism program, Tallahatchie County has to build a tourism infrastructure, including lodging and food options. Right now, the county is only positioned for pass-through tourism, as visitors will have to stay and eat in adjacent counties. Nearby Tunica County provides an example of how a county can go from little infrastructure to a multi-million dollar tourism industry; through the 1980s, Tunica was one of the poorest counties in the US, but today it is a major gaming destination, with hotels, restaurants, and other amenities. Civil rights tourism in Tallahatchie County will probably not be as significant a draw as gambling in Tunica, but Tallahatchie does have a unique heritage resource. With vision and collaboration Tallahatchie County can develop its own tourism-based industrial development, and in the process contribute to how Americans view the extension of civil rights to all citizens.

Conclusion

Tourism for reconciliation is a relatively new idea and a difficult undertaking. It requires a cohesive narrative that can be marketed to a target audience. More importantly, and thornier, reconciliation tourism requires a willingness to challenge people's perceptions and demand that people consider a civil rights perspective and a worldview that represents society's disenfranchised and marginalized members.

To do so, tourism planners, managers, and providers, as well as residents in the host area may have to ask themselves hard questions. In the process, though, both the story and the process of reconciliation can lead to a transformative sense of healing to accomplish what Freya Higgins-Desbiolles (2003) defines as the task of reconciliation tourism: "tourism healing divided societies!"

Overall, Tallahatchie County has initiated a tourism effort that should contribute to reconciliation in the global sense—they have the means to tell a compelling civil rights story representing the local perspective. People who visit Tallahatchie County can view first-hand the environment that both produced the Emmett Till verdict, and that has resulted from that case. The Commission's actions may also lead to reconciliation at the local level, which is equally important in conveying the narrative of Emmett Till's legacy. Both elements of reconciliation contribute to equity and social justice in the county and in the nation, and as such build the foundation for a sustainable tourism industry in the Mississippi Delta.

Acknowledgments

The authors thank the members of the Emmett Till Memorial Commission of Tallahatchie County, MS for graciously collaborating on this research. We appreciate the helpful comments from Katie Kerstetter, Deborah Moore and two anonymous reviewers on a previous draft. We thank Subu Swaminathan and the Delta State University Center for Interdisciplinary Geospatial Information Technologies for their assistance.

Notes

1. Michaels (2006) argues that attention to culture comes at the expense of structure. A focus on diverse identities ignores the real issue, economic inequality. We do not mean to detract from the importance of economic equality, but we view equality as multifaceted, involving more than just economics.
2. In alternative spring breaks, common at many American universities, students forego a week on the beach to engage in community development projects (Bermudez, 2008). The gap year, a concept more common in Europe than North America, refers to a year of travel between high school and college, and some "gappers" are finding time to work on community development projects in lieu of or while backpack touring through places like Southeast Asia or South America (Simpson, 2004).
3. On the USHMM's webpage (http://www.ushmm.org/museum/mission/), part of the description of the museum's mission is: "With unique power and authenticity, the Museum teaches millions of people each year about the dangers of unchecked hatred and the need to prevent genocide. And we encourage them to act, cultivating a sense of moral responsibility among our citizens so that they will respond to the monumental challenges that confront our world." This call to action exemplifies the transformative experience that the museum seeks to provide for visitors.
4. For more information on the Emmett Till case, see Beauchamp (2005), Beito & Beito (2004), Huie (1956), Popham (1955), Russell (2006), Segall & Holmberg (2003), Sparkman (2005), and Whitfield (1988).
5. About three months after the verdict was handed down in the Emmett Till murder, Rosa Parks refused to give up her seat on a Montgomery, Alabama bus, which led to an extended bus boycott by the city's African Americans. Mrs. Parks' actions have been widely recognized as sparking the civil rights movement, but Mrs. Parks also acknowledged that she was inspired by Emmett Till as she remained seated on the bus (Segall & Holmberg, 2003).
6. One complaint we did not hear, but that was common during the 1950s and even part of the strategy used by the defense lawyers during the Emmett Till trial, was that the NAACP and other outside groups were using the murder of Emmett Till as a way of undermining "the Southern way of life" (Popham, 1955). While some residents are concerned about the appearance of exploiting Emmett Till's personal tragedy, the

notion that outsiders are exploiting it for political gain does not seem to be a prevalent view in the county today.

7. The brochure can be viewed at http://www.etmctallahatchie.com/pages/et-brochure.htm
8. The text of the statement can be viewed at http://www.etmctallahatchie.com/pages/news-archives.htm

References

Adams, J., & Gorton, D. (2006). Confederate lane: Class, race and ethnicity in the Mississippi Delta. *American Ethnologist, 33*(2), 288–307.

Allman-Baldwin, L. (2006, July 20). Ebony escapes! On African American heritage tours. *New York Amsterdam News, 97*(30), pp. 24, 31.

Andrews, K.T. (1997). The impacts of social movements on the political process: The Civil Rights Movement and black electoral politics in Mississippi. *American Sociological Review, 62*(5), 800–819.

Asch, C.M. (2008). *The senator and the sharecropper: The freedom struggles of James O. Eastland and Fannie Lou Hamer*. New York: The New Press.

Associated Press. (2008, October 27). Vandals destroy sign marking Emmett Till murder site. *USA Today*. Retrieved November, 2008 from http://www.usatoday.com/news/nation/2008-10-27-emmett-till_N.htm

Austin, S.D.W. (2006). *The transformation of plantation politics: Black politics, concentrated poverty, and social capital in the Mississippi Delta*. Albany, NY: State University of New York Press.

Austin, S.W., & Middleton, R.T. (2006). Racial politics of casino gaming in the Delta: The case of Tunica County. In D. von Herrmann, *Resorting to casinos: The Mississippi gambling industry* (pp. 47–66). Jackson, MS: University Press of Mississippi.

Babbie, E. (1986). *Observing ourselves: Essays in social research*. Prospect Heights, IL: Waveland Press.

Barretta, S. (2009, March 2). Sonny Boy marker erected, Bronzeville blues, Blues Hall of Fame inductees announced. *Highway 61 Radio*. Retrieved March, 2009 from http://www.highway61radio.com/?p=1392

Barton, A.W. (2005). *Attitudes about heritage tourism in the Mississippi Delta: A policy report from the 2005 Delta Rural Poll*. Cleveland, MS: Center for Community and Economic Development, Delta State University.

Barton, A.W. (2007). *Visitation to heritage tourism sites by residents of the Mississippi Delta*. Cleveland, MS: Center for Community and Economic Development, Delta State University.

Beauchamp, K. (2005, February). The murder of Emmett Louis Till: The spark that started the Civil Rights Movement. *Black Collegian, 35*(2), 88–91. Retrieved March, 2008 from http://www.black-collegian.com/african/till2005-2nd.shtml

Beito, D.T., & Beito, L.R. (2004, April 26). Why it's unlikely the Emmett Till murder mystery will ever be solved. *George Mason University's History News Network*. Retrieved March, 2008 from http://hnn.us/articles/4853.html

Berg, B.L. (2004). *Qualitative research methods for the social sciences* (5th ed.). Boston, MA: Allyn and Bacon.

Bermudez, C. (2008). Working vacation. *Chronicle of Philanthropy, 20*(9), 1.

Brown, M.F. (2003). *Who owns native culture?* Cambridge, MA: Harvard University Press.

Carrier, J. (2004). *A traveler's guide to the Civil Rights Movement*. Orlando, FL: Harcourt, Inc.

Clifton, J., & Benson, A. (2006). Planning for sustainable ecotourism: The case for research ecotourism in developing country destinations. *Journal of Sustainable Tourism, 14*(3), 238–254.

Cobb, C.E., Jr. (2008). *On the road to freedom: A guided tour of the civil rights trail*. Chapel Hill, NC: Algonquin Books.

Cohen, E. (1988). Authenticity and commoditization in tourism. *Annals of Tourism Research, 15*(3), 371–386.

Collins-Kreiner, N. (2006). Graves as attractions: Pilgrimage-tourism to Jewish holy graves in Israel. *Journal of Cultural Geography, 24*(1), 67–89.

Dewan, S.K. (2004, August 10). Civil rights battlegrounds enter world of tourism. *New York Times*. Retrieved October, 2007 from http://www.nytimes.com/2004/08/10/us/civil-rights-battlegrounds-enter-world-of-tourism.html?sec=travel&&scp=1&sq=civil%20rights%20battlegrounds&st=cse

Eadington, W.R., & Smith, V.L. (1992). Introduction: The emergence of alternative forms of tourism. In V.L. Smith & W.R. Eadington (Eds.), *Tourism alternatives: Potentials and problems in the development of tourism* (pp. 1–14). Philadelphia: University of Pennsylvania Press.

Edelman, P. (2005). Where race meets class: The 21st century civil rights agenda. *Georgetown Journal on Poverty Law and Policy*, *12*(1), 1–12.

Edson, G. (2004). Heritage: Pride or passion, product or service? *International Journal of Heritage Studies*, *10*(4), 333–348.

Edwards, A.R. (2005). *The sustainability revolution: Portrait of a paradigm shift*. Gabriola Island, BC, Canada: New Society Publishers.

Ellis, C. (2003). When volunteers pay to take a trip with scientists—Participatory environmental research tourism (PERT). *Human Dimensions of Wildlife*, *8*(1), 75–80.

Fischer, M.A. (1989). The practice of community development. In J.A. Christensen & J.W. Robinson, Jr. (Eds.), *Community development in perspective* (pp. 136–158). Ames, IA: Iowa State University Press.

Flora, C.B., & Flora, J.L. (2008). *Rural communities: Legacy and change* (3rd ed.). Boulder, CO: Westview Press.

Frank, A.G. (1986). The development of underdevelopment. In P.F. Klaren & T.J. Bossert (Eds.), *Promise of development: Theories of change in Latin America* (pp. 111–123). Boulder, CO: Westview Press.

Gallardo, J.H., & Stein, T.V. (2007). Participation, power and racial representation: Negotiating nature-based and heritage tourism development in the rural South. *Society and Natural Resources*, *20*(7), 597–611.

Gatewood, J.B., & Cameron, C.M. (2004). Battlefield pilgrims at Gettysburg National Military Park. *Ethnology*, *43*(3), 193–216.

Gentleman, A. (2006, May 7). Slum tours: A day trip too far? *The Observer*. Retrieved January, 2009 from http://www.guardian.co.uk/travel/2006/may/07/delhi.india.ethicalliving/print

Grant, E. (2005). Race and tourism in America's first city. *Journal of Urban History*, *31*(6), 850–871.

Greene, J.C. (1990). Three views on the nature and role of knowledge in social science. In E.G. Guba (Ed.), *The paradigm dialog* (pp. 227–245). Newbury Park, CA: Sage Publications.

Hasty, J. (2002). Rites of passage, routes of redemption: Emancipation tourism and the wealth of culture. *Africa Today*, *49*(3), 46–76.

Haywood, K.M. (1988). Responsible and responsive tourism planning in the community. *Tourism Management*, *9*(2), 105–118.

Hemming, S.J. (1993). Camp Coorong—Combining race relations and cultural education. *Social Alternatives*, *12*(1), 37–40.

Higgins-Desbiolles, F. (2003). Reconciliation tourism: Tourism healing divided societies! *Tourism Recreation Research*, *28*(3), 35–44.

Higgins-Desbiolles, F. (2008). Justice tourism and alternative globalisation. *Journal of Sustainable Tourism*, *16*(3), 345–364.

Hill, M. (2007, December). The economic status of African-Americans in Mississippi. *Mississippi Economic Review and Outlook*, *21*(2). Retrieved February, 2008 from http://www.mississippi.edu/urc/economics.html

Hitchcock, M., & King, V.T. (2003). Discourses with the past: Tourism and heritage in South-East Asia. *Indonesia and the Malay World*, *31*(89), 3–15.

Howard, P. (2002). The eco-museum: Innovation that risks the future. *International Journal of Heritage Studies*, *8*(1), 63–72.

Huie, W.B. (1956, January 24). The shocking story of approved killing in Mississippi. *Look*, *20*(2), 46–50.

Jubera, D. (2007, October 2). Decades later, an apology: Once an icon of racism, town plans to say it's sorry near where Emmett Till's killers were freed. *Atlanta Journal Constitution*. Retrieved March, 2008 from http://www6.lexisnexis.com/publisher/EndUser?Action=User DisplayFullDocument&orgId=574&topicId=100020422&docId=l:678257167&start=15

Kelner, S. (2001). Narrative construction of authenticity in pilgrimage touring. Paper presented to the 96th annual meeting of the American Sociological Association, Anaheim, CA.

Kirtsoglou, E., & Theodossopoulos, D. (2004). 'They are taking our culture away': Tourism and culture commodification in the Garifuna community of Roatan. *Critique of Anthropology, 24*(2), 135–157.

Klein-Viehhauer, S. (2009). Framework model to assess leisure and tourism sustainability. *Journal of Cleaner Production, 17*(4), 447–454.

Lancaster, J. (2007, March). Next stop, squalor. *Smithsonian, 37*(12), 96–105. Retrieved January 2009 from http://www.smithsonianmag.com/people-places/squalor.html

Lang, C. (2004). Between civil rights and black power in the Gateway City: The Action Committee to Improve Opportunities for Negroes (ACTION), 1964–75. *Journal of Social History, 37*(3), 725–754.

Malkin, R. (1999, July/August). The pioneers. *The UNESCO courier, 52*(7), 24–25. Retrieved February, 2009 from http://www.unesco.org/courier/1999_08/uk/somm/intro.htm

Markey, E. (2007, July 20). Tourism with a conscience. *National Catholic Reporter, 43*(32), 12.

McIntosh, A.J., & Zahra, A. (2007). A cultural encounter through volunteer tourism: Towards the ideals of sustainable tourism? *Journal of Sustainable Tourism, 15*(5), 541–556.

Michaels, W.B. (2006). *The trouble with diversity: How we learned to love identity and ignore inequality*. New York: Metropolitan Books/Henry Holt and Company.

Miles, M.B., & Huberman, A.M. (1994). *Qualitative data analysis: An expanded sourcebook* (2nd ed.). Thousand Oaks, CA: Sage Publications.

Mississippi Department of Archives and History. (2009). *Review board makes Nat'l Register recommendations*. Retrieved January, 2009 from http://mdah.state.ms.us/admin/news/preservation.html

Moore, S., & Jie Wen, J. (2009). Tourism employment in China: A look at gender equity, equality, and responsibility. *Journal of Human Resources in Hospitality & Tourism, 8*(1), 32–42.

Murphy, P.E., & Andressen, B. (1988). Tourism development on Vancouver Island: An assessment of the core-periphery model. *Professional Geographer, 40*(1), 32–42.

National Agricultural Library. (2008). *Promoting tourism in rural America*. Baltimore, MD: National Agricultural Library, Agricultural Research Service, U. S. Department of Agriculture. Retrieved February, 2009 from http://www.nal.usda.gov/ric/ricpubs/tourism.html#tourismdevelopment

Parker, S. (2001, June 20). African American's heritage set in stone. *Christian Science Monitor*. Retrieved March, 2009 from http://www.csmonitor.com/2001/0620/p3s1.html?s=widep

Patton, M.Q. (1990). *Qualitative evaluation and research methods* (2nd ed.). Newbury Park, CA: Sage Publications.

Pearce, D.G. (1992). Alternative tourism: Concepts, classifications, and questions. In V.L. Smith & W.R. Eadington (Eds.), *Tourism alternatives: Potentials and problems in the development of tourism* (pp. 15–30). Philadelphia: University of Pennsylvania Press.

Pierre, J. (2009). Beyond heritage tourism: Race and the politics of African-diasporic interactions. *Social Text, 27*(1), 59–81.

Popescu, R. (2007, October 15). A boom in 'poorism.' *Newsweek, 150*(16), 12. Retrieved February, 2009 from http://www.newsweek.com/id/42482

Popham, J.N. (1955, September 23). Mississippi jury acquits 2 accused in youth's killing. *New York Times*. Retrieved March, 2008 from http://www.nytimes.com/packages/pdf/magazine/till4.pdf

Porter, B.W., & Salazar, N.B. (2005). Heritage tourism, conflict, and the public interest: An introduction. *International Journal of Heritage Studies, 11*(5), 361–370.

Povoledo, E. (2008, September 7). Searching for the roots of a deep faith. *New York Times*. Retrieved September, 2008 from http://www.nytimes.com/2008/09/07/travel/07journeys.html

President's Committee on the Arts and the Humanities. (2005). *A position paper on cultural heritage tourism in the United States.* Washington, DC: U.S. Department of Commerce. Retrieved February, 2009 from http://www.pcah.gov/pdf/05WhitePaperCultHerit Tourism.pdf

Ragin, C.C. (1994). *Constructing social research: The unity and diversity of method.* Thousand Oaks, CA: Pine Forge Press.

Rao, K. (2009, March 11). 'Slumdog' success calls attention to tours in Mumbai. *New York Times.* Retrieved March, 2009 from http://globespotters.blogs.nytimes.com/2009/03/11/slumdog-success-spawns-tours-in-mumbai/?scp=2&sq=slumdog%20tours&st=cse

Raymond, E.M., & Hall, C.M. (2008). The development of cross-cultural (mis)understanding through volunteer tourism. *Journal of Sustainable Tourism, 16*(5), 530–543.

Richards, G., & Hall, D. (2000). The community: A sustainable concept in tourism development? In G. Richards & D. Hall (Eds.), *Tourism and sustainable community development* (pp. 1–14). London: Routledge.

Robinson, M. (1999, July/August). Is cultural tourism on the right track? *The UNESCO courier.* Retrieved February, 2009 from http://www.unesco.org/courier/1999_08/uk/somm/intro.htm

Robinson, M. (2000). Collaboration and cultural consent: Refocusing sustainable tourism. In B. Bramwell & B. Lane (Eds.), *Tourism collaboration and partnerships: Politics, practices and sustainability* (pp. 295–313). Clevedon, UK: Channel View Publications.

Russell, M.M. (2006, Spring). Justice delayed: Reopening the Emmett Till case. *Santa Clara Magazine.* Retrieved March, 2008 from http://www.scu.edu/scm/spring2006/justice.cfm

Scheyvens, R., & Momsen, J.H. (2008). Tourism and poverty reduction: Issues for small island states. *Tourism Geographies, 10*(1), 22–41.

Schultz, M. (2007). *The rural face of white supremacy: Beyond Jim Crow.* Urbana, IL: University of Illinois Press.

Segall, R., & Holmberg, D. (2003, February 3). Who killed Emmett Till? *The Nation.* Retrieved March, 2008 from http://www.thenation.com/doc/20030203/segal

Sharpley, R. (2001). Tourism in Cyprus: Challenges and opportunities. *Tourism Geographies, 3*(1), 64–86.

Silver, I. (1993). Marketing authenticity in Third World Countries. *Annals of Tourism Research, 20,* 302–318.

Simpson, K. (2004). 'Doing development': The gap year, volunteer-tourists and a popular practice of development. *Journal of International Development, 16*(5), 681–692.

Sparkman, R. (2005, June 21). The murder of Emmett Till: The 49-year-old story of the crime and how it came to be told. *Slate.* Retrieved March, 2008 from http://www.slate.com/toolbar.aspx?action=print&id=2120788

Thomas, P. (2009). The trouble with travel. *Geographical, 81*(2), 50–52.

US Census Bureau. (2009a). *Mississippi: Population of counties by decennial census: 1900 to 1990.* Retrieved February, 2009 from http://www.census.gov/population/cencounts/ms190090.txt

US Census Bureau. (2009b). *County quickFacts: Tallahatchie County, Mississippi.* Retrieved February, 2009 from http://quickfacts.census.gov/qfd/states/28/28135.html

US Census Bureau. (2009c). American Factfinder: Glendora Village, Mississippi. Retrieved March, 2009 from http://factfinder.census.gov/servlet/SAFFFacts?_event=Search&geo_id=&_geoContext=&_street=&_county=glendora&_cityTown=glendora&_state=04000 US28&_zip=&_lang=en&_sse=on&pctxt=fph&pgsl=010&show_2003_tab=&redirect=Y

US Commission on Civil Rights. (2001). *Racial and ethnic tensions in American communities: Poverty, inequality, and discrimination—Volume VII: The Mississippi Delta report.* Washington, DC: U.S. Commission on Civil Rights. Retrieved May, 2004 from http://www.usccr.gov/pubs/msdelta/pref.htm

Weiner, E. (2008, March 9). Slum visits: Tourism or voyeurism? *New York Times.* Retrieved March, 2008 from http://www.nytimes.com/2008/03/09/travel/09heads.html?_r=1&scp=1&sq=slum%20visits&st=cse

Whitfield, S.J. (1988). *A death in the Delta: The story of Emmett Till.* Baltimore, MD: Johns Hopkins University Press.

Woods, M. (2000). *Diversifying the rural economy: Tourism development.* Mississippi State, MS: Southern Rural Development Center. Retrieved February, 2009 from http://srdc.msstate.edu/publications/woods.pdf

World Commission on Environment and Development. (1987). *Our common future*. New York: Oxford University Press.

World Travel & Tourism Council. (2008). *World Travel & Tourism Council: Progress and priorities, 2008/09*. London, UK: WTTC. Retrieved February, 2009 from http://www.wttc.org/bin/pdf/original_pdf_file/progress_and_priorities_2008.pdf

Yin, R.K. (1984). *Case study research: Design and methods*. Beverly Hills, CA: Sage Publications.

An exploratory analysis of factors mediating community participation outcomes in tourism

Sherma Roberts

Department of Management Studies, The University of the West Indies, Cave Hill Campus, Barbados

It is now widely acknowledged in the contemporary tourism literature that community participation is crucial to sustainable tourism development, the latter of which emphasizes local participation in the decision-making process. The rationale for resident involvement is that it helps minimize the negative social impacts of tourism development, it increases the level of buy-in into tourism projects and it creates an environment for the host community to receive optimal benefits from the industry. These assumptions have been challenged based upon the heterogeneous nature of communities and the power differentials in participation which can often undermine expected beneficial outcomes. While acknowledgment of these issues is crucial to any discussion on community participation initiatives and outcomes, this paper argues that there are other factors that mediate the extent to which communities are able to access the benefits of community participation initiatives. These factors have been identified in this study as clear and consensual objectives, sustained interest and institutional support. The study was conducted using interviews and a focus group among residents of a small community on the island of Tobago.

Introduction

The seminal work of Peter Murphy (1985)—*Tourism: A community approach* provided the impetus for tourism policy makers and academics to begin to consider the involvement of local residents in the decision-making process related to tourism development planning. Murphy's argument for this approach to tourism planning was based upon an explicit recognition that experts cannot judge the perception, preferences and priorities of residents, and that those most affected by tourism should have a say in how it evolves. Some have even gone further, arguing that a tourism industry that ignores community input can lead to soured host-tourist encounters and the eventual decline of tourism in the destination (Haywood, 1988; Zhang, Inbakaran, & Jackson, 2006). For many developing countries whose economies are premised upon the profitability of the tourism industry and by extension amicable relations between visitor and resident, this observation is crucial.

In fact, Doxey's Irridex (Swarbrooke, 1999) proposes that host-guest encounters can move from euphoria to outright antagonism if not well managed. One way of ensuring a positive visitor experience and the sharing of equitable benefits among all stakeholders is for the local community to share in the decision-making process.

This approach to community involvement in tourism decision-making has been further legitimised by the introduction and broad acceptance of the Brundtland Report and later by Local Agenda 21 (Baker, 2006; World Commission on Environment and Development, 1987) which stresses that development must be sustainable if the livelihoods of future generations are to be safeguarded. Sustainable tourism development has therefore emphasised and encouraged local involvement in the planning process, and the ability of communities to help shape their future (Choi & Sirakaya, 2006; Hall & Jenkins, 1995; Santhanam, 1993; World Tourism Organisation [WTO], 1996). From the early 1990s, community participation was seen as a critical tool in tourism development planning, the approach was regarded as more sustainable and more democratic than the traditional top-down, often exploitative and externally imposed tourism planning.

While acknowledging the *potential* of this new approach to transform tourism planning, the assumption that "equitable involvement" would lead to "equitable benefits" has not gone unchallenged (Blackstock, 2005; Haywood, 1988; Joppe, 1996; Taylor, 1995; Tosun, 2000). The reasons for this chasm have centered around two main ideas, one being the political nature of participation and the other, the heterogeneous nature of communities (Hall & Jenkins, 1995; Haywood, 1988; Joppe, 1996). Tosun (2000) adds to this debate, albeit in a polemical fashion and using secondary sources, by identifying operational, structural, and cultural factors that can undermine participation outcomes particularly in developing countries. It is now agreed that an understanding of the politics of participation and the contradictions of community are critical to any discussion on community participation; however, this paper seeks to explore in more detail, specific micro factors that can impact upon participation outcomes. Moreover, the paper builds upon Tosun's (2000) more conceptual work, by looking empirically at a community participation initiative within the context of a developing country. The paper considers three factors including clear and consensual objectives, sustained interest and institutional support and the way they inadvertently mediated outcomes of this particular tourism community participation initiatives. The ensuing discussion considers some of the main narratives related to community participation in tourism; a further literature review will focus on the factors under consideration; the study context and methodology will then be briefly discussed. The paper ends by examining the findings of the case and proposing some recommendations for policy and research.

Community participation in tourism

As indicated above, local, bottom- up approaches to tourism planning were articulated by Agenda 21 for the Travel and Tourism Industry (WTO, 1996) and embraced by tourism researchers and practitioners. However, its neglect of the political nature of participation as impacting upon participation outcomes has been widely challenged (Blackstock, 2005; Doorne, 1998; Keogh, 1990; Tosun, 2000). In highlighting the politics of participation, Joppe, (1996) points to instances where well-resourced developers align themselves with the political directorate and certain interest groups that are supportive of the development in order to claim "community support" or even consultation. Case studies undertaken by Wyllie (1998) and Doorne (1998) support the argument. For example, Doorne (1998) shows how subtle questionnaire biases were used to support a pro-development agenda when residents felt that their views were being genuinely sought. Thus, the processes and the outcomes of consultation may therefore serve to entrench the powerful position of some stakeholders, often the local elite (Willis, 1995) rather than lead to shared decision-making, new social bargaining tables and equitable benefits.

Arnstein (1969) argues that any consideration of public or community participation cannot neglect that it is a fundamentally political process. She contends that there is a critical difference between going through the empty ritual of participation and having the real power needed to affect the outcome of the process. To demonstrate that there are "genres of participation" Arnstein developed an eight rung ladder of citizen participation moving through three stages from non-participation through degrees of tokenism and then to degrees of citizen empowerment—as one goes further up the ladder, real power in terms of ability to influence decisions increases. Midgley (1986) also emphasizes the centrality of power in public participation and produces a framework of analysis that examines structured versus unstructured, authentic versus pseudo, and sanctioned versus independent participation.

Within tourism, the politics of community participation and its attendant outcomes is exacerbated by the reality that communities are not homogenous but are made up of individuals and organizations who may have different values, aims and objectives (Fagence, 1977; Joppe, 1996; Midgley, 1986). In this regard, typologies of tourism communities have been developed to highlight the disparate interests of various groups within a geographical bounded community and to demonstrate that participation outcomes may often not reflect the interests of the majority. Madrigal (1994) identified three types of community clusters comprising "tourism realists, haters and lovers." According to him these groupings can occur as a result of the perception in the disparity of economic benefits or in other words "others get the benefit, not me." Similarly, Ryan and Montgomery (1994) proposed a community typology based upon "enthusiasts, sceptics and the non-committed." Discussions about the community dynamic are further complicated by the fact that those who appear to gain most or have their voices heard may not actually be part of the community. They may be "offcomers" or strangers who import qualities and have positional power (Blackstock, 2005; Taylor, 1995; Taylor & Davis, 1997) both of which are used in ensuring that they get the outcomes that they desire.

The typologies and cases presented above are a clear recognition that "community" is a complex notion; with communities often clustering beyond their municipalities or geographical boundaries based on their assessment of the value of working together. In this regard, the term "community" has been contextualized or defined in a variety of ways. The sociologist Bernard (1973 cited in Milne, 1998, p. 40) distinguishes between "the community" which is an aggregation of people at a particular locale and "community" which is characterised by social interaction, intimacy, moral commitments, cohesion and continuity through time. Rotham et al. (1995 cited in Telfer & Sharpley, 2008, p. 116) view "community as a territorial organization of people, goods and services, and commitments that are important subsystems of society where locally relevant functions occur." Milne (1998) puts a different complexion on the debate by noting that advancements in technology may also have the impact of redefining community beyond spatial boundaries. According to him,

> [...] the earth is being criss-crossed afresh by invisible threads uniting individuals who differ by all conventional criteria, but who are finding that they have aspirations in common. (Milne 1998, p.40)

Indeed, this proposition challenges the traditional conceptual foundations of "community" and even the value and significance of protocols such as LA21, so that one would need to concur that geographical boundaries may not necessarily be the glue which keeps individuals feeling part of the same cohesive community. Still, as Hillery (1955) and Urry (1995) submit, most definitions identify three current threads that can be used to provide a conceptual frame for "community." One is the geographical boundaries of a community. Two, is a sense of social organization connecting people and institutions and three, the existence of some level of social interaction implying a sense of belonging and personal ties. It is these characteristics of community that form the definitional basis for the discussion in this paper.

While the concept of genuine community participation in tourism has been challenged based upon its inherent assumption that all communities, whether located in developed or developing countries, are the same in terms of composition, values and interests, and that there is a pluralistic allocation of power within a community which will allow for equity in decision-making and equity in benefits, the discussion needs to be taken further to examine how these and other factors impact upon participation outcomes. After all, the expected result of any community participation initiative is not shared decision-making but that expected outcomes or benefits accrue to all stakeholders. The following considers how some of these factors—clear and consensual objectives, sustained interest, and institutional support—can exacerbate or improve participation outcomes, such that residents feel that they are either being taken for granted or being given an opportunity to shape their destiny.

Clear and consensual objectives

Sanoff (1992) stresses that it is important for community groups to articulate a clear vision from the start as a failure to do so can impede progress and undermine anticipated outcomes. Thus, planning for a successful participation program involves a great deal of thought and analysis prior to the first public meeting. Issues such as what do we expect out of participation; what are the objectives of the specific participation initiative is it to – generate ideas, identify attitudes, disseminate information, resolve conflict, determine costs and benefits – need to be identified and agreed upon by the stakeholders (Sanoff, 1992). The premise of this approach is that when participation goals and objectives are not clearly identified and articulated at the onset, and realistic objectives are not made clear, participants will have different expectations of what the exercise is to achieve. For example, Reed (1997) shows how the development of a tourism plan in Squamish Canada, was protracted as a result of power relations and competing objectives and expectations. The heterogeneous community will seldom allow for unanimity in setting objectives; neither does clarity of objectives mean that the participation process will not be railroaded and expected outcomes not achieved because of internal and external occurrences as Parker (2000) demonstrates in the case of Bonaire. However, what both cases (Bonaire and Squamish) reveal is that once residents coalesce around particular objectives fairly early in the process, some favorable outcomes are possible (Ritchie, 1993). The importance of setting clear objectives must be juxtaposed against the fact that the convenors of power are "likely to be purposeful, goal-oriented actors that use their power to their own purposes" (Reed, 1997, p. 589).

Sustained interest

The question of continuous participation possibly presents a big challenge for the type of outcomes that communities receive. According to Goodwin (1998) apathy, non-participation or participation attrition arises where there is uncertainty over the motives of organisations in participatory initiatives to address what *residents* consider to be the "real" issues. In this regard, people perceive their participation as a cost to themselves with no anticipation of their involvement being rewarded. As a result many residents choose neither to speak out nor participate. Thus, where there is poverty of expectations *coupled with* mistrust of the authoritative organisation, residents either withdraw or fail to participate. For this reason Lankford, Knowles-Lankford, and Povey (1996, p. 330) conclude that "critical to achieving high levels of participation is the creation of an environment where stakeholders believe that they have a stake in the course of events and that their participation can effect the course of events." O'Riordan (1977) however sees the process of attrition as an endemic feature of participation noting that only the devoted "hard core" will remain. With respect to participation initiatives in developing countries Tosun (2000) attributes high attrition to the fact that the poor are often preoccupied with "bread and butter" issues and do not have the luxury of time to attend meetings over a prolonged period, especially in the absence of incentives to participate. It is unquestionable that community participation is very time consuming for all parties involved and while according to some authors (Mowforth, Charlton, & Munt, 2008; Sewell & Coppock, 1977) there may be no correlation between high levels of participation and positive outcomes, the interests of the community cannot be well represented, if its residents are absent or are represented by only a few.

Institutional support

The literature suggests that governments are critical to the survival of the tourism industry (Elliott, 1997) and they alone can provide the institutional framework for participatory tourism planning (Hall & Jenkins, 1995). In this regard, Bates and Linder-Pelz (1987, cited in Willis, 1995) suggest that there are two factors necessary for ensuring favorable participation outcomes. One is that the government must be fully committed (both at the political and administrative levels) to ensuring that community participation in tourism planning is not merely a window-dressing exercise; and two, that there must be a belief that participation or the addition of other, often non-expert voices would lead to improvements. For communities located in peripheral spaces and developing countries, the need to create meaningful institutional support is even more crucial since local capacity in terms of knowledge and resources may be minimal or absent. This issue is highlighted in Cole's (2006) work on communities in East Indonesia where community benefits were stymied by the Department of Tourism's failure to provide the community with adequate training and information which would have prepared them to at least "bridge the gap between local and expert understandings" (Goodwin, 1998, p. 7).

Desai (1995, p. 40 cited in Tosun 2000, p. 619) suggests that the reason for this lies in the "lack of political will to implement participation because of the implications for the distribution of power and resources." Added to that, is the time taken in reaching a decision, which inevitably increases the costs of planning. What often therefore emerges is what Arnstein (1969) refers to as non-participation and Midgley (1986) labels manipulative or incremental modes of government involvement in participation where communities are not given any real power to change or influence the decision-making process (non-participation and tokenism). Rather, the process is seen as a political weapon (manipulative) or given official support but with a level of ambivalence that would ensure poor outcomes or failure (incremental).

Study context

The Lowlands community is located on the island of Tobago, the smaller of the unitary state of Trinidad and Tobago. The primarily service led economy of Tobago has a population of about 55,000 (http://www.cso.gov.tt, Central Statistical Office of Trinidad and Tobago, 2008) with tourism accounting for 56.8% of the island's employment and 39% of overall Gross Domestic Product (WTTC, 2005). Over the last three decades the island has experienced modest growth in its stay over and cruise arrivals and a notable increase in its room stock. To date the biggest development on the island has been a 750 acre five-star resort owned by Tobago Seaside Limited (TSL).[1] The resort, located in Lowlands on what was once a coconut estate, began construction in late 1998 and opened in November 2000.

The community participation initiative between the developers and the community was kick-started by a community activist who felt that the community was being disadvantaged and marginalized by TSL. The "call" for the first meeting was done through house visits, information pamphlets and broadcasting via a public address system and was intended to mobilize and organise the community into a formal entity, so that they could identify collectively the problems affecting them as a result of the construction of the resort. It was at this first meeting held in February 1999 that the Lowlands Community Action Group (LCAG) was formed and a Committee comprising of a President, Vice President, Secretary and Treasurer was elected. With the exception of the Treasurer, representation on this Committee was biased in favor of older residents, those who considered themselves "true Lowlanders." Subsequent to this first meeting where only residents of the community were in attendance, there were approximately 10 other meetings held on the second Thursday of every month—the schedule presumably agreed by TSL and the LCAG Committee. In attendance at some of these meetings were the local government representatives of the Tobago House of Assembly (the body responsible for the internal affairs of Tobago albeit with limited power) and the Public Relations Officer of TSL. At the initial consultation, the agenda seemed to be largely set by the Committee of the LCAG rather than by joint consultation; however the balance of power shifted once the developer and the government representatives understood the interests and needs of the community. Maximum attendance at meetings totaled 42 residents with the attendance fluctuating over the course of the consultation.

The Lowlands community exhibits some complexities in terms of its social and physical (geographical) structure, which may have affected the level of participation at the public consultation meetings. Physically, the community is divided into two parts by a highway. On the Eastern side are the people that have lived in Lowlands for over 30 years with the exception of a few newcomers. Most of the "Easterners" are retired public servants, some with adult children who no longer reside in the community. Their homes are situated directly opposite the Tobago Seaside Development (TSL) and were therefore the most affected by dust, bad roads and noise pollution from the construction. On the Western side, are the newcomers, who have been living in Lowlands for under 15 years; again with a few exceptions. The "Westerners" comprise mostly working class people with school-aged children; who had bought land from a developer in the late 1980s and have now built homes and relocated to Lowlands from other parts of Tobago. There is also another much smaller group in the community regarded mostly as transients or temporary residents who are for the most part working on construction sites or have other short-term employment.

Methodology

This study was conducted in March 2000 and utilized a combination of qualitative research techniques including semi-structured interviews and a focus group (Roberts, 2000). These methods were chosen because unlike quantitative techniques, they provide the space for the interviewees to articulate their perceptions, feelings and understanding (Sekeran, 2000) concerning the factors they felt impacted upon the outcomes of the community participation initiative, while still allowing the researcher to cover the issues of interest to the enquiry. The research was carried out in three stages; stage one included interviews with residents, stage two included interviews with officials of TSL and the Tobago House of Assembly who were involved in the consultation and the final stage included a focus group with the Executive Committee of the Lowland Community Action Group (LCAG). This approach borrows from Babbie (1998) who advises that obtaining official views first can have the effect of influencing researcher bias. Critical to the success of this staged approach to data collection, was the LCAG Executive Committee and in particular the President, who provided the researcher with access to the community both in terms of the use of the register of attendance and the use of her name to get residents to share their experience and views.

A total of 22 interviews were conducted with residents of the Lowlands community, 17 with residents who attended the meeting and consented to be interviewed and five with residents who did not attend the meeting and volunteered to be interviewed. Two elite interviews were also conducted—one with two officials of TSL and the other with the Secretary for Tourism of the THA respectively. The labeling of these interviews as elite is underpinned by the fact that these individuals were well-informed with regards to the development and were influential in facilitating the consultation as well as its outcomes. In other words, these respondents may be considered corporate and political elites based upon their position relative to the residents. While access to the TSL officers was fairly easy, access to the Secretary of Tourism had to be negotiated using the researcher's institutional affiliation and positioning the research in such a way that it appeared relevant and non-threatening. A focus group was also conducted with the Executive of the LCAG to garner their views on the consultation process and outcomes and to understand their role in the initiative. The Executive was quite cooperative although the researcher had to deliberately manage the session as it could have been easily dominated by the President or descend into the Executive probing the researcher to find out what were residents' perspectives on the initiative. Analysis of the data used thematic analysis where similar and recurrent words and phrases are indexed and coded and then grouped into smaller categories reflective of the patterns or themes which emerge (Collis & Hussey, 2003). The themes in this study related to factors impacting upon participation outcomes. The findings and discussion considers the demographic of the resident participants, their expectations and the outcomes of the consultation between TSL and the Lowlands community. The factors mediating the outcomes will be examined and discussed.

Findings and discussion

The majority of the participants at the consultation were those who had been living in the community for over 15 years. This is also the case with those who attended the meeting and consented to the interview. These individuals consider themselves as the "true Lowlanders," and feel that they are the ones who know what is best for the community and by extension, have the right to speak on its behalf. Those who did not attend any of the consultations reported that they did not know about them, did not feel a genuine member of the community, did not need a job, were not interested or viewed TSL as insincere. It is noteworthy that these individuals had been residents of the community for either less than five years or between 5–10 years. Although the size of the interview sample is too small for a specific analysis of class to be made, the diversity of opinions expressed in the interviews suggest that there is some underlying tension that is class-based. In terms of participant demographic, only one participant was from the 16–25 age group. The remainder of participants were either between 33–55 or retired public servants (see Table 1 for a profile of residents interviewed). At least three of the residents interviewed attributed the absence of the young people at the consultation to a lack of community youth leadership and the composition of the Executive Committee of the LCAG—none of whom were in the 16–25 age group. As one interviewee commented "it takes youth to draw youth." The failure of the young people to participate in the consultation seemed also to have been a source of frustration for many of the older participants who felt that they were negotiating for jobs for a constituent that were at best apathetic.

The list of concerns put forward by the residents can perhaps best be categorized into short term and long term or more sustainable concerns. The short term concerns related to the bad conditions of the roads caused by the frequency of use by trucks; dangerous driving by the truckers; dust levels and 24 hour noise pollution due to construction. The more long term "wish list" coalesced around employment; training for employment in the hotel; access to the beach that was once a recreation area for the youth of Lowlands; environmental protection; fostering of a partnership with TSL; development of a recreational/sports facility.

Expectations that their concerns would be addressed were given legitimacy when at one of the initial meetings; TSL was quoted as saying they were going "to adopt the Lowlands Community." The text of the announcement included some of the more sustainable objectives of the community, for example, employment for residents, hospitality training and the development of a recreational space for the community. However, what resulted in the end was a chasm between the community's expectations and participation outcomes. The Public Relations Officer of TSL admitting during the interview that while promises of first preference for jobs and training in hospitality services (she refered to it as an Apprenticeship Program)

Table 1. Profile of residents interviewed.

Code	Gender	Length of residence (years)	Occupation	Participated***
1	M	>20	Retired local	Y
2	M	>20	Retired local	Y
3	F	<5	Retired expatriate	N
4	F	>20	Retired local	Y
5	M	>20	Public servant	Y
6	F	>20	Public servant	Y
7	M	>20	Self-employed	Y
8	F	>20	Professional	Y
9	M	10–20	Public servant	Y
10	F	10–20	Housewife/husband	Y
11	F	<5	Retired local	Y
12	M	10–20	Self-employed	Y
13	F	10–20	Professional	Y
14	M	10–20	Self-employed	Y
15	F	5–10	Professional	Y
16	M	<5	Professional	N
17	M	<5	Retired expatriate	N
18	M	>20	Public servant	Y
19	F	5–10	Housewife/husband	N
20	F	10–20	Self-employed	N
21	F	>20	Retired local	Y
22	F	10–20	Student	Y

Notes: Participated***: Y – attended 1 or more meetings, N – attended no meetings.
Source: adopted and modified from Wilson (1999).

had been made, the organization was unable to deliver. According to her, TSL's conventional interpretation of "adopting the community" is the provision of cash donations, assisting schools in repairs and other outreach programs, and lecturing the community on the benefits of tourism.

Another expectation that residents had, particularly men, was that TSL would give some firm commitment to the use of the beach area—traditionally used for bathing, fishing and hunting crabs—but was now rendered inaccessible to residents due to the development. According to one respondent, "this (beach access) is now a very sore point in Tobago where foreign concerns are fencing off hitherto used beaches from locals. TSL is another one (foreign concern limiting access). They skirted around the issue and up to now have not given any word to residents about it."

At the end of the consultation, Tobago Seaside Limited did not deliver on its promise for training, did not give preference to the residents of Lowlands in terms of employment opportunities, provided only temporary reprieve in terms of road fixing, speeding trucks and dust control, and still had the beach cordoned off by a chain-link fence, thus denying residents any access. The factors that mediated these largely unfavorable outcomes will be discussed in the following section.

Clear and consensual objectives

The list of concerns presented to TSL reflected that of individual households or a segment of the community rather than a consensus position of the community. For example, some households shared common concerns given their proximity to the construction site of the development. What was therefore put before TSL as a common agenda of community concerns was in fact an itemization of individual or faction requests. Not surprisingly, when residents on the Eastern side found that the dust and emissions problems were not being dealt with quickly enough by the developers, they resorted to blocking the roads as a form of protest. The result was that the LCAG quickly segregated into two camps: Easterners versus Westerners, where the latter felt that this action was not necessary—even though they were not directly affected by the development but had expressed solidarity over the need to have the environmental impacts mitigated. Three of the participants from the Eastern side strongly felt that their plight was not properly represented by the Committee members and the solidarity expressed by their fellow residents was not translating into action. One resident commented that this unwillingness to side with them in protest was because two of the Committee members were getting what was considered "the lion's share" from TSL in the form of property rental and key positions in the company. Notwithstanding, one of the short-lived outcomes of the protest was that TSL had arranged for the potholes in the roads to be filled and the road surface to be wet twice per day, thus temporarily alleviating the dust problem. In addition, the truckers were instructed to use an alternative route which was monitored by the police to curb speeding. These measures were not lasting and according to one interviewee "things reverted to normal."

Another manifestation of the divided community interests and agendas was that after some residents obtained some relief, albeit temporary, they stopped attending the meetings. In one resident's words, "they [residents] preferred temporary relief rather than permanent gain." This statement raises the question of genuine commitment to improving the community and realizing some of the long-term objectives from the initiative. Philosophically, many of the residents who were directly affected understood that tourism development provides employment and other indirect benefits but they have no need for these jobs as many are retired with adult kids. Not surprisingly, their focus of attention was on solving the problems that disrupted their daily lives rather than working towards shared community benefits.

The failure of the LCAG to find consensus and articulate clear objectives at their initial meeting resulted in temporary relief of short term concerns and non-realization of long term goals such as employment, training etc. One resident suggested that this failure may be due in part to the Executive Committee's lack of understanding of the preparation and process of consultations; therefore, they went into the initiative thinking that once issues were identified and presented in a formal setting, there would be some favorable outcomes. What was not anticipated were the fractured and variegated interests developing within the community, such that individuals' needs superseded any form of shared community vision (Prentice, 1993). When asked for reasons why the community did not achieve its goals, at least 10 residents responded that it was because the meetings in general were lacking in focus. What is instructive here is that despite most residents including the Committee members, being concerned about the same things to varying degrees, in a congregated forum they were unable to articulate how they were going to bargain with TSL to achieve these aims. Thus, according to these residents "the same things were being said over and over again." Moreover, some of these residents reported that local opinion was dominated by the views of key and professional figures within the community. One resident attributed the failure of the group to achieve more tangible community outcomes to the age and inexperience of the group. To a large extent this assessment may be correct. What transpired however is that TSL's Public Relations Officer translated the competing interests among residents as "the people of the community do not know what they want" and dismissed the group as disorganized opportunists.

Sustained interest

The lack of sustained interest among many residents meant that the lobby to secure the long term outcomes of the consultation was severely reduced. Of the 17 residents who attended the consultation, four attended only once, five at least three times and the remainder attending most of the times, with intermittent absences. The most common answers to "why did you stop attending the meetings?" were that expectations were not met, other commitments, sense of being unable to influence outcomes, and inadequate and untimely dissemination of information. Significantly all the persons who did not participate and were interviewed stated that an inability to influence outcome was their main reason for not attending the meetings. Thus, whilst non-participation may be interpreted as apathy or even ignorance, it could also be regarded as residents' skepticism of participatory initiatives that do not address the "real" issues. In this regard, people perceive their participation as a cost to themselves with no anticipation of their involvement being rewarded (Goodwin, 1998). As a result many residents chose neither to speak out nor participate. Thus, where there is a poverty of expectations and mistrust of the authoritative organization, residents either withdraw or fail to participate. These responses reveal in part that people's receptiveness and response to information is shaped by their sense of agency, that is, the feeling that they can make some real difference to the outcome (Goodwin, 1998; Lankford et al., 1996).

Time to participate coupled with inadequate and untimely dissemination of information also led interviewees to abandon attendance at the meetings. All residents interviewed reported that they heard about the initial meeting from the radio, via flyer or by word of mouth, but information concerning the time andvenue of subsequent meetings seemed to have been vicariously distributed. The Secretary of the LCAG felt strongly that TSL could have provided some sort of incentive for the community to be active and devoted participants. This view is supported by O'Riordan (1977) who believes that in the absence of incentives to encourage participation only a few people will be mobilized to play their part.

It may be a moot point to say that participation requires the involvement of people to be successful. The results indicate that over 50% of the interviewees (less than nine) dropped out between the first and the fourth meeting either because their problems were solved or because of disillusionment. It is contended that the realization of long-term goals requires commitment to the participatory process. While it is not a measurement that the participation process will be successful, commitment can serve as an indicator to the other party that the community "means business." Continuous participation rests on indications that some useful purpose is being served. Members of the community involved in planning need to feel that they are participating in something that is likely to have tangible results. When such confidence declines so also does the motivation for involvement (Sewell & Coppock, 1977). Indeed, many of the participants felt that TSL was "mamaguying" (Tobago dialect for making false promises) the residents so that they chose not to go to the meetings after a while. In particular the issues of access to the beach and preferential employment were identified as "pacifying tactics" which never materialized.

Institutional support

At least eight of the residents interviewed believed that one of the factors that affected the outcomes was the neglect by the Tobago House of Assembly (THA) to properly educate and equip the residents prior to the start of the Development. Most felt that the THA should have held information workshops on the ways in which the community could successfully negotiate with TSL to ensure that their concerns were met with more action. According to one resident, even though members of the THA attended some of the meetings, it seemed as if the agenda was to put residents against TSL rather than assist residents during the meetings.

Interviews with TSL's representative and the Secretary for Tourism also revealed that there was indeed some underlying (or perhaps overt) disagreement between these two parties. The former conceded during the interview that the Assembly is too parochial in view and territorial in operation; meaning that they (the THA) wanted to have some control over the development rather than have the decision to move ahead with the development brokered by the Trinidad based Central government. For their part, the THA felt slighted that their involvement in the formal negotiations was only marginal. Given this tension, it would not be peculiar for the THA representatives to attempt to co-opt the participation process to suit their agenda.

Thus, rather than assist the community in securing optimal benefits and outcomes through adequate institutional support such as training in negotiation, assistance in articulating their objectives, assignment of a Community Tourism Liaison Officer and so on, the consultation in part became a war of words between Tobago Seaside Limited and the Tobago House of Assembly, with the community being the most disadvantaged. In this regard, it would be fair to say that the THA was operating within the incremental and manipulative modes of community participation, for while they provided official verbal support for the initiative, there was an ambivalence of how it should be implemented in the community (incremental). This coupled with the fact that the process (incremental) was used as a political weapon (manipulative) (Midgley, 1986). For their part, the Executive Committee of the LCAG, while having good intentions that led to the initiation of the consultation between TSL and the residents, were themselves poorly prepared for taking the consultation beyond the identification of issues.

The mode of participation reflected in this initiative can be considered pseudo participation or vacillating between non-participation and degrees of tokenism on Arnstein's (1969) ladder of citizen participation. According to Arnstein (1969, p. 219) "if participation is restricted to this level what citizens achieve in all this activity is that they have participated in participation." What powerholders achieve is the evidence that they have gone through the required motions of involving "those people."

Conclusion

It is axiomatic that residents deciding to participate in any form of community participation initiative do so because either they have some interest to protect or wish to know how they will be impacted by the particular development. They therefore attend the participation initiatives with some degree of expectation. The translation of these expectations into tangible and beneficial outcomes is however not simple and often mediated by a number of factors. This study has considered some of these factors impacting upon participation outcomes in a consultation initiative in the community of Lowlands, Tobago. The residents of this community went into the consultation with specific concerns and expectations that at the end were not realized. The reasons for this were bound up not only in the heterogeneous nature of communities and the unequal power often present in participation but also in other what can be considered "micro issues" such as the absence of a shared vision and clear objectives, lack of sustained interest, poor institutional support and so on. While the findings are not generalizable to other settings, the study raises awareness that merely engaging a participatory approach to tourism development ought not to be assumed to deliver positive outcomes. Such an assumption masks the pivotal role that the actions of individuals and official agencies can have on outcomes. It also masks some inherent complexities that may exist in communities.

If community participation is seen as mandatory for progressing destinations towards sustainable tourism development then it is necessary to go beyond moral and ideological sentiments about participation, and find pathways to ensuring that the outcomes are beneficial to the residents who are integral to the success of the tourism industry. Reflecting on this specific case, three policy recommendations are proposed for making outcomes more favorable towards residents. One is that the Assembly needs to develop a policy on community participation which should spell out what the authorities mean by community participation, what are the objectives, what are the various modes, how and when the affected community should become involved, what is the institutional role of the Assembly, what are the possibilities, challenges etc. This policy document would provide a framework of action for participation, acting as a guide while having some flexibility, recognizing that even within the same geographical space, communities will differ. Relatedly, it is proposed that the Assembly provide a resource person, for example, a Community Tourism Liaison Officer, that would work with communities in understanding the benefits and costs of tourism development and educate them on how to negotiate so that they emerge from community participation with significant wins. It is also suggested that community participation initiatives work through existing non-governmental organizations and community groups which may already have the trust of community members, are bound by common interests and have built up some level of capacity and/or possess the *savoir-faire* to access various resources. The case of the LCAG demonstrated that the formation of a new group with its members having varying degrees of concern but without clear and consensual intent or objectives was insufficient to garner the respect and attention of the powerful TSL. Moreover, the capacity required with respect to skills—organizing, negotiating etc. was not resident among the community group and made them appear ill-prepared. Finally, sustaining community interest is premised upon residents' sense that their input matters and that they can influence the outcome. Another school of thought suggests that communities need incentives to participate (O'Riordan, 1977). A two-pronged approach is therefore being proposed where the community is equipped with the requisite information and skills to participate and if necessary, provided incentives by the Assembly to attend.

Further research in other types of tourism settings should consider the type of factors that mediate participation outcomes that are advantageous to residents. A panoply of factors can then allow us to evolve a framework that can assist planners and policy makers as they attempt to move sustainable tourism development from rhetoric to reality.

Note

1. The name of the developer has been changed for reasons of anonymity.

References

Arnstein, S.A. (1969). Ladder of citizen participation. *Journal of American Institute of Planning*, *35*, 216–224.

Babbie, E. (1998). *The practice of social research* (8th ed.). Ontario: Wadsworth.

Baker, S. (2006). *Sustainable development*. London: Routledge.

Blackstock, K. (2005). A critical look at community based tourism. *Community Development Journal*, *40*(1), 39–49.

Central Statistical Office of Trinidad and Tobago. (2008). *Population data*. Central Statistical Office of Trinidad and Tobago. Retrieved June 22, 2009, from http://www.cso.gov.tt.

Choi, H., & Sirakaya, E. (2006). Sustainability indicators for managing community tourism. *Tourism Management*, *27*, 1274–1289.

Cole, S. (2006). Information and empowerment: The keys to achieving sustainable tourism. *Journal of Sustainable Tourism*, *14*(6), 629–644.

Collis, J., & Hussey, R. (2003). *Business Research: A practical guide for undergraduate and postgraduate student* (2nd ed.). New York: Palgrave-Macmillan.

Doorne, S. (1998). Power, participation and perception: An insider's perspective on the politics of the Wellington Waterfront Redevelopment. *Current Issues in Tourism*, *1*(2), 129–166.

Elliott, J. (1997). *Tourism, politics and public sector management*. London: Routledge.

Fagence, M. (1977). *Citizen participation in planning*. Oxford: Pergamon.

Goodwin, P. (1998). Hired hands or local voice: Understandings and experiences of local participation in conservation. *Transactions*, *23*(4), 481–499.

Hall, C.M., & Jenkins, J.M. (1995). *Tourism and public policy*. London: Routledge.

Haywood, K. (1988). Responsible and responsive tourism planning in the community. *Tourism Management*, *9*(2), 105–118.

Hillery, G.A. (1955). Definitions of community: Areas of agreement. *Rural Sociology*, *20*, 111–123.

Joppe, M. (1996). Sustainable community tourism development revisited. *Tourism Management*, *17*(7), 475–479.

Keogh, B. (1990). Public participation in community tourism planning. *Annals of Tourism Research*, *17*, 449–465.

Lankford, S., Knowles-Lankford, J., & Povey, C. (1996). Instilling community confidence and commitment in tourism: Community planning and public participation in government camp, Oregon, USA. In L. Harrison & W. Husbands (Eds.), *Practicing responsible tourism – international case studies in tourism planning, policy and development* (pp. 330–349). New York: Wiley.

Madrigal, R. (1994). Resident perceptions and the role of government. *Annals of Tourism Research*, *22*(1), 86–102.

Midgley, J. (1986). Community participation: History, concepts, and controversies. In J. Midgley with A. Hall, M. Hardiman & D. Narine (Eds.). *Community participation, social development and the State* (pp. 13–44). London: Methuen.

Milne, S. (1998). Tourism and sustainable development: the global- local nexus. In M. Hall & A. Lews (Eds.), *Sustainable tourism: A geographical perspective* (pp. 35–48). Essex: Longman.

Mowforth, M., Charlton, C., & Munt, I. (2008). *Tourism and responsibility: Perspectives from Latin America and the Caribbean*. London: Routledge.

Murphy, P. (1985). *Tourism: A community approach*. London: Methuen.

O'Riordan, T. (1977). Citizen participation in practice: Some dilemmas and possible solutions. In W. Sewell & J. Coppock (Eds.), *Public participation in planning* (pp. 159–172). London: John Wiley.

Parker, S. (2000). Collaboration on tourism policy making: Environmental and commercial sustainability of Bonaire, NA. In B. Bramwell & B. Lane (Eds.), *Tourism collaboration and partnerships: Politics, practice and sustainability* (pp. 78–97). Clevedon: Channel View Publications.

Prentice, R. (1993). Community driven tourism planning and residents' preferences. *Tourism Management, 14*, 219–227.

Reed, M. (1997). Power relations and community-based tourism planning. *Annals of Tourism Research, 24*(3), 566–591.

Ritchie, J.R. (1993). Crafting a destination vision-putting the concept of resident-responsive tourism into practice. *Tourism Management, 14*(5), 379–389.

Roberts, S. (2000). *Community participation in tourism planning – an examination of some of the factors that contribute to participation outcomes*. Unpublished M.Sc. dissertation. UK: The University of Surrey.

Ryan, C., & Montgomery, D. (1994). The attitudes of Bakewell residents to tourism and issues in community responsive tourism. *Tourism Management, 15*(5), 358–369.

Sanoff, H. (1992). *Integrating programming, evaluation and participation design: A theory z approach*. Aldershot: Avebury.

Santhanam, M. (1993). Community participation for sustainable development. *Journal of Public Administration, 39*(3), 413–423.

Sekeran, U. (2000). *Research methods for business*. New York: John Wiley and Sons.

Sewell, W.R.D., & Coppock, J.T. (1977). A perspective on public participation. In W. Sewell and J. Coppock (Eds.), *Public participation in planning* (pp. 1–14). London: John Wiley.

Swarbrooke, J. (1999). *Sustainable tourism management*. Wallingford, UK: CAB International.

Taylor, G. (1995). The community approach: Does it really work? *Tourism Management, 16*(7), 487–489.

Taylor, G., & Davis, D. (1997). The community show: A mythology of resident responsive tourism. In M.J. Stabler (Ed.), *Tourism sustainability - principles to practice* (pp. 323–334). Wallingford, UK: CAB International.

Telfer, D., & Sharpley, R. (2008). *Tourism and development in the developing world*. London: Routledge.

Tosun, C. (2000). Limits to community participation in the tourism development process in developing countries. *Tourism Management, 21*, 613–33.

Urry, J. (1995)*Consuming places*. London: Routledge.

Willis, K. (1995). Imposed structures and contested meanings: Policies and politics of public participation. *Australian Journal of Social Issues, 30*(2), 211–227.

World Commission on Environment and Development. (1987). *Our common future*. New York: United Nations.

World Tourism Organisation. (1996). *Agenda 21 for the travel and tourism industry: Towards environmentally sustainable development*. Madrid: World Tourism Organization.

Wyllie, R. (1998). No tin my backyard: Opposition to tourism development in a Hawaiian community. *Tourism Recreation and Research, 23*(1), 55–64.

Zhang, J., Inbakaran, R., & Jackson, M. (2006). Understanding community attitudes towards tourism and host-guest interaction in the urban-rural border region. *Tourism Geographies, 8*(2), 182–204.

Tourism planning and power within micropolitan community development

William L. Obenour and Nelson Cooper

Department of Recreation and Leisure Studies, East Carolina University, Greenville, NC 27858, USA

The purpose of this research is to investigate the community planning processes associated with the development of a new and iconic attraction in a micropolitan community. The four sources of evidence in the case study research were communication with community leaders, planning documents, newspaper articles, and observations. Two hypotheses were formulated with the first phrased as planning for a proposed iconic tourist attraction is heavily swayed by power networks for immediate gains in economic development and was not being supported by the research. The rival hypothesis was phrased as planning for organic growth of selected recreational assets into tourist attractions is realized through collaborative power networks and public involvement based on long-term sustainability was supported. Analytic generalization applies to power networks, planning processes, and tourism integration in community development. The analyses contained two power networks termed iconic and integrative. An illustration incorporating power networks and a planning continuum is presented.

Community development includes planning for tourists' experiences within metropolitan population centers as well as micropolitan communities with established tourist attractions such as Branson, Missouri (USA) or with existing natural attractions such as Hilton Head Island, SC (USA). In the United States, attention on tourism has been on the metropolitan centers of the larger cities in the United States which include 83% of the population compared to micropolitan areas with 10.3% (Mackun, 2005). Micropolitan communities are a rural county with an urban cluster with between 10,000 and 49,999 people and a total area population of up to 249,999 (Mackun, 2005). The micropolitan designation was officially incorporated in the United States in 2003 and provides a uniform definition for differentiating non-metropolitan areas from metropolitan areas (Brown, Cromartie, & Kulcsar, 2004).

Development of tourism attractions is one economic strategy for micropolitan areas that are faced with the loss of employment in primary sectors such as manufacturing, slow growth in population of 1.6% between 2000 and 2003, a decrease in the net migration of residents, and a need to diversify its economy (Vias, Mulligan, &

Molin, 2002). New tourist attractions for the 560 micropolitan statistical areas in the United States (Mackun, 2005) are sought to spur consumption, job creation, and further economic development (Gartner, 2005).

There is scant literature on the integration of tourism and attraction development within community planning for micropolitan communities. Public monies are increasingly spent to spur the development of tourism attractions and diversify a small town's economy. The rational is similar to metropolitan areas whose leaders provide economic stimulation by building tourism infrastructure with public monies to produce a prominent place image to lure more visitors, residents, and businesses to the area (Law, 2002). Metropolitan areas have greater experience with tourism development initiated by entrepreneurs and expertise in planning than micropolitan communities. Within micropolitan communities, planning for tourism attractions become enmeshed within power structures and a contested purpose of planning within government (Bramwell & Meyer, 2007; Cheong & Miller, 2000; Ingamells, 2007). This paper contributes to research on tourism and community development by applying the concepts of planning and power networks (Reed, 1997) to the process of developing a tourist attraction in a micropolitan community.

The purpose of this research is to investigate power within the community planning processes associated with the development of a new and iconic attraction in a micropolitan community. Case study research provides a technique to analyze the purpose statement because it is a holistic situation involving multiple concepts (Verschuren, 2003), it also utilizes multiple sources (Yin, 1993), focuses on a process over a period of time (Mitchell, 1983), and comprises a unique and complex phenomenon (Stake, 1995). Yin (1993) suggests that the use of analytic generalizations in case study research with two hypotheses. In this case study, the first hypothesis is planning for a proposed iconic tourist attraction (i.e., a celebrity named theater) is heavily swayed by power networks for immediate gains in economic development. The second and rival hypothesis is that planning for organic growth of selected recreational assets into tourist attractions is realized through collaborative power networks and public involvement based on long-term sustainability.

Literature review

Micropolitan community development

Comprehensive community planning became institutionalized in the 1920s as part of the governmental reform movement to provide a framework for goals and objectives for community development. A comprehensive community plan was a requirement for zoning and incorporated a wide range of areas including: land-use, transportation, environmental, park and open-space, utilities and infrastructure, school facilities, neighborhoods, historic preservation, social and regional issues. Separate from the comprehensive plan but related are auxiliary plans for economic development, parks and recreation, downtown, corridor, housing, neighborhood, annexation, transportation, and infrastructure (Kelly & Becker, 2000). Hudson (1979) has criticized comprehensive planning because of the inability to consider all elements in a community at once. Other modes of planning have been advocated such as incremental planning processes resulting in the formulation of smaller decisions for mid-level managers (Hudson, 1979).

Currently, there is little uniformity in the integration of tourism within the community planning process, although models of tourism development exist for possible integration (Butler, 1980; Law, 2002; Pearce, 1989). In Law's model, tourism is a change agent to advance growth in social, physical, and economic spheres, although a greater emphasis in the model is on the economic results. Creating a private sector tourism attraction can improve the place image of the micropolitan, leading to increased visitation, a greater number of relocated businesses, and a rising number of new residents. Historically the main catalyst and owner of the tourist attraction is the entrepreneur (Veal, 2002) who is a commercial entity that takes risks and bears the consequences of either profit or losses.

Governmental units are becoming more entrepreneurial by taking risks to further economic growth, utilizing tax incentives, partnering with private enterprise, cultivating a place and destination image, and competing with other destinations for the visitor (Ingamells, 2007; McCarthy, 1997). Post-industrial communities especially in the United States must contend with reductions in federal subsidies to cities since the 1970s, the relocation of residents which reduces the amount of property taxes, the accompanying flight of retail businesses decreasing the sales tax, and a loss of manufacturers creating fiscal distress for municipalities (McCarthy, 1997). In this post-industrial economic system, tourism's role progressively becomes more important as an economic growth and development strategy (Singh, 2005). Communities seek to bid or even lure private sector entrepreneurs who have proposals for attractions to bring visitors for overnight stays and increasing sales and hotel room tax revenues, property values, and employment. The community and government must react to new initiatives and innovations in tourism attractions, especially if the government is to go the beyond traditional functions of building infrastructure to contribute to tax subsidies (Joppe, 1996). These developments may lack community participation outside of certain business and cultural interests (Joppe, 1996) and a comprehensive analysis of tourism impacts (Reid, Mair, & George, 2004).

Planning models

The boundaries between tourism and recreation are indistinct as both share facilities and spaces (Baud-Bovy & Lawson, 1998) and strive for prominence within the micropolitan planning system. Planning in public recreation agencies has traditionally been limited in definition and interpretation. Public recreation professionals discuss planning in the context of property and space acquisition or development. Developing and acquiring park and recreation facilities involves extensive planning and one can understand how discussions of planning can become viewed in a single context. While park development motivates planning, many other park and recreation issues and activities also demand planning. Evolving issues such as risk and performance management and agency activities such as personnel management, fiscal management, and marketing can all impact the frequency and content of recreation plans.

Planning is defined as a future oriented, proactive, dynamic, and fluid process that results in agency road maps (Burch, 1996). Agency planning is a mindful and structured activity that uses rational analysis to assess the current state of affairs, choose realistic goals, and determine objectives to meet those goals (Burch, 1996). While the process of planning is analytical, the information it uses comes from scientific data and the experiences, insights, intuition, and common sense of the agency professionals (Burch, 1996).

Planning theory has traditionally been defined in two frameworks; Rational Comprehensive Planning (RCP) and Incremental Planning (IP). Rational Comprehensive Planning contains four classical elements (Hudson, 1979): (1) goal-setting; (2) identification of policy alternatives; (3) evaluation of means against ends; and (4) implementation of policy. The RCP process commands constant and accurate information regarding issues, alternatives, and consequences. Achieving this requires constant citizen input and assessment. The RCP process is thorough but requires regular attention, is the dominant framework for planning and often the basis for other planning frameworks (Hudson, 1979).

IP was defined by Charles Lindblom who claimed that RCP processes were unrealistic, especially for systems such as bureaucratic governmental departments (cited in Hudson, 1979). IP occurs when high-level decisions are made based upon expedited consultations and previous experience, resulting in smaller decisions being distributed to mid-management and front-line personnel to form alliances and contribute to administrative goals (Macleod, 2007). RCP and IP illustrate polarized concepts of planning processes and procedures. They also suggest a continuum of how planning may occur in public and non-profit recreation agencies (Figure 1).

Recreation professionals commonly cite a lack of resources, expertise, or political differences as reasons for not engaging in comprehensive planning activities. Boyne, Gould-Williams, Law, and Walker (2004) assessed technical and political factors within municipalities that relate to a local government's ability to conduct rational planning. The study sample was local government agencies in the United Kingdom that had implemented a mandated rational planning process. The process resulted in a government entity producing a performance plan and an action plan. Results showed that municipalities with greater resources for planning and more extensive expertise in the planning process were more likely to produce planning documents with minimal difficulty. The researchers did not find a difference in planning success when considering political factors. The study suggests that planning challenges are more frequently technical than political.

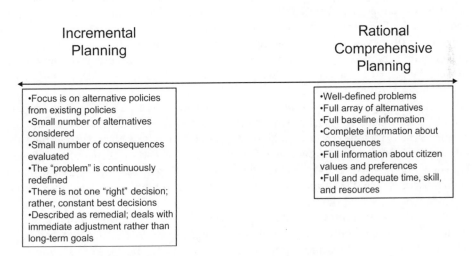

Figure 1. Planning continuum.

Power networks and planning

Tourism system models (Mill & Morrison, 1985; Murphy, 1985; McIntosh, Goeldner, & Brent Ritchie, 1995) and planning models (Gunn, 1979; Inskeep, 1991) define tourism as controllable, formally coordinated, initiated through a top-down approach, and result in collaborative goals (McKercher, 1999). The models imply a deterministic approach, assume stakeholders are equal and participate, and are managed by public sector planners (McKercher, 1999). The models for planning explain what should happen, however power determines what does happen. Power determines discourses circulated in the community to determine how and if plans are processed and implemented, if tourist assets are developed, and relations among stakeholders. Power facilitates the process of decision-making in networks (Pickett, 2005). Networks are described as the observable pattern of social relationships among individuals and groups (Abercrombie, Hill, & Turner, 2006a) and are an essential foundation in Foucault's power (Abercrombie, Hill, & Turner, 2006b), community development (Ingamells, 2007) the making of place (Bradshaw, 2008), and tourism (Dredge, 2006; Reed, 1997). Power impacts the processes related to community tourism planning (Joppe, 1996) and the enforcement of rules and regulations in a municipality (Bourdieu, 2005).

One interpretation of power is by Foucault (1979) who states that: "Power produces reality and the domains of objects and rituals of truth" (p. 194). Foucault views democracies as governing through invisible power by shaping the discourses of citizens' identities and goals which is more important to Foucault than the formal structure of society's institutions such as governments exerting power. Cheong and Miller (2000) interpret Foucault's perspective on power as a relationship among stakeholders created by the structure of knowledge. Within this concept, power is regulated through the presence of discourse, or the use of social language and messages. Power is continually in flux among stakeholders, rather than an asset used to dominate by an institution or a fixed property held by class or individuals (Pickett, 2005).

Cheong and Miller (2000) summarize three key components of Foucault's power as it relates to tourism. First, power is an outcome from conflict between various actors, as opposed to a mechanism used to dominate (Cheong & Miller, 2000; Pickett, 2005). Second, power is more fluid and becomes a relationship that flows in multiple directions, as opposed to formal laws and rules used by one dominant group. Third, power is reinforced by knowledge, which contributes to social language and messages. Foucault refers to power as precluding the agency since power is first required for the agent to acquire knowledge in the world. Only after power is engaged to acquire knowledge can an agent decide to act, which is the foundation of agency (Pickett, 2005; Rossi, 2004).

There are four features of Foucault's vision of power relationships which involve targets and agents in social situations (Cheong & Miller, 2000). First, the omnipresence of power is everywhere in tourism including when attractions are developed. Power networks have agents embedded with certain forms of knowledge (Dredge, 2006; Rossi, 2004). Various power networks generate discourses with no single discourse truer than another as it pertains to community, growth, recreation, tourism, planning, and development.

A second feature builds on the omnipresence of power by indicating that power is both repressive and productive amid the actors, agents and brokers (Cheong & Miller, 2000). Discourses are formulated through power networks and linguistic devices that structures knowledge. The structures of knowledge pre-determines the ways development projects are "allowed" to function and practitioners are "allowed" to act in specific contexts (Rossi, 2004).

The third feature of power situates tourism within networks consisting of agents divided into private and public sectors and local residents and tourists as targets. Cheong and Miller (2000) distinguish private brokers as agents deriving a living from tourism production. Private sector brokers include entrepreneurs in real estate, hotel owners and employees, chambers of commerce, and vendors. Entrepreneurs in attraction and real estate development are also termed chaos-makers who innovate by proposing new attractions for a destination (Russell & Faulkner, 1999). The second type of agents is public sector brokers comprising politicians, city planners, and other quasi-governmental entities such as convention and visitor bureaus. Planners and regulators are seen as dampeners whose actions moderate or control changes (Russell & Faulkner, 1999). Local residents are agents as well as market researchers, academics, journalists and travel writers. Tourists are targets and positioned within a relational network with agents, brokers, and locals. This does not necessarily mean that commercial entities have a repressive force of control over tourists but instead power produces the relational network and the reality within which the network exists (Cheong & Miller, 2000). This reality is structured through the discourses of agents, brokers and locals in the power network. Power relations are established and maintained through symbolic discourses such as verbal exchanges and written documents that frame development and planning.

A fourth feature of Foucauldian power is the touristic gaze that assists in the development of and maintenance of power relationships (Cheong & Miller, 2000). Agents construct and exert knowledge on what is a successful tourism attraction worthy of the tourists' gaze. Tourists chose spaces defined by their social relations and desire to gaze upon the features of landscape and townscape separate from everyday experience (Urry, 1990, 1992). The destination becomes a space that is designed for pleasure, spectacle, and consumption of the tourists' gaze (Urry, 1992).

Method

The case study is as an empirical inquiry into a phenomenon within a real-life context, when the boundary is not clearly evident between phenomenon and context and comprises multiple sources of evidence (Yin, 1989). This case is bounded by the phenomenon which is the planning process and the context is a micropolitan area in the Southeastern United States (Creswell, 1994). This single case design is justifiable because it represents a critical examination of power in the community planning of tourism, the case is a rare and unique event in tourism attraction development, and serves a revelatory purpose (Yin, 1989). The micropolitan's name and other identifiers (e.g., name of local newspaper and websites) are suppressed to empower local leaders to provide more insights. The micropolitan is designated as the Southeastern Micropolitan Community (SMC) and the websites, documents, and newspapers are identified only with SMC or local, to enable the researchers to gather more insights into the planning process.

The evaluative criteria for the case study research include a form of construct validity and reliability suggested by Yin (1989). Yin characterizes one form of construct validity for case study research as identifying and applying the appropriate procedures for the stated purpose statement and includes the sources, conceptual framework, and two hypotheses for analytic generalization. The researchers utilize

Yin's version of analytic generalization which applies the results of the single case to relate to the relevant theories and concepts of the purpose statement. Case study reliability is formulated through multiple data sources (i.e., four sources of data) to develop patterns and explanations, documented procedures for data collection, consensus building between two researchers using the same theoretical and conceptual background, and incorporating conceptual analysis in the interpretation of the data (i.e., Carmel, 1999).

The case study utilized four discourses of evidence suggested by Yin (1989), the discourses were used to examine the exercise of Foucauldian power (Power, 2006) in the way public and private agents, targets, and tourist gaze were self-imprisoned within a power network. The four discourses consisted of the following: (a) personal communication with four community leaders (current city manager, ex-city manager and economic developer, and directors of recreation and tourism who were directly involved with the planning process; (b) planning documents and websites with planning information; (c) local newspaper articles from the 2001 to 2008; and (d) reflexive comments from the researchers' direct observations of the tourism attractions (i.e., Ingamells, 2007). Personal communication is cited in the results section. The planning documents analysis provided information on the type of planning utilized. The analysis of the local newspaper articles were from 2001 to 2008, including the editor's opinion section. We searched the local newspapers website with keywords such as theater, the celebrity's name, and four existing local attractions. This produced a total of 249 articles which were read and reviewed by the researchers. An analysis used the concept of "framing the issue" to locate key articles. The analysis revealed 46 reporter's articles and six editor's opinions dated between April 2005 and April 2009 which are essential frames to identify the key content and incorporated in the chronological narrative of the result's section (Abrudan, & Mucundorfeanu, 2009; Menashe & Siegel, 1998).

The case study results were written as a chronological narrative within the context of a mircopolitan community in the US. In the results section, the context is further described, along with the phenomenon. The planning process is interpreted via the concepts for attraction development and two power networks in community planning. At the end of the results section, the researchers illustrate with a diagram the interaction and continuum of the power networks within community planning of tourism. Based on the results, the competing hypotheses previously identified are evaluated in the discussion section.

Case study results

The micropolitan development context

The SMC had a slight increase in population between 1990 and 2000 and a projected annual growth rate of less than 1%. Eventually this will result in a reduction in population because of the negative outflows of residents (SMC State Economic Data, 2009). From 2000 to 2002, unemployment was over 12% as manufacturers closed their plants and agriculture was less profitable in the area (SMC State Bureau of Labor Statistics, 2009).

The supply of tourism attractions in the SMC traditionally focused on a core of four existing resources, which included a historic town site, a wildlife preserve, a state park, and a history museum and trail (director, personal communication, 5 January 2009). This SMC is situated on a major highway where approximately

100,000 cars per day pass by it is also in an accessible location positioned within a 100 mile trade area of approximately six million people (local land developer's website, 2009). These advantages, plus a theater attraction have grown the hotel supply to approximately 1500 rooms (SMC County Tourism Brochure, 2009). In the 1980s a county tourism bureau was formed, tourism expenditure in 2007 gradually increased to approximately $75 million, generating over three million in state tax receipts, and over one million in local tax receipts (SMC State, 2009; SMC Tourism Bureau, 2008). This was an increase of over 8% from 2006 as tourism increasingly garnered attention by community leaders, developers, and entrepreneurs.

The community leaders such as the mayor, tourism director, and city manager sought to create tourism and retail employment, stem the outflow of residents, broaden the image of the community, attract non-tourist businesses, and increase housing demand (ex-city manager, personal communication, March, 2009). An additional advantage to developing tourism was the reduced needs for governmental services by tourists as compared to new residents (Ex-city manager, personal communication, March 2009). Public and private partnerships resulted in a Wal-Mart Supercenter shopping complex. Considering the accessible location and quality of the county's four recreational attractions, tourists were already staying overnight and an opportunity existed to increase this through a major tourist attraction (Directors, personal communication, 5 January 2009). Economic development was a prime need for this SMC and they were hopeful for additional opportunities based on its prime location for a mass audience.

Attraction opportunity

A new opportunity for a tourist attraction was announced by the city council at a public gathering in 2005. The tourist entertainment district was estimated as a one hundred million dollar investment with a net positive income flow to the government of almost two million dollars. In phase one, the district would have 2500 jobs and additional phases were planned on 700 acres. In essence, the SMC would invest ten million of tax dollars over a ten year lease for the 15 acres needed for the first theater in the entertainment district and leases the theater back to the developer and a celebrity's entertainment company to recoup $11.8 million in revenues over ten years. The SMC awarded an incentive grant valued at $351,000 over a six-year period to the entertainer. One city councilman revealed a diagram of the first phase showing two motels, four restaurants, five theaters and a 400,000 square foot outlet-style shopping facility. As indicated in the local newspaper, the meeting was to gain support from the local government for the economic incentive package. The announcement of the plan emphasized the thousands in job losses in the county since 1997 and the poverty rate being twice as high as the state average. The message emphasized that the music theater destination would produce positive economic impacts, little negative environmental impacts, and limited community expenses that occur with new residents. The paper's journalist mentioned just a few non-supportive comments from a surrounding landowner and one resident.

Iconic power network

The power network, designated as iconic, was created in the process of planning for the unique tourism attraction and eventually to build the theater. This type of attraction relies on agents who are private sector entrepreneurs. The developer of the land formed a partnership with the public sector agents such as the governmental leaders and tourism bureau to bid on the right to develop a theater complex (directors, personal communication, 5 January 2009). The bid process was initiated by a regional economic development planner who sought out a celebrity entertainer and producer to be the marquee attraction for the theater complex. The economic planner and celebrity entertainer then sought competitive bids from communities for the project (directors, personal communication, 5 January 2009).

Russell and Faulkner (1999) describe the role of a chaos-maker which in this case is the celebrity entertainer and production company, who generates an unforeseen opportunity that is outside the realm of long-range community planning documents. This was obviously seen as a great opportunity to utilize tourism and change the economic fabric of the SMC. As far as risk for the government, there was a feasibility study by a university along with approvals by the regional governmental unit of the plan and especially the financing. Repeated analogies with another micropolitan, Branson, Missouri and its 47 theaters increased the perception that entertainment is a successful avenue for tourism. According to a Branson tourism leader interviewed in an article, this growth required the right mixture of attractions and entertainment, substantial infrastructure, and the difficulty of one developer replicating a Branson destination.

The first public announcement on 7 April 2005 started the process for approval to annex the property, authorization for an incentive package, and completion of a feasibility project for a proposal to the state and interested parties. The editor of the local paper supported the project and broadcast the need for quick progress as the SMC was bidding against six additional communities. Russell and Faulkner (1999) refer to planners and regulators as dampeners who moderate changes. In today's post-industrial communities the role of economic development planners has become more entrepreneurial instead of a dampener. Even the former SMC city manager, had a pro-active role as an economic developer for the SMC for the project (ex-city manager, personal communication, 6 March 2009). Public sector economic planners actively engaged entrepreneurs to form reactionary power networks which differ from the power networks established around comprehensive community planning.

An iconic power network is based on relational power that is reactive toward an ephemeral symbolism presented by a celebrity entrepreneur. The iconic power network formed the discourse that focused on the economic and societal benefits of the tourism project. The power network initially consisted of a small number of agents. There were challenges in preparing the proposal in a short time because power relationships were quickly formed between the private developer, the entertainment, various governmental entities, and potential investors.

Foucauldian targets are positioned within a relational network with agents, brokers and locals (Cheong & Miller, 2000) and in this case the target was the proposed attraction to lure new tourists. The power network was aligned to support the theatrical attraction as a target for tourists. The theater as an attraction was meant to satisfy the gaze from new tourists and produce revenues and jobs. For the economic developer and current city manager (personal communication, 6 March 2009), the iconic celebrity's name was a crucial factor for the development to succeed. While other community leaders believed the theater complex would succeed on its own merit (directors and ex-city manager, personal communication, January 5;

March 6, 2009). The governmental risk in an iconic power network is the ability to correctly predict the tourist demand for the theater which is a complex challenge.

Some elements of the power network were not visible to the public, for example, the celebrity entertainer was not revealed until after the project was shown to the public and private developer. Another issue became the entrepreneur's proprietary information which necessitated certain financial information was not made public (current and ex-city managers, personal communication, 6 March 2009) and reduced the public transparency of the process.

The announcement to award the SMC with the theater development was made by the iconic power network comprised of the private development partners, the city government of SMC, the regional economic development partnership, and the county tourism bureau. A university research institute formulated an economic impact study which was touted in the media and relied upon by government officials in deciding the feasibility of this distinctive attraction. A master plan was created for the project without opposition to rezoning of the land. A conditional use permit was passed by the city council for phase one of the plan consisting of a theater, a waterfront park, an avian sanctuary, a public green and amphitheater, a water feature and fountain, a live feed video sign, two hotels, an outlet retail/commercial area, traffic loop, a hotel with ground floor retail, water park, promenade, aquarium, and a service station.

The city council then pursued the financing for the project by designating a financial district and financing plan which included state level governmental grant monies for the tourist bureau to market the theater, $3.7 million for roads, $1.9 million for water and sewage, and $13 million in micropolitan bonds that would be used to build the theater. The $13 million in bonds would be paid back through tax increment financing using lease payments from ticket sales and then real estate tax revenues from the project or citywide sales tax and supposedly not from SMC wide property taxes. Before a public hearing on the financing, an updated financing plan was announced with the following: SMC committed $14.65 million to the construction of the theater with approximately $6.85 million more for capitalized interest, required debt reserve funds and issuance costs for a total of $21.5 million. In a February 2006 newspaper article, the SMC city manager is quoted as saying if the theater fails the city and its taxpayers are obligated to pay the debt service, but this was the only opportunity available for the community and there was too much at stake to let it fail.

The artist fee paid to the celebrity entertainer was $750,000 which was to be paid from the entire year's revenue for the theater. Next, the operating expenses for the theater were paid, including the annual debt service. There is another possible $750,000 artist fee after all these expenses are paid and if there were additional revenues. These payments were essential because of the competition among communities in the Southeastern United States for the celebrity led theater development.

The SMC economic development manager indicated it was unusual for rural areas to pursue this level and complexity of development necessitating feasibility studies of the marketing and tax increment funding and numerous lawyers to negotiate the contracts. An opinion piece appeared in the local newspaper detailing contract changes that were not well publicized in the media when made in March 2007 regarding the artist fee, initial lease payments from SMC financed reserve fund, and the delay in opening. The theater finally opened to rave reviews in the local newspaper.

One aspect of this power network is the issue of proprietary information which included financial records concerning the $3 million reserve fund. As reported in the paper, this fund was to be awarded to the celebrity entertainment company to be used for initial promotion, development and operation of the theater. The company and city asserted that the uses for these funds were proprietary and that the company submitted financial records to receive the monies.

The iconic power network is centered on the popularity of the celebrity who has financial means, legal expertise, name recognition and some force to control the situation. The original contract in 2007 gave the celebrity virtually no liability or accountability and gave the city little to no control in the operation of the theater. After the theater failed to bring in revenues, a renegotiated contract forgave money the celebrity owed to the city, paid an artist fee for the celebrity's appearances, and the city assumed thousands of dollars in liabilities owed by the celebrity. After the renegotiation, the celebrity's organization retained the right to approve any theater sale which continued to curtail the options available to the micropolitan city's leaders. Finally, as the theater's losses continued, another negotiation terminated the control of the celebrity over the theater, cost the city government hundreds of thousands of dollars but saved additional monies and time in the settlement.

Numerous characteristics of the iconic power network contributed to the initial failure of the theater project. The SMC sought the star power of a celebrity icon (city manager, personal communication, 6 March 2009), but in reality the celebrity lacked the iconic capital to generate a substantial and profitable number of visitors to the theater every week of the year. There was a lack of public transparency. Reasons for this included low attendance at public meetings, contractual obligation of the micropolitan city to protect the proprietary and commercial information, and use of tax increment financing as a basis for the theater construction bond, which does not need a public referendum as do general obligation bonds. Management issues plagued the theater complex; the celebrity icon was never fully vetted by the city as being an entrepreneur who was capable of operating and marketing the theater. Management issues continued as the celebrity icon was removed and temporary management were hired, then fired, with the economic developer filling the gap without the necessary experience.

Integrative power network

With the celebrity entrepreneur gone from the theater and power being fluid and relational, the discourse on the planning and development of the entertainment district experienced a change. This new power network is termed integrative and includes similar agents, brokers and locals plus additional agents, especially local residents and leaders contributing to the power network. Comments and opinions in the paper mostly indicated that the theater is and always was a good idea.

After the dissolution of the celebrity icon's contract, the integrative network using the fluidity of power focused on the next major task which was to find either a management company or an owner for the theater. In this process, the integrative power network became much more transparent as some actors changed their actions, such as the city government and mayor who advocated transparency and openness in every aspect of governance from the budget to the theater. The 2009 recession created more economic hardships for the community—an increase in sales tax was proposed for 2009. A primary reason for the sales tax proposal was the city's long-term debt of $21.5 million from the bond obligation for the theater. This was announced during a citizens' open forum soliciting financial ideas for the community. These ongoing citizen forums, which had four people from each district on a panel, shaped and influenced the integrative power network.

Additional acts of transparency included a theater advisor committee that was formed and populated by business leaders, along with a mayor's advisory committee of local business and civic leaders. The mayor addressed the public through an interview in the local newspaper and described the financial problems of the city in 2008 which were mostly caused by the theater problems. However, the mayor reminded the public of the lack of opposition at the two public hearings on the theater proposal, plus the value of the land had risen because of the theater, the new hotel, and the recreational vehicle park. This was a long-term project that would produce additional tax revenues projected at $1.5 million and tourism jobs in the future for a community which did not have many job creating opportunities. In 2007, the local tax rate had not increased for years but a proposal for a five cent increase to keep normal recreation center hours and salaries was made for 2008 and the final tax increase was over 8%.

A search was conducted for bids and proposals for selling or managing the theater and 15 bids were submitted. After a private firm was hired to evaluate the proposals, one bid for a lease-purchase agreement was viewed as the front-runner by the theater advisory committee. In addition, two public hearings were held in October 2008 and an open council meeting in January 2009 to discuss the proposals. Eventually the bid was accepted for the theater and the city's obligation was finally reduced.

The bank which issued the bond financing for over 21 million dollars took transparent action by attending the citizen meetings. As the bank's representative indicated at the forum, due diligence was important on the part of the prospective owner about the theater but also by the SME on the prospective owner. The theater advisor committee visited other developments of the prospective owner in the Midwest and reviewed financial documents which were also reviewed by the city council and lawyers. An audit indicated how complicated the theater agreement was for all parties involved and difficult for a city with a low reserve fund. Even after a lease-purchase agreement with the new owner the agreement would leave the taxpayer with nearly $9 million in bond debt, with an $800,000 a year payment by the city. The contract depended on the new owners using their operational, marketing, and entertainment expertise to book events. The new owner sought to expand the theater to 5000 seats with a variety of shows and entertainment such as rodeos and children's shows, gospel, rock, rhythm and blues. The new owner asked for community support and was willing to publicize some financial information about the theater, although a specific business plan would not be made public because of competitive reasons and the proprietary nature of the information within the plan.

The target of the integrative power network now consisted of a built theater, but also a core four of attractions within the county to further stimulate overnight stays and tourist arrivals. Integration of the theater with the existing county attractions began in 2006 for the benefit of increased tourism arrivals, synergy with the core four attractions, especially with tour operators, and enhanced cooperation with the tourism authority to make the theater a success.

Summary

A unique observation surfaces with the shift in power networks that occurred. The micropolitan planning for the tourist attraction initially occurred under an iconic power network, which experienced a disruption in development and progress, and evolved into an integrative power network. Based on Foucauldian power (Cheong & Miller, 2000) an additional continuum is formulated with the extremes being iconic power and integrative power (see Figure 2).

The planning continuum and the power continuum exist parallel to each other in the context of the case study, suggesting that incremental planning occurs in the iconic power structure and rational comprehensive planning occurs in the integrative power structure. When the two continuums are imposed together, a construct is presented that further illustrates this co-existence (Figure 3). Using Figure 3, the SMC began its tourism planning efforts in quadrant C and shifted to quadrant B. While the shift to a rational comprehensive planning approach often advances at a slower pace, the increase in transparency, accountability, and shared power produces a buy-in and sustainable success.

Discussion

The researchers' conclusions pertain to the two hypotheses that were previously formulated. The first hypothesis is planning for a proposed iconic tourist attraction

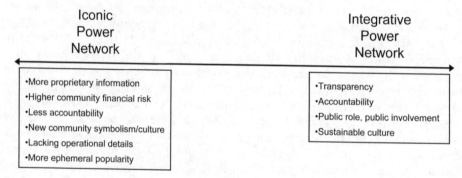

Figure 2.   Power continuum.

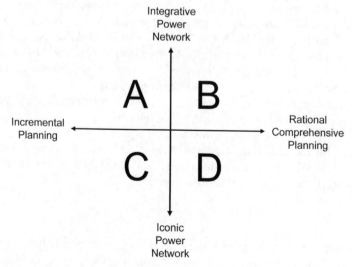

Figure 3.   The planning and power relationship.

(i.e., a celebrity named performing arts center) and heavily swayed by power networks for immediate gains in economic development. The resulting power network was termed iconic, and based on the use of proprietary information from entrepreneurial chaos-makers, higher financial risk for the community, less accountability, the creation of a new community symbolism and culture, the generation of immediate gains with hopes of substantial long-term payoffs in employment and tax revenues, a lack of operational structures, and based on the ephemeral status of a celebrity as an attraction. However, the immediate gains were consumed by the celebrity without the resulting popularity that emanates from a truly iconic entity with long-term sustaining symbolic capital. The private sector brokers, public sector brokers, and residents perceived this development as a long-term economic endeavor for the community, partly because of necessity and the current economic conditions which are not favorable for new attractions. The first hypothesis is not supported as analyzed through the conceptual framework of power networks and the continuum of the planning processes.

The rival hypothesis is planning for organic growth of selected recreational assets into tourist attractions is realized through collaborative power networks and public involvement based on long-term sustainability. This integrated approach to planning is progressive with neither the attention nor power affiliations for the rapid elevation of the recreation assets into distinctive tourism attractions. The power network consists of a more stable form of relational power among the agents and brokers of the SMC. In addition, this network and its attributes of transparency, accountability, public involvement role, and sustaining a long-term and socio-cultural environment subsumed the remnants of the iconic power network as it dramatically shifted to being more transparent with community participation. Even the new theater owner had a plan that depended less on name recognition and more on management, operations, and marketing expertise in entertainment. This rival hypothesis is supported by the case study research. The four existing attractions were vetted through a strategic and master planning process and adopted for economic and social-cultural benefits.

The analytic generalization from this case research applies to the power network concept, planning continuum, and tourism integration in micropolitan and community development. The researchers identified this connection through four illustrative points. First, tourism integration within community development gathered increased momentum as the theater lost its drawing power. The integration of tourism within community development was achieved through resident participation, collaboration among more public and private sector brokers and the potential for synergy of the theater with the four existing attractions to extend the overnights of tourists. As shown in the case study, a micropolitan leadership using the comprehensive planning model does not have a planning structure for the expedient and effective analysis of unique tourism attractions that are presented by a chaos-maker such as an entrepreneur. A micropolitan community and its leaders need the ability to react quickly to prioritize and evaluate attraction proposals. Micropolitan communities may consider more incremental planning versus the comprehensive rational planning approach to prepare for entrepreneurial chaos-makers. Reid et al. (2004) call an attraction a process catalyst that may not be fully vetted on all its impacts, even though the attraction fits within the current land use plans. A preliminary framework interconnecting power and the planning continuum is developed based on the research in the case study. As the case study unfolded, the SMC moved from quadrant C to quadrant B in Figure 3.

Second, post-industrial public sector brokers of micropolitan areas are under pressure to facilitate economic generation. For these public leaders and planners the power network promotes the use of entrepreneurial strategies such as risk-taking in the use of public monies for a tourism attraction. This role contrasts with Russell and Faulkner (1999) concept of public sector planners and government directors traditionally seen as moderating change or controlling change through the formation and implementation of plans. Economic development planners are traditionally more schooled in business attraction and retention instead of tourism attraction development or the organic growth of local resources for tourism (Muske, Woods, Swinney, & Khoo, 2007).

Third, an iconic power network that enables attraction and development may not include the operational details that provide the key to initial and long-term success as a unique tourist attraction. An emphasis on the celebrity's ability to lure visitors was a primary focus but there are few icons that possess this innate power of attraction for long periods of time. A system that popularizes a celebrity through image marketing was not part of the operational expertise of the performer and hence the ability to draw tourists waned. In addition, the iconic power network relied on planning processes that veered toward the incremental end of the continuum as seen in Figure 1, although long-term growth goals required a more comprehensive approach for this form of development.

Fourth, there is great diversity in the economic base for micropolitans. Many micropolitans have received attention because of the improved quality of life and reduced congestion and crowding associated with suburban metropolitan areas (Vias et al. 2002). The fastest shrinking micropolitan areas are almost entirely in the South. This site was without a distinctive set of amenities that drive the economies of tourism micropolitans such as Moab, Utah (Berube, Katz, & Lang, 2006). With the population growth in the Southeast, this site had a terrific location accessible to millions and prospects for growth. Many metropolitan locations are dependent on their location and with similar issues in attraction development faced by this micropolitan. The major differences are the micropolitan has less resources and expertise in evaluating distinctive tourism attractions based on tourist demand. In addition, the risk is greater from a failed attraction because of the smaller tax base and the repercussions on the cash reserves of a micropolitan.

References

Abrudan, M., & Mucundorfeanu, M. (2009). Brand and nation branding in the case of Romania. *Journal of Media Research*, (5), 89–100.

Abercrombie, N., Hill, S., & Turner, B. (2006a). Network/social network. *Credo Reference*. Retrieved 19 February 2009 from http://www.credoreference.com/entry/penguinsoc/network_social_network

Abercrombie, N., Hill, S., & Turner, B. (2006b). Power. *Credo Reference*. Retrieved 19 February 2009 from http://www.credoreference.com/entry/penguinsoc/network_social_network

Baud-Bovy, M., & Lawson, F.R. (1998). *Tourism and recreation handbook of planning and design: Handbook of planning and design*. Oxford, UK: Architectural Press.

Berube, A., Katz, B., & Lang, R. (2006). *Redefining Urban and Suburban America: Evidence from Census 2000*. Washington, DC: Brookings Institution Press.

Bourdieu, P. (2005). *The social structures of the economy*. Cambridge, UK: Polity.

Boyne, G.A., Gould-Williams, J.S., Law, J., & Walker, R.M. (2004). Problems for rational planning in public organizations: An empirical assessment of the conventional wisdom. *Administration & Society*, 36(3), 328–350.

Bradshaw, T.K. (2008). The post-place community: Contributions to the debate about the definition of community. *Community Development, 39*(1), 5–16.

Bramwell, B., & Meyer, D. (2007). Power and tourism policy relations in transition. *Annals of Tourism Research, 34*(3), 766–788.

Brown, D.L., Cromartie, J.B., & Kulcsar, L.J. (2004). Micropolitan areas and the measurement of American urbanization. *Population Research and Policy Review, 23*(4), 399–418.

Burch, H.A. (1996). *Basic social policy and planning: Strategies and practice methods.* Binghamton, NY: The Haworth Press.

Butler, R.W. (1980). The concept of a tourist area cycle of evolution: Implications for management of resources. *The Canadian Geographer, 24*(1), 5–12.

Carmel, E. (1999). Concepts, context and discourse in a comparative case study. *International Journal of Social Research Methodology, 2*(2), 141–150.

Cheong, S.-M., & Miller, M.L. (2000). Power and tourism: A Foucauldian observation. *Annals of Tourism Research, 27*(2), 371–390.

Creswell, J. (1994). *Research design: Qualitative and quantitative approaches.* Thousand Oaks, CA: Sage.

Dredge, D. (2006). Policy networks and the local organisation of tourism. *Tourism Management, 27*(2), 269–280.

Foucault, M. (1979). *Discipline and punish: The birth of the prison* (A. Sheridan, Trans.). Oxford, UK: Vintage.

Gartner, W.C. (2005). A synthesis of tourism trends. In J. Aramberri & R. Butler (Eds.), *Tourism development: Issues for a vulnerable industry* (pp. 3–26). Clevedon and Buffalo: Channel View.

Gunn, C.A. (1979). *Tourism Planning.* New York: Crane Russak.

Hudson, B.M. (1979). Comparison of current planning theories: Counterparts and contradictions. *Journal of the American Planning Association, 45*(4), 387–398.

Ingamells, A. (2007). Community development and community renewal: Tracing the workings of power. *Community Development Journal, 42*(2), 237–250.

Inskeep, E. (1991). *Tourism planning: An integrated and sustainable development approach.* New York: John Wiley & Sons.

Joppe, M. (1996). Sustainable community tourism development revisited. *Tourism Management, 17*(7), 475–479.

Kelly, E.D., & Becker, B. (2000). *Community planning: An introduction to the comprehensive plan.* Washington, DC: Island Press.

Law, C.M. (2002). *Urban tourism: The visitor economy and the growth of large cities* (2nd ed.). London: Thomson Learning.

Mackun, P.J. (2005). Population change in metropolitan and micropolitan statistical areas: 1990–2003. *Summer.* Retrieved 25 January 2007 from http://www.census.gov/prod/2005 pubs/p25-1134.pdf

Macleod, D. (2007). Planning theory. Retrieved August 18, 2007 from http://www3. sympatico.ca/david.macleod/PTHRY.HTM

McCarthy, J. (1997). Revitalization of the core city: The case of Detroit. *Cities, 14*(1), 1–11.

McIntosh, R.W., Goeldner, C.R., & Brent Ritchie, J.R. (1995). *Tourism principles, practices, philosophies (7th ed.).* New York: John Wiley.

McKercher, B. (1999). A chaos approach to tourism. *Tourism Management, 20*(4), 425–434.

Menashe, C.L., & Siegel, M. (1998). The power of a frame: An analysis of newspaper coverage of tobacco issues US, 1985–1996. *Journal of Health Communication, 3*(4), 307–326.

Mill, R., & Morrison, A. (1985). *The Tourism System: Tourism planning, policies, processes and relationships.* Englewood Cliffs, NJ: Prentice-Hall International.

Mitchell, J.C. (1983). Case and situation analysis. *The Sociological Review, 31,* 187–211.

Murphy, P.E. (1985). *Tourism: A Community Approach.* London and New York: Routledge.

Muske, G., Woods, M., Swinney, J., & Khoo, C.-L. (2007). Small businesses and the community: Their role and importance within a state's economy. *Journal of Extension, 45*(1). Online. Retrieved 19 February 2009 from http://www.joe.org/joe/2007february/rb4.php

Network/social network. (2006). In *The Penguin Dictionary of Sociology.* Retrieved from http://www.credoreference.com/entry/penguinsoc/network_social_network

Pearce, D.G. (1989). *Tourist Development (2nd ed.)*. New York: Longman Scientific & Technical.

Pickett, B. (2005). *On the use and abuse of Foucault for politics*. Lanham: Lexington Books.

Power (2006). In *The Penguin Dictionary of Sociology*. Retrieved from http://www.credoreference.com/entry/penguinsoc/power

Reed, M.G. (1997). Power relations and community-based tourism planning. *Annals of Tourism Research, 24*(3), 566–591.

Reid, D.G., Mair, H., & George, W. (2004). Community tourism planning: A self-assessment instrument. *Annals of Tourism Research, 31*(3), 623–639.

Rossi, B. (2004). Revisiting Foucauldian approaches: Power dynamics in development projects. *Journal of Development Studies, 40*(6), 1–29.

Russell, R., & Faulkner, B. (1999). Movers and shakers: Chaos makers in tourism development. *Tourism Management, 20*(4), 411–423.

Singh, T.V. (2005). Tourism and development: Not an easy alliance. In R.N. Ghosh, M.A.B. Siddique, & R. Gabbay (Eds.), *Tourism and economic development: Case studies from the Indian Ocean region* (pp. 30–41). Burlington, VT: Ashgate.

SMC County Tourism Bureau (2009). SMC county tourism brochure for 2009.

SMC County Tourism Bureau (2008). SMC county's tourism bureau annual report for 2007.

SMC State (2009). SMC state economic data. Retrieved from website of state economic development office on 19 February 2009.

SMC State Bureau of Labor (2009). SMC data. Retrieved from state bureau of labor statistics on 15 March 2009.

Stake, R.E. (1995). *The art of case study*. Thousand Oaks, CA: Sage Publications.

Urry, J. (1990). *The tourist gaze: Leisure and travel in contemporary societies*. London: Sage.

Urry, J. (1992). The tourist gaze "revisited," *American Behavioral Scientist, 36*(2), 172–186.

Veal, A.J. (2002). *Leisure and Tourism Policy and Planning (2nd ed.)*. New York: CABI.

Verschuren, P.J.M. (2003). Case study as a research strategy: some ambiguities and opportunities. *International Journal of Social Research Methodology, 6*(2), 121–140.

Vias, A.C., Mulligan, G.F., & Molin, A. (2002). Economic structure and socioeconomic change in America's micropolitan areas, 1970–1997. *The Social Science Journal, 39*(3), 399–417.

Yin, R.K. (1989). *Case study design and methods* (Revised ed. Vol. 5). Newbury Park: Sage.

Yin, R.K. (1993). *Applications of case study research* (Vol. 34). Newbury Park, CA: Sage.

Community understanding of the impact of temporary visitors on incidental destinations

Ken Simpson[a] and Phil Bretherton[b]

[a]Department of Management, Unitec Institute of Technology, Private Bag 92-025, Auckland, New Zealand; [b]School of Law and Business, Charles Darwin University, Darwin, NT, Australia

Influential changes in global economics have posed important survival and sustainability questions for small urban communities. In response, many such communities have turned to the tourism industry as a potential economic saviour, and have thus embarked on a developmental journey that has been exhaustively examined in the tourism literature of the past thirty years. However, this literature is all but unanimous in examining the benefits and costs of community tourism *after* the event, when those costs and benefits have become clearly evident and significantly entrenched. In seeking to evaluate the extent to which residents of four small cities are aware of potential costs and benefits, *before* the advent of any significant tourism activity, this paper analyses the content of 782 responses to a written survey procedure. Results indicate a generally realistic local awareness of the economic aspects of increased tourism activity, but an over-optimistic assessment of environmental impacts, societal impacts, and the ability of local stakeholders to successfully manage the process of tourism industry development.

There are no evil monsters ... there are only humans who think, feel, and act irrationally, sometimes out of confusion, sometimes out of insecurity (Switzer, 2001)

In commenting on Nobel prize-winner J.M. Coetzee's 1980 novel "Waiting for the Barbarians," Chris Switzer highlights the degree to which human beings are typically able to maintain an enhanced level of positivity in the prelude to an anticipated event. Particularly in environments that are perceived as less than optimal, we have all experienced a conviction that somehow things will get better—when the government changes, when the weather improves, or when we acquire a higher level of qualification. The unifying feature in all of these situations is a somewhat irrational belief that the future unknown will necessarily be an improvement on the currently known—that the grass of the future will inevitably be greener than the grass of the present.

To some extent, this is the promise of community development for, as Theodori (2005, p. 662) has aptly observed, "time and again, community development has been prescribed as a popular means of improving the social, economic, and environmental quality of life for residents of a community." In order to achieve this ambition, there is an inevitable process of optimistic futurism associated with the community development model, in which multiple strands of potential quality of life improvement are presented to community residents as an enticement to take part in some form of programmed behavior change. As Theodori goes on to say, however, this admirable objective can often founder through a lack of understanding of what "community" actually is, and an imperfect knowledge of the processes necessary to transform a theoretical model into a practical outcome.

In this respect, there are significant parallels and overlaps with many of the well established principles that populate the tourism literature. Just as community development continues to promise improvement in societal, economic, and environmental conditions, so the gradual evolution of paradigmatic thinking in relation to a burgeoning tourism industry has arrived at a conclusion that true sustainability in tourism development (if, indeed, there is such a thing) can only be realised in circumstances where economic, societal, and environmental implications are taken into account (Weaver & Lawton, 2002). These coincidental streams of reasoning have found an outlet for their expression in the concept of community-based tourism, the process by which the principles and practices of domestic and/or international tourism are used as a vehicle to facilitate local community development (Addison, 1996).

The basic premise of a tourism-based model of community development is that sustainable improvements in economic, societal, and environmental conditions can be realised in situations where a local community is actively involved in the design, implementation, management, and review of its own local visitor industry (Fleischer & Felsenstein, 2000). In this context, "active involvement" implies that local citizens will participate in the process of opportunity identification and evaluation (Sautter & Leisen, 1999), the design of an overarching policy and strategy (Bramwell & Sharman, 1999), the operational monitoring of visitor industry activities (Hardy & Beeton, 2001), and the mitigation of any negative outcomes that arise (Choi & Sirakaya, 2006). Indeed, there are a significant number of instances in which this process has been at least superficially undertaken, and a catalogue of common benefits and costs has emerged as a result (Zhang, Inbakaran, & Jackson, 2006).

Again reflecting the principles of both community development and tourism management, these benefits and costs have traditionally been presented as a triad of economic, societal, and environmental impacts. Though the scope and scale of impact is thought to continuously evolve in response to changing patterns of visitor volumes, tourist types, and activities undertaken, there is a well-supported view that tourism offers substantial (though selectively distributed) economic benefits to a community, often severe and sometimes debilitating environmental costs, and something of a mixed bag of both positive and negative societal adjustments (Hall & Lew, 1998). From this perspective then, appropriate management of any community venture into tourism appears extremely desirable, as does an improved under-standing of the ways in which community tourism is thought to develop.

However, it is important to note that the majority of these evolutionary processes have been described in retrospect. In other words, there has been a predominant focus on determining the overall costs and benefits of tourism development *after* the event, when it may well be too late to seek any real adjustment to the policies and processes by which benefits are accrued and distributed; and certainly too late to avoid the apparently inevitable negatives that are thought to accompany such economic improvements. Thus, the literature has been much more effective in identifying "what went wrong" than it has been in equipping communities with the strategies necessary to anticipate and adapt to the dangers that are predicted to lie ahead.

In an attempt to address this anomaly, this paper initially reviews the theoretical propositions that have emerged from thirty years of academic investigation into the development of tourism in high-profile destination areas, concluding that a broadly predictable model of community tourism development can readily be isolated and described. The paper then applies the principles that underpin that model to a range of communities in which tourism has yet to fully establish itself. Introducing the concept of "incidental destinations," the paper seeks to measure the extent to which those communities have reached an accurate understanding of the implications of visitor activity, and the extent to which this understanding translates to a level of support for (or opposition to) future visitor industry developments.

In pursuit of this goal, a parallel program of research activity was undertaken in four small city communities in England, Ireland, Australia, and New Zealand, in an effort to establish the degree to which these communities might have absorbed the experiences of those who have already progressed much further along the tourism development continuum. The outcomes of this research are therefore expected to be of interest to all members of such early-stage tourism development communities, but more specifically those who are entrusted with the responsibility of delivering maximum economic benefits alongside minimized environmental and/or social side effects.

Tourism-based community development

The previously posited parallels and overlaps between community development (CD) and tourism management (TM) suggest that both bodies of knowledge may well have relevant contributions to make to any consideration of tourism-based community development. From a broader CD perspective, authors such as Di Stefano (2004) have acknowledged the underlying need to build a sustainable future for communities through attention to the aforementioned triad of developmental perspectives, and a number of alternative drivers for this type of development have been identified—encompassing a range of disparate economic engines such as science and technology (Hommen, Doloreux, & Larsson, 2006), the arts (Phillips, 2004), clothing and textiles (Marcinczak & van de Velde, 2008), and the so called "knowledge economy" (Yigitcanlar & Velibeyoglu, 2008). However, irrespective of the specific economic driver selected, a clear unifying element for the community development process is the need to ensure that as wide a range of community stakeholders as possible is involved in the design and implementation of that process.

Indeed, the powerful emphasis that the CD literature has traditionally placed on the empowerment of communities and their residents is regarded as a fundamental condition of ultimate success. In this paradigm, recognition of citizen concerns around economics, societal issues, and environmental purity, and the establishment of a process that supports citizen control of the decisions related to these concerns, is fundamental—and intended developments that are undertaken without the whole-hearted participation and support of the community concerned are almost certainly destined to fail. As Simpson (2007, p. 186) has commented, in relation to tourism-based community development, the key challenge is to "develop economically viable enterprises that provide livelihood benefits to local communities while protecting indigenous cultures and environments."

Some researchers working in the CD field have however seen a need to question the ability, and indeed the desire, of tourism industry advocates to meet the essential benchmark conditions necessary to breathe life into a tourism-based CD initiative. For example, Blackstock (2005) has cast doubt on the ability of tourism to provided any meaningful or lasting benefit to the local communities that succumb to its appeal, noting that much of the thrust of the community-based tourism literature can be seen as an attempt to legitimise the business of tourism in the eyes of community, rather than to maximise the cost-benefit equation from a community resident perspective. Similarly, de Beer & Marais (2005) point to a fundamental tension between CD's desire to maximise community prosperity and TM's focus on creating shareholder wealth. For these authors, rather than achieving the claimed partnership between community stakeholders and commercial interests, the typical community involvement initiative can often be little more than an elaborate public relations exercise.

Yet there have been instances where the interests of CD and tourism have apparently coincided. Di Stefano (2004) cites the example of Whitefish, Montana, a town that responded to the gradual decline of traditional industry by introducing a new, and highly successful, visitor industry based on winter sports; and Gotham (2005) points to the invaluable contribution made by tourism to the transformation of New Orleans from a regionally to a globally recognized and respected city. Thus, there are clearly evident positives and negatives associated with a move into tourism-based community development, and the extent to which these elements are influential has become a frequent topic of discussion in the tourism literature.

In the early literature on tourism development, a so-called "advocacy" approach prevailed, in which the relatively new commercial activity of tourism was presented as a pollution free alternative to declining primary and extractive industry. From this perspective, Page (2003) notes that the introduction of a new local tourism industry held the promise of significant income generation and employment creation, along with an encouragement of increased entrepreneurial behavior across a more equitably balanced portfolio of economic activity. Similarly, tourism was held to be largely beneficial to the local society, introducing enhanced levels of sophistication to the local culture, providing an impetus for the creation of new infrastructure which was subsequently accessible by local people, and leading to an expanded range of recreational facilities available to all. Even environmental impacts were seen in a positive light, visitors being held responsible for a range of "clean-up" exercises intended to present the character of the destination in the most favorable way possible.

As academic consideration of tourism's influence intensified, a more cautionary approach emerged in the literature, as researchers began to uncover the reverse side of the tourism coin. Page (2003) goes on to say that the economic transformation wrought by tourism could potentially result in an over-dependence on visitors as a sole source of income, a subsequent exposure to what might well prove to be a highly seasonal activity, a high level of financial leakage outside of the community to pay for necessary imports and repatriation of corporate profits, and the introduction of inflationary pressures to real estate and commodity markets. From a societal perspective, a high influx of visitors could lead to the exclusion of local people from traditional open-access sites and activities, the commodification of local culture to meet the time-poor requirements of transient visitors, and higher levels of socially undesirable and often criminal practices (Pearce, 1989). Finally, the enormous potential for environmental destruction was belatedly conceded, and a highly negative ecological cost-benefit equation established. Tourism was now seen to indeed be a viable alternative, but pollution-free it certainly was not— Table 1 below summarizes the contradictory nature of these observations.

Identification of these conflicting issues has largely resulted from research carried out in highly tourism-intensive environments like the Hawaiian Islands (Liu & Var, 1986), the city of York, England (Snaith & Haley, 1999), the Gold Coast region of Australia (Tomljenovic & Faulkner (1999), and the Mediterranean island of Cyprus (Akis, Peristianis, & Warner, 1996). In these and similar cases, the level of tourism development, socio-cultural characteristics of the dominant visitor profile, and subsequent attitudes expressed by both individual residents and the "community at large" have been presented as contributing elements to a generic and broadly specified theory of tourism's primary costs and benefits as summarized in the final column of Table 1. Thus, as destinations continued to develop along with a continued expansion of world-wide tourism, some reasonably consistent principles have become accepted as germane to the underlying resident-visitor relationship. In this respect, local residents of high profile tourism destinations are frequently judged to have:

- A sound understanding of tourism's contribution to the local economy.
- A less accurate understanding of tourism's *relative* economic importance.
- Difficulty in identifying personal benefits—what's in it for me?
- An appreciation of tourism's contribution to improved community infrastructure and services.
- A perception of tourism as a negative influence over environmental purity.
- A perception of tourism as a positive influence over local society and lifestyle.
- Considerable faith in local planners' ability to successfully manage tourism.
- An overall marginally positive attitude to further tourism development.

However, given the tourism-intensive sites in which these previous investigations were conducted, it is relevant to speculate on whether similar results would necessarily have been obtained had the research been carried out *prior* to the advent of any significant tourist activity. Would the same portfolio of principles hold true, even though the physical and environmental surroundings were different? Would local attitudes towards visitors change in a circumstance where tourist activity was much less prominent, where the community in general did not fully understand the extent of their influence? These are the questions that have underpinned the overall approach to the research described in this paper.

Method

Though there have been a number of well-received attempts to develop an authoritative assessment scale to measure community attitudes to tourism—notably those developed by Lankford & Howard (1993), and Ap & Crompton (1998)—it was decided to reject the use of these and similar scales in favor of a direct test of respondents' level of agreement with each of the eight principles of resident attitude identified earlier. This approach was adopted to reflect a belief that the current research did not set out to gather resident opinion per se; rather it set out to assess

Table 1. Summarized benefits and costs of tourism development.

Type of impact	Positives	Negatives	Summary
Economic impacts	Generation of income for local economy Creation of new employment Improved "balance" in local economy Encouragement for entrepreneurial activity	Potential for economic over-dependence Inflationary pressures Growing dependence on imported resources High degree of seasonality in demand High levels of import leakage Employment often low skilled and poorly paid Demand is price and income elastic	Tourism does indeed generate significant income, but that income is inequitably distributed. Tourism operators (often non-local) and a vaguely cited "overall economy" are primary beneficiaries, local people much less so.
Socio-cultural impacts	Enhanced levels of sophistication in the local culture Creation of new infrastructure Expanded range of recreational facilities	Commodification of culture Inwards migration places pressure on infrastructure Changes in occupational structure towards low-skilled, female, seasonal employment Higher levels of community turnover Increased crime and anti-social behavior	Influx of visitors is exciting and contributes much to community social life. There are some notable negatives that considerably dilute this level of positivity.
Environmental impacts	Greater controls on environmental conservation More funds for environmental maintenance Heightened awareness of importance of environment	Water, visual, architectural, and noise pollution Unplanned ribbon development Traffic and human congestion Land erosion and loss of faunal habitat Segregation of tourists in visitor zones	Visitors are sometimes more considerate of the natural environment than local people. However, overall visitor impact is strongly negative.

Source: Page, 2003.

the attitudes and beliefs of a range of case study communities *in comparison with* a synthesis of attitudes and beliefs established by earlier research. In effect, the primary objective of the research was to gather resident opinion in a range of communities that were NOT well known for their appeal to visitors, and to subsequently compare those opinions with the assessed view of tourist destination community residents as discussed in the previous section. As such, the advantages of simplicity offered by a brief eight item survey were thought to outweigh the greater levels of reliability available through application of a more complex instrument.

Each of the previously identified "principles of resident opinion" was initially translated into a direct attitude statement as presented below, with potential responses guided by a seven point Likert scale that was anchored by "completely disagree" as score option 1 and "completely agree" as score option 7.

- Visitors make a valuable contribution to the local economy.
- Our visitor industry is just as important as other industries to our economy.
- Visitors to our community increase individual residents' wealth.
- Visitors to our community help provide improved local facilities.
- Visitors to our community have a positive effect on the natural environment.
- Visitors to our community have a positive effect on our local lifestyle.
- Careful planning of visitation to our community can overcome possible negative effects.
- We should encourage more visitors.

These eight statements were then incorporated into a paper survey instrument, with the addition of demographic questions relating to length of community residence, gender, age, education level, personal participation in a tourism-related occupation, and income. The survey was pre-tested for potential ambiguity with a small convenience sample of the researchers' colleagues and students, before implementation in four study sites in England, Ireland, Australia and New Zealand. The Irish and New Zealand versions of the survey were mailed to 1000 individuals randomly selected from the local register of electors, with a request to complete and return within a ten day time span. The survey was accompanied by a reply-paid return envelope, and an incentive to complete was offered in the form of a gift of petrol vouchers to a randomly drawn respondent. In Australia, the same questions were included in a large scale annual social survey exercise, and administered by telephone interview to 400 local residents selected at random from the landline telephone directory—in order to reduce the size of the Australian sample to the (approximately) 200 targeted at the other three sites, random selection was used to discard 50% of the initial data set and to retain the remaining 50% for subsequent analysis.

At the English site, due to localized resource constraints, the survey was administered through the implementation of an intercept interview process with patrons of a major shopping mall located in the heart of the community concerned. A random sampling process was used, at a fixed spatial location within the shopping mall, to collect resident opinion over a five day period—as such, the number of completed responses is significantly lower than in the other three sites. A summary of the overall and sectional response statistics is shown in Table 2 below.

Data collected via this process were evaluated through the application of SPSS software, and the following statistical processes conducted:

Table 2.   Survey response statistics.

Criterion	England	Ireland	Australia	New Zealand	Overall
Surveys completed	147	217	207	211	782
Male/female	30%–70%	46%–54%	50%–50%	40%–60%	42%–58%
Mean age (years)	42.12	43.18	49.61	52.81	47.63
Mean education level (1–6 scale)	2.64	3.07	3.02	2.89	2.93
Tourism-related occupation	83%	32%	38%	26%	36%
Income level (1–7 scale)	1.87	2.75	2.08	3.14	2.51

- Calculation of basic descriptive statistics for the sample and each sub-sample
- Calculation of mean response to each of the eight principles of resident attitude
- Application of Analysis of Variance (ANOVA) to identify any significant opinion differences within and between resident groups

Due to the subjective nature of the authors' interpretations of the literature, as presented in Table 1, it was not possible to carry out statistically rigorous comparisons of survey data with assessed academic opinion. However, these comparisons were performed on an informal basis, and a qualitative description of the resulting outcomes is presented in a later section of the paper.

Study sites

In order to meet the overall objectives of the wider survey project, it was deemed desirable to conduct this research in four reasonably comparable communities that nevertheless reflected varying stages of tourism intensity development. As such, the communities of Buxton (England), Waterford (Ireland), Rockhampton (Australia), and Whangarei (New Zealand) were selected as broadly comparable entities. As such, all four communities are presented as market towns that act as a service center for a surrounding rural community; all four are located in relatively close proximity to major population centers; and all four are (to a degree) transit stops between those large population centers and iconic tourism destinations of international repute. A summarized comparison of site characteristics is presented in Table 3 below.

Results

The primary descriptive statistics associated with respondent results are shown in Table 4 below, with responses to each of the eight evaluative questions shown as an overall mean and as a separate mean for each of the four study sites.

Discussion

Respondents clearly claim to understand the economic promise that tourism offers their communities, though the impact of this promise is somewhat less prominent in the Australian sample—implementation of an ANOVA over the relevant responses confirmed a statistically significant difference between the Australian data and those

Table 3. Study site characteristics.

Criterion	England	Ireland	Australia	New Zealand
Study Site	Buxton	Waterford	Rockhampton	Whangarei
Urban population	25,000	45,000	65,000	45,000
Rural population	75,000	30,000	100,000	25,000
Economic drivers	Agriculture, tourism	Agriculture, light manufacturing	Mining, agriculture	Agriculture, light manufacturing
Relative prosperity	Moderate	Moderate	Moderate	Moderate
Iconic visitor attractions	High Peak National Park	Waterford Crystal	None	None
Nearby urban conurbations	Several, approx. population 15 million	Dublin, 1.6 million	Brisbane, 1.8 million	Auckland, 1.4 million
Nearby tourism icons	Several	Ring of Kerry	Great Barrier Reef	Bay of Islands
Level of tourism activity	High	Moderate to low	Low	Low

Table 4. Summarized results.

Visitor Criterion (maximum agreement = 7.00)	Overall	England	Ireland	Australia	New Zealand
Visitors make a valuable contribution to the local economy.	5.90	6.07	6.14	5.43	5.99
Our visitor industry is just as important as other industries to our economy.	5.12	5.28	5.22	5.10	4.91
Visitors to our community increase individual residents' wealth	3.80	4.35	3.75	3.47	3.81
Visitors to our community help provide improved local facilities.	4.32	3.80	4.46	4.38	4.49
Visitors to our community have a positive effect on the natural environment.	5.12	5.01	5.22	5.12	5.09
Visitors to our community have a positive effect on our local lifestyle	5.16	5.18	5.18	5.16	5.13
Careful planning of visitation to our community can overcome possible negative effects.	5.94	5.60	6.30	5.78	5.99
We should encourage more visitors.	5.90	5.56	6.23	5.70	5.99

from the other three study sites ($F = 5.589$, $p < .01$). Further analysis of the entire data set revealed a direct link between scores for the variables "visitors make a valuable economic contribution to the local economy" and "we should encourage more visitors"—the Pearson coefficient for this relationship was a statistically moderate .406—and there does therefore seem to be a degree of causality between perceived economic benefits and enthusiasm for further expansion.

Interestingly, our informal prediction that respondents would under-estimate the relative economic importance of tourism to their communities was not supported in the data, though New Zealand respondents appeared rather less positive than those in the other study sites. This can of course be interpreted as a reflection of current reality, as tourism is not yet a major force in any of these communities, but can equally well be seen as a failure to recognize the full industrial-economic implications of growing non-resident activity in the area. On the other hand, respondents appear to have a pragmatically realistic set of expectations in terms of potential for improvements in their own personal wealth. Here, it is interesting to note the higher level of confidence expressed by English respondents in response to this question, attributable at least in part to these respondents' much higher levels of direct involvement with visitors—there is a statistically significant Pearson coefficient of .306 between the variables "I am employed in a tourism related occupation" and "Visitors to our community increase individual residents' wealth." It appears then that familiarity, in this instance at least, breeds greater understanding rather than increased contempt!

If the data does tend to suggest a reasonably accurate understanding of the ways in which economic positives may be expected to flow from increasing visitor activity, a vastly different picture emerges from resident perceptions of non-economic impacts. In the first instance, there is a significant lack of appreciation of the degree to which a healthy visitor industry demands the provision of updated recreational infrastructure, which then at least equally benefits the resident population in terms of better parks and gardens, shopping, food and beverage options, and entertainment etc. More important perhaps is the consistently positive view of tourism as an environmental and social benefactor that can be successfully managed to the elimination of negative impacts. As much of the extant literature would seem to indicate, this is by no means coincident with the past experiences of communities with higher levels of past visitor industry involvement.

In a number of other respects though, sub-sets of respondent opinion were very much in alignment with the types of attitude expected in visitor-intensive communities. When a series of ANOVA procedures were conducted to assess the impact of demographic variables on respondent opinion, no significant variation could be attributed to respondents' years of residence in the community, gender, or income levels. However, those who claimed direct involvement with the local tourism industry were understandably more positive about industry contributions to individual wealth ($F = 11.222$, $p < .01$), and were also more supportive of any attempts to attract more visitors ($F = 4.799$, $p < .01$). This desire was not, however, supported by older residents ($F = 5.5506$, $p < .01$) or the better educated ($F = 3.303$, $p < .01$). These findings are very much in line with the experience of past researchers cited earlier in this paper, again suggesting that the level of conceptual understanding in these incidental tourism communities may in fact be relatively well developed in some respects.

Overall, although there is an obvious element of subjective interpretation involved in any such judgements, it appears possible that these communities' lack of any major past exposure to the realities of the tourism industry has permitted the evolution of a "rose coloured glasses" perception of what tourism can do for the local community, and of what the attendant costs of these benefits might be. As such, the four study sites may already be exhibiting the classic symptoms of what Smith & Krannich (1998) called "hungry" communities—high economic expectations, albeit tempered with a realistic scepticism of the degree of personal benefit, allied to an apparent belief that both societal and environmental concerns can be effectively managed in the interests of minimum change.

If this is indeed the case, the likely future evolution of tourism in these communities is clearly, and not altogether positively, signposted in the literature—"hungry" community attitudes drifting in a steady downwards spiral through ambivalence and into saturation, and a corresponding shift in resident attitudes from embracement to withdrawal. So what can these communities do now to avoid or at least mitigate the negatives that appear to lie ahead? One answer to this question would appear to lie with a revised response to the management of expectations, a commitment by local government and other peak body stakeholders to an objective and transparent presentation of the realities of tourism industry development—*before* such development becomes "official" community policy. If this more realistic approach to representing the potential impacts of tourism is adopted, we argue that community planners' language may then be expected to move from the conventional and largely expected version represented in the left column of Table 5; and towards a more pragmatic and ultimately more honest representation presented in the right column.

Community development practice is replete with examples of local projects that have been "sold" to residents via an amalgam of established fact, inadvertent oversight, and deliberate misrepresentation, and the potential relevance of this judgement to local community tourism development is not difficult to imagine. Though it may perhaps be unfair to describe this practice as typical, the left column of typical 5 represents a by no means unusual "push" strategy that conceptualizes tourism as a development initiative that must therefore be actively promoted to

Table 5. Two developmental rationales for community tourism.

Conventional rationale	Recommended rationale
Community tourism means much higher levels of income flowing into the local economy	Community tourism means an increase in the number of people available for local businesses to market to
Community tourism means that individuals will become more prosperous	Community tourism offers an opportunity to build relationships that will be economically beneficial for all organizations and individuals concerned
Community tourism means that we will need to build better local infrastructure for use by residents and visitors alike	Community tourism means that we may have to rethink our infrastructural development priorities, and to assess the positives and negatives that reprioritization implies
On balance, an increase in visitor numbers will have a negligible impact on our natural environment	Visitors may have a different value system than local people in relation to the natural environment—the more visitors we have, the greater care needs to be taken to sustain our own local value system
On balance, an increase in visitor numbers will have a positive impact on our local lifestyle	Temporary visitors and permanent residents have radically different expectations in relation to lifestyle elements—the more visitors we have, the greater care needs to be taken to sustain our own local value system
Whatever the benefits and costs of increased community tourism, damage to our community can be minimized or eliminated by careful local government planning	Commitment to increased levels of community tourism places ever greater demands on local planners to exhibit high levels of professional care and attention in a largely unfamiliar planning milieu

residents in pursuit of community acceptance and endorsement—an intrinsically beneficial strategy that needs only to be invested in, promoted, and subsequently tolerated by all concerned. In contrast, we argue that the right column of Table 5 represents a superior "pull" strategy that sees tourism as a significant agent of change that will substantially alter the character of the community, and something that must therefore be carefully managed in pursuit of maximum benefit with minimum side effects—an intrinsically high risk strategy that communities cannot afford to treat with anything but the utmost care and attention.

The enhanced degree of honesty, transparency, and equity that characterizes the right column of Table 5 constitutes, to us, the most persuasive argument for its adoption. On the one hand, residents who are more accurately aware of what lies ahead for any given community venture are more likely to offer informed opinions on that venture's desirability, exhibit enhanced levels of participation and ownership, and commit to high level determination to succeed. More pragmatically, and whatever the motivation, it is the opinion of the current authors that the right side of Table 5 is, in fact, a much more effective "selling" proposition than the more commonly evident advocacy position reflected in the left column—telling the truth, the whole truth, and nothing but the truth remains as powerful a strategy as it ever has been.

Conclusions

This paper has investigated the extent to which local communities on the brink of committing to the development of a tourism industry are fully aware of the conventionally accepted ramifications of such a move. In summary, the authors propose that such communities are frequently encouraged to enter into such an activity by the (involuntary or deliberate) promise of high level economic benefit, accompanied by manageable social and environmental change. It is further suggested that communities who accept this equation as an accurate representation of what they might reasonably expect from tourism are largely doomed to disappointment—tourism is infinitely more complex than a simple economic equation might suggest, and early acceptance and understanding of this reality is a useful contributor to enhanced prospects of successful industry development in the community.

For local community administrations, the essential message—commitment to over-promise and under-delivery— is a simple though superficially challenging proposition to adopt. It has traditionally been accepted practice for local government and other development project sponsors to err on the side of optimism when presenting a rationale for developmental direction change—however, it is the central contention of this paper that this may be a short sighted approach that greatly enhances the possibility of ultimate disappointment whilst doing little or nothing to enhance local community support for the project in question. If this is indeed the case, we urge local government administrations in those communities who currently qualify as "incidental destinations" to consider their options extremely carefully, and to ensure that they and their residents are fully acquainted with the past history of local tourism development, before electing to invest scarce local resources in this most intricately complex of activities. The rewards of success are by no means clearly established, but the penalties of failure have been writ large for all to see.

References

Addison, L. (1996). An approach to community based tourism planning in the Baffin region, Canada's Far North. In L.C. Harrison & W. Husbands (Eds.) *Practising responsible tourism: International case studies in tourism planning, policy and development.* New York: John Wiley & Sons.

Akis, S., Peristianis, N., & Warner, J. (1996). Residents' attitudes to tourism development: The case of Cyprus. *Tourism Management, 17*(7), 481–494.

Ap, J., & Crompton, J.L. (1998). Developing and testing a tourism impact scale. *Journal of Travel Research, 37*(2), 120–130.

Blackstock, K. (2005). A critical look at community based tourism. *Community Development Journal, 40*(1), 39–49.

Bramwell, B., & Sharman, A. (1999). Collaboration in local tourism policy making. *Annals of Tourism Research, 26*(2), 392–415.

Choi, H.C., & Sirakaya, E. (2006). Sustainability indicators for managing community tourism. *Tourism Management, 27*, 1274–1289.

Coetzee, J.M. (1980). *Waiting for the Barbarians.* London: Secker and Warburg.

De Beer, F., & Marais, M. (2005). Rural communities, the natural environment and development – some challenges, some successes. *Community Development Journal, 40*(1), 50–61.

Di Stefano, D. (2004). Tourism, industry, and community development: Whitefish, Montana, 1903–2003. *Environmental Practice, 6*(1), 63–70.

Fleischer, A., & Felsenstein, D. (2000). Support for rural tourism: Does it make a difference? *Annals of Tourism Research, 27*(4), 1007–1024.

Gotham, K.F. (2005). Tourism from above and below: Globalisation, localisation, and New Orleans' Mardi Gras. *International Journal of Urban and Regional Research, 29*(2), 309–326.

Hall, C.M., & Lew, A.A. (1998). *Sustainable tourism – a geographical perspective.* New York: Addison Wesley Longman.

Hardy, A.L., & Beeton, R.J.S. (2001). Sustainable tourism or maintainable tourism: Managing resources for more than average outcomes. *Journal of Sustainable Tourism, 9*(3), 168–192.

Hommen, L., Doloreux, D., & Larsson, E. (2006). Emergence and growth of Mjarvedi Science Park in Linkoping, Sweden. *European Planning Studies, 14*(10), 1331–1361.

Lankford, S.V., & Howard, D.R. (1993). Developing a tourism impact attitude scale. *Annals of Tourism Research, 21*(1), 121–139.

Liu, J.C., & Var, T. (1986). Resident attitudes towards tourism impacts in Hawaii. *Annals of Tourism Research, 13*, 193–214.

Marcinczak, S., & van der Velde, M. (2008). Drifting in a global space of textile flows: Apparel bazaars in Poland's Lodz region. *European Planning Studies, 16*(7), 911–923.

Page, S. (2003). *Tourism management: Managing for change.* Amsterdam: Butterworth-Heinemann.

Pearce, D.G. (1989). *Tourism development.* Hartlow: Longman.

Phillips, R. (2004). Artful business: Using the arts for community economic development. *Community Development Journal, 39*(2), 112–122.

Sautter, E.T., & Leisen, B. (1999). Managing stakeholders: A tourism planning model. *Annals of Tourism Research, 26*(2), 312–328.

Simpson, M.C. (2007). An integrated approach to assess the impacts of tourism on community development and sustainable livelihoods. *Community Development Journal, 44*(2), 186–208.

Smith, M.D., & Krannich, R.S. (1998). Tourism dependence and resident attitudes. *Annals of Tourism Research, 25*(4), 783–8702.

Snaith, T., & Haley, A. (1999). Residents' opinions of tourism development in the historic city of York, England. *Tourism Management, 20*(1), 595–603.

Switzer, C. (2001). Waiting for the Barbarians Review. Turtleneck – an online journal of literary culture. Retrieved on 10 October 2009 from http://turtleneck.net/summer01/tweedjacket/coetzee2.htm

Theodori, G.L. (2005). Community and community development in resource-based areas: Operational definitions rooted in an international perspective. *Society and Natural Resources, 18*, 661–669.

Tomljenovic, R., & Faulkner, W. (1999). Tourism and older residents in a sunbelt resort. *Annals of Tourism Research*, *27*(1), 93–114.

Weaver, D., & Lawton, L (2002). *Tourism management* (2nd ed.). Milton, Australia: John Wiley and Sons.

Yigitcanlar, T., & Velibeyoglu, K. (2008). Knowledge based urban development: The local development path of Brisbane, Australia. *Local Economy*, *23*(3), 195–207.

Zhang, J., Inbakaran, R.J., & Jackson, M. (2006). Regional community attitudes towards tourism: identification of community clusters in Murrindini Shire, Victoria. *Proceedings of 16th annual CAUTHE conference*. Melbourne, 6–9 February, pp. 1257–1271.

Sustainable practices of community tourism planning: lessons from a remote community

Oksana Grybovych[a] and Delmar Hafermann[b]

[a]Division of Leisure, Youth, and Human Services, University of Northern Iowa, Cedar Falls, IA 50614-0241, USA; [b]Graduate Program in Public Policy, University of Northern Iowa, Cedar Falls, IA 50614-0241, USA

This article examines community tourism planning practices through the theoretical framework of deliberative democracy, and provides an example of best practices of integrating tourism planning and development into community comprehensive planning. It illustrates how a small remote community on Vancouver Island, Canada embraced practices of participatory dialogic planning in its official community planning process. Having faced a threat of tourism development going out of control, this community decided to take a proactive stance and collectively design a policy framework to guide potential developers. Fresh and innovative planning and policy approaches not only helped safeguard community and social capitals, but exemplified fresh unconventional practices of embedding community based tourism planning into broader sustainable community planning efforts.

Introduction

The decline of traditional industries and agriculture in recent times has forced many urban and rural areas to turn to tourism as a field of opportunities on the way to economic growth and diversification (adapted from Hall & Mitchell, 2000; Hall, 2005). As a result, tourism is now one of the target industries for communities of all sizes wishing to integrate it into their overall comprehensive plans (Blackstock, 2005; Murphy & Murphy, 2004). The promise of tourism is especially apparent in rural areas experiencing economic instability and disintegration of the local fabric (adapted from Gannon, 1993). While rural tourism development alone is not the panacea to the ailments of rural regions, it has a great potential when integrated in broader community development efforts. The latter scenario often means diversification of the economic base, provides opportunities for social, economic, environmental, and cultural development, and also ensures greater security for the community (Gannon, 1993; Murphy & Murphy, 2004).

This study is part of a larger research project presented by the authors at the 2008 CDS Conference in Saskatoon, Canada.

For such an endeavor to be successful and sustainable, it has to be both *community-led* and *participatory*[1]. Significant community development takes place only when local residents are committed to investing themselves and their resources in the effort (Kretzmann & McKnight, 1993); when it comes to rural tourism development and planning, the most successful examples of tourism occur in communities in which there is broadly based resident participation in the planning and development of tourism projects (Butler & Hall, 1998; Cooke, 1982; Godfrey & Clarke, 2000; Marien & Pizam, 1997; Pearce & Moscardo, 1999; Tosun & Timothy, 2001). In other words, for tourism or community development to be sustainable, local control over public decision making and planning is needed (Gibbs, 1994). This community based participatory planning and decision making implies a process of interaction within the community, which ultimately leads to the development of community (adapted from Marcus & Brennan, 2008). This process can be further enhanced by a policy framework at the national and regional levels that would favor the development of sustainable community based tourism practices (World Tourism Organization, 1994). Such a policy would also encourage successful partnerships of public, private and nonprofit sectors within the broader resident population, ensuring sustainability of outcomes and policy and financial support of community-backed initiatives.

While this sounds a rather complex task to undertake, examples of successful community tourism planning practices are readily available. This paper discusses the experiences of one such community through the theoretical framework of deliberative democracy. Following review of pertinent literature, we will examine new and unconventional practices of embedding community based tourism planning into broader sustainable community planning efforts.

On rural reflation, asset-based community development, and appreciative inquiry

During the 1950s, the United Nations' report *Social progress through community development* introduced *community development* as a "process designed to create conditions of economic and social progress for the whole community with its active participation and the fullest possible reliance on the community's initiative" (United Nations, 1955, p.6). In essence, community development was envisioned as a set of tools and techniques communities could use to improve their physical, social, and economic life conditions (Christenson, Fendley, & Robinson, 1989). In practice, it often involved organized efforts to involve a broad range of stakeholders in a process of public decision making regarding issues considered of critical importance to the community (adapted from Hutchison & Nogradi, 1996). Over time, community development came to be seen as a process encompassing citizen involvement and utilizing local resources for solving issues of local concern (Alinsky, 1971; Rothman, 1995). More recently the United Nations, World Bank and World Tourism Organization, among other important bodies, have also emphasized sustainable, rural and community development (as well as participatory governance efforts) in their funding and policy priorities. While keeping outcomes in sight, the focus has been on the *process* of bringing community residents together in a cooperative and collaborative fashion (Hutchison & McGill, 1992) with the purposeful attempt to improve communities under democratic conditions of participation (Phifer, List, & Faulkner, 1989). Some even argued that the development of community has become synonymous with the process of (or a restoration of) democracy (Stormann, 1996).

Review of community development literature reveals several themes of importance to this paper: (1) citizen participation and community involvement in decision making are essential to community development (Bridger & Luloff, 1999; Hutchison & Nogradi, 1996; Phifer et al. 1989); (2) there are numerous barriers to effective and sustainable community development (Bridger & Luloff, 1999); and (3) effective and sustainable community development demands a considerable investment in effort and needs to be rooted in the development of local capacities and place-based strategies rather than imposing standard cut-and-dry models from elsewhere (Day, 1998). Among others, two theoretical approaches stand out providing guidance to those seeking answers on how exactly can local community capacities be developed, namely *rural reflation* and *asset-based community development*[2].

In 1989, Fendley and Christenson put forth an idea of *rural reflation* as a process of developing the character and abilities of rural communities in the global economy. Times had changed, they argued, so the community development practices must change as well. For communities wishing to affect the change rather than be affected by it, rural reflation provided "the dual attempt at building a community market in the world economy while maintaining and solidifying a community identity" (p.106). The process emphasized the role of leadership and favorable policy framework, local government involvement, and an active probusiness interest group with the will to act and effect change; these provided the necessary conditions for developing a niche in the world economy through organizing and maximizing the use of community's human and financial capital. Among a wide range of opportunities for rural reflation, authors emphasized development of service industries (including tourism) as especially lucrative for creating unique area identity.

In 1993, Kretzmann and McKnight expanded rural reflation theory by suggesting a process of building communities "from inside out." Instead of traditional practices of creating what they termed "client neighborhoods," they advocated for an approach to neighborhood regeneration that would capitalize on local assets— individuals, associations and institutions, harnessing them for local development purposes. As such, an *asset-based community development* approach appeared, advocating the view of tangible and intangible community assets as strengths to be appreciated and used to create new economic and social opportunities. Today, an asset-based community development provides a framework for a broad range of community development projects (see, for example, *Asset based approaches to rural community development* project of the Carnegie Trust UK and the International Association for Community Development).

Finally, over the last decade community development practitioners and organizations such as the International Institute for Sustainable Development have been advocating the *appreciative inquiry (AI)* model of community development—arguing that *asset-based community development* and *appreciative inquiry* hold the greatest potential for a grass-roots community change. Modified from the fields of action research and organizational development, appreciative inquiry theory identifies the best of "what is" to pursue dreams and possibilities of "what could be," therefore focusing on community strengths to advance sustainable development at the community level (Flora & Flora, 2008; International Institute for Sustainable Development, 2000).

While providing parallel guidelines for community development practitioners, all these models emphasize the role of citizen participation and collective action in achieving significant community development goals. Rural tourism planning and development, as argued earlier, has a promise of assisting communities achieve these goals—but only if it is being integrated in broader comprehensive community development practices.

On community tourism planning and citizen participation

Community based tourism planning has recently attracted a fair amount of attention. This can be explained by a number of factors. As Hibbard (1999) pointed out, rural communities in the United States have undergone a process of "devolution," or a shift of responsibility from higher to lower levels of government support of local control of planning and decision making. Existing ideology of "expertism" and failure of traditional "top-down" planning approaches have further contributed to the growing interest in alternative integrated, comprehensive, sustainable and community-driven planning and development models (adapted from Durant, 2001). Finally, an increased recognition that this new community oriented approach requires genuine and extensive public participation and relies on the input from a broad range of stakeholders (Fuller & Reid, 1998; Harrill, 2004; Hibbard & Lurie, 2000; Jamal & Getz, 1999).

Tourism in this sense is in a unique position—like no other industry, it relies heavily on the goodwill and cooperation of host communities (Murphy, 1985). It therefore becomes increasingly important to ensure that those who will have to live with tourism outcomes are involved in every stage of the tourism planning and decision making process. Involvement of those affected in the planning process not only helps ensure public support, it can also help build bridges of trust and confidence among planners, the general public, and the private industry (Loukissas, 1983). Community oriented approaches to tourism planning and development can provide valuable guidelines for policy makers (Liu & Var, 1986), whereas without public participation tourism growth may make little contribution to the objectives of development (Tosun & Timothy, 2001). In other words, tourism development which is a part of a community is generally more successful than development set apart from a community (Pearce & Moscardo, 1999). Even more so, tourism development which is not integrated with community can be disastrous (Butler & Hall, 1998). In order to achieve this decentralized, integrated and dynamic community-led tourism planning and development, the practice of tourism planning needs to shift the focus from economic growth and marketing—traditional approach to understanding and implementing tourism projects in rural areas—to community input (Butler, 1991; Fuller & Reid, 1998; Godfrey & Clarke, 2000; Loukissas, 1983; Marcouiller, 1997; Murphy, 1985; Reid, 2003).

Over time, a number of tourism planning models and approaches have been developed, all emphasizing sustainability, citizen involvement, and community-led development. Among them—integrated and integrative tourism planning (Butler, 1991; Gunn, 1994; Ioannides, 1995; Inskeep, 1991; Marcouiller, 1997; Pearce & Moscardo, 1999), responsible and responsive tourism planning (Haywood, 1988; Ritchie, 1993), comprehensive and balanced tourism planning (Madrigal, 1993; Murphy, 1985), collaborative tourism planning (Jamal & Getz, 1995; Reed, 1997; Sautter & Leisen, 1999; Williams, Penrose & Hawkes, 1998), participatory tourism planning (Timothy, 1999), inclusive tourism planning (Madrigal, 1995; Prentice, 1993), and dialogic tourism planning (Jamal, Stein & Harper, 2002). One of the most recent efforts has been to expand existing participatory community tourism planning models by utilizing the framework of *deliberative democracy* (Grybovych, 2008).

Deliberative democratic planning and decision making appears to address most of the weaknesses traditional planning approaches have suffered from, and differs from existing participatory models by the breadth and quality of participation. It emphasizes an ongoing inclusive and dialogic participatory process of learning and shared decision making based on what Yankelovich (1991) called "public judgment" (Weeks, 2000). Applied in practice, deliberative democratic processes aim to ensure transparency, representativeness of public planning and decision making, with dialogue as a necessary prerequisite to an effective and meaningful exercise of participatory governance.

On deliberative democracy

The study of deliberation is not new by any means. In fact, a brief review of the literature on deliberation will take the reader back to the works of Aristotle (384 BC–322 BC), Jean-Jacques Rousseau (1712–1778), and John Dewey (1925, 1930, 1938, 1939). Often defined as a transformative process of social learning (Chrislip, 2002; Farrelly, 2004; Forester, 1999), deliberative democracy feeds upon two main theories of learning—reflective pragmatism of John Dewey (1930), and relationships of knowledge and power of Paulo Freire (1970, 1985; Forester, 1999). This emphasis on learning distinctively differentiates deliberative democracy from other democratic forms of governance, and explains the rising interest in deliberative practices, born out of frustration with adversarial politics (Karpowitz & Mansbridge, 2005).

In the field of political theory and planning the most known and influential interpretation of deliberative democracy belongs to Jürgen Habermas (1984, 1987). *Deliberative democracy*, in his view, opens governmental institutions and laws to free reflection and discussion by the public. It therefore offers a new way of engaging citizens in deciding upon the matters that directly affect their lives, and by doing so fosters the creation of livable communities characterized by community cohesion, existing norms of trust and reciprocity, civic engagement, and participatory governance. Habermas (1984, 1987) defines deliberation as a process of seeking consensus and persuasion of one's opponents by civil argumentation rather than force or coercion. Decisions reached consensually through the deliberations of multiple stakeholders, because there are good reasons for them rather than because of the economic or political power of participants, are viewed then as communicatively rational (Innes, 1996). Habermas's (1984, 1987) theory of *communicative rationality* implies an uncoerced and undistorted interaction among competent individuals—an ideal process that aspires to perfection of an "ideal speech situation." Not only can such participatory discourse bring about the ideal of communicative rationality (Webler, 1995), but conditions of this genuine participatory process form the core characteristics of deliberative democratic processes. Webler (1995) further argues that Habermas's (1984, 1987) communicative rationality gives impetus to fair and competent ideal speech situation or what he calls "right" citizen participation.

Weeks (2000) outlines the following characteristics of a sound deliberative democratic process: (1) broad and representative public participation; (2) informed public judgment; (3) deliberative public participation, and (4) highly credible and methodologically sound outcomes/results. Principles of deliberative democracy, he argues, are not a pure theoretical construct, a method, or a project, but rather a philosophy of governance (Weeks, 2003). Case studies have illustrated how principles of deliberative democracy can be applied to help communities address the most critical issues. These examples showcase how deliberative democratic tools can be used to facilitate the eliciting of broad public participation in a process which provides citizens with an opportunity to consider the issues, weigh up the alternatives, and express judgment about which policy is preferred (AmericaSpeaks, 2004; Hartz-Karp, 2005; Lukensmeyer & Torres, 2003; Stein, Imel, & Henderson, 2004; Weeks, 2000).

The goals of deliberative democracy—to revitalize civic culture, improve the nature of public discourse, and generate the political will necessary to take effective action on pressing problems (Weeks, 2000)—are strikingly similar to the goals of community development discussed previously. The framework of deliberative democracy therefore provides a very interesting angle from which community planning and development initiatives can be examined. Setting high standards for community planning processes, it provides important guidance for designing and implementing processes that would ensure meaningful citizen involvement in tourism planning and development.

Methodology

This project applied a case study approach in order to gain an in-depth understanding of community tourism planning practices. Merriam (1988) recommends a case study approach for addressing problems in which understanding is sought in order to improve practice, for this understanding can have influence on policy, practice, and further research. Yin (1994, p.1) adds that case studies "are the preferred strategy when 'how' or 'why' questions are being posed." Selin and Beason (1991) argue that case study research is particularly appropriate for examining the dynamic process-oriented nature of collaborative planning processes.

Case study research is inherently multimethod in nature and often involves qualitative techniques of interviewing, observing, and analyzing documents and records (Denzin & Lincoln, 2005). Qualitative case study is also characterized by "researchers spending extended time on site, personally in contact with activities and operations of the case, reflecting, and revisiting descriptions and meanings of what is going on" (Stake, 2005, p.450). This study utilized three main methods of data collection including: (1) analysis of administrative, planning and legal documents and records, as well as census data, media reports, and others; (2) in-depth phone and face-to-face interviews (both formal and informal) with planners, developers, researchers, university and college students, and residents who had first-hand experience participating in community tourism planning processes; and (3) observations to support/improve interpretations of the interview findings (Angrosino, 2005).

The community we are about to examine—the District of Ucluelet—is located on the west coast of Vancouver Island, Province of British Columbia, Canada (see Figure 1 in the following section). It has recently been spotlighted as a community applying unconventional participatory planning approaches that ultimately brought it national and international recognition. The purpose of this research project was to apply the framework of deliberative democracy to examine the lessons this community learned as it attempted to apply deliberative democratic principles in practice.

Figure 1. Map of the Province of British Columbia and location of Ucluelet. Source: Super, Natural British Columbia.

Initial contacts for this study were established through Vancouver Island University (formerly known as Malaspina University-College) and the planning department of the District of Ucluelet. In total, 26 individuals were interviewed (this excludes a number of informal interviews), half of them—more than one time, with interviews lasting from half an hour to several hours. Most of the interviews were recorded (later transcribed) and documented with extensive and detailed notes; post-interview and observational notes were taken following a number of informal conversations about the project.

Most of the conversations were initiated by asking broad questions about the nature of changes in the community, social and economic context of the process, participants' background and role/participation in the process, as well as their perceptions, attitudes and beliefs. Although an interview guide was used, conversations were free-flowing and open ended. The interviews took place in locations selected by the participants, usually in their homes and workplaces. Study participants represented diverse and at times conflicting interests. They were elected officials, business owners, developers and real estate agents, environmental and advocacy group members, community volunteers, as well as citizens—all of them had first-hand experience in community tourism planning processes in the District of Ucluelet.

Ultimately, the merit and worth of any research lies in its interpretations and assertions. This is especially critical in qualitative inquiry where the researchers are not only (re)constructing other's realities, but should also realize and embrace the full responsibility their actions and assertions entail. To address these issues, investigator and methodological triangulation were used providing another perspective to consider, and interview notes were compared with observational notes taken during the interviews and the site visit. At the same time, as in any other qualitative study of a similar nature, while most assertions made are substantiated by the secondary sources, many of the findings are co-created with the participants through interviews and observations. The latter approach directly feeds on Stake's (2005) argument that in our assertions we should not only "expect [our] readers to comprehend [our] interpretations but to arrive, as well, at their own" (p. 450). Gallagher (1995) referred to this as a study's "believability" and further explained that it "does not mean that one applied method accurately; it means that one accounts for his or herself honestly and with integrity so that the readers can judge the believability of the work" (pp. 32–33). In an effort to produce believable assertions, however, we should not forget that the final outcome is "hidden mix of personal experience, scholarship, and assertions of other researchers" (Stake, 1995, p.12).

Lessons from a remote community

The District of Ucluelet is located on the west coast of Vancouver Island (Province of British Columbia, Canada), on the west side of Barkley Sound, south of the Long Beach Unit of the Pacific Rim National Park Reserve, within the boundaries of the Clayoquot Sound Biosphere Reserve (see Figure 1). The region is characterized by miles of sandy beaches interrupted by rocky headlands and fringed by an old growth temperate rainforest, and is isolated from the rest of Vancouver Island by the long spine of the Vancouver Island Range (District of Ucluelet, 2005). Archaeological evidence indicates the presence of First Nations in the area for at least 4300 years; European and Japanese fur traders and fishermen settled here in 1870, lured by the promises of gold, abundant fishing, and rich forest resources. In 2006, the direct population of Ucluelet was estimated at 1487; the surrounding region, also serviced by Ucluelet, totaled about 3000 additional residents (BC Stats, 2007; District of Ucluelet, 2005).

Historically, the region depended on forestry and fishing. With both industries declining, today its economy is shifting to include other value added and service industries such as tourism, real estate, retail, construction and development, and fish processing. In 2001, the unemployment rate for Ucluelet was 9.7%, with major employers being service industries (accommodation, food services and retail trade), resource-based industries (to include fish processing and logging), and construction (BC Stats, 2001).

Over the past several decades, the District has undergone major economic and social changes. Its transformation has been rather radical—from the community known for its unsustainable logging practices (Ucluelet was in the epicenter of anti-logging protests during the so called "War in the Woods" of 1993), to one recognized nationally and internationally for its sustainable and participatory planning and policy practices (among many awards to Ucluelet is the United Nations' endorsed International Award for Liveable Communities including a Gold Award for the Official Community Plan, a Silver Award for "Most Liveable Community" with a population of under 20,000, and the overall award for Community Sustainability). This journey to sustainability has been neither fast nor easy, and required extensive community participation, passion and commitment of the District staff, as well as partnerships and collaborations in order to establish the framework for achieving community vision. It all started in the late 1990s when the District of Ucluelet added a planner to its civic staff and initiated its first glass-roots review of the Official Community Plan (OCP)—an official guide for decisions on planning and land use management (Government of British Columbia, 1996). The OCP process gathered public input through a series of open houses (public hearings), introduced a number of important development policy changes, and served as a turning point that brought confidence to developers and encouraged all kinds of new developments in the town including Tauca Lea resort construction in 1998 and the Reef Point development in 1999.

While providing a general framework for planners and developers, Official Community Plans are designed to be amended and modified in order to provide a "safety net" for the communities. While the OCP of 1998 provided such protection, it needed additional "smart growth" policies and environmental guidelines in order to give Ucluelet leverage over rezoning or development issues. With this in mind, the District of Ucluelet initiated a review of its OCP in 2003. At the same time, while the town was protecting itself from unwanted development, there were no new development projects on the horizon. Existing tourism initiatives did not provide a sufficient tax base for any infrastructure improvements or community development projects; the District needed more. The promise of an increased tax base materialized in 2004 with the release of 800 acres of rainforest area adjacent to the District from the forest land reserve (Tree Farm License TFL44)[3]. Almost overnight, the District of Ucluelet saw a huge land mass opening for development; now, the decision had to be made as to what would be the best use of the released lands, and that decision had to be incorporated in District zoning bylaw as a part of the Official Community Plan.

These new developments introduced an element of the unexpected to the community. How the lands were to be developed would inadvertently impact everyone's "backyards," therefore the District needed to engage in extensive community dialogue to gauge resident attitudes and opinions towards the future of the community. As it appeared, tourism would be an integral component of that future. Over a short time period, the District saw a number of tourism development proposals ranging from high end tourism projects including resorts and golf courses, to multi-purpose land use projects including single- and multi-family residential areas, affordable housing, parks, trails, and community amenities. The challenge was to identify what mix would best fit within the District's vision, and how the community would benefit from any of these projects.

The planning process that followed was unique in many aspects. From day one, the District of Ucluelet utilized principles of solid sustainable planning and community development in order to "tap into" the community and ensure that not only the most vocal would get involved, but also the "average Joes." While keeping the outcomes/final product in mind, it was the planning process that was placed at the forefront. As in any deliberate process, the OCP revision and rezoning of Weyerhaeuser lands were lengthy and intense, and attempted on informing the community and engage each and everyone in the process of dialogue. For the District planner, the process also presented a challenge of negotiating with a broad range of stakeholders while remaining impartial, keeping focused, and not losing touch with his constituencies. This was largely addressed by engaging the students from Malaspina University-College who were viewed as a "neutral" third party, hence had community trust and support. Mediating skills of the planner aside, it was the grass-roots nature and transparency of the process that played a critical role in opening the doors to the community.

It is difficult to keep things secret in Ucluelet. The small size of the community means neighbors discuss issues their community is facing, share their ideas, and are far from intimidated to speak to their Council or express their opinions during community open houses. To facilitate the process, the District appointed a Steering Committee within which they attempted to include a broad range of representative stakeholders—from high school students and nurses, to educators, retailers, and logging and fishing industry representatives. A number of venues allowing for public input were nowhere near the traditional "public hearings" scenario: there were notice boards in grocery stores and coffee house meetings, local festivals and events, there were public questionnaires and public picnics at the beach, there were flyers and community newsletters, banners on the streets, advertising on the TV and in the local newspaper, an interactive Internet website, and traditional open houses and comment cards. In addition, during the process of rezoning Weyerhaeuser lands, scientists and environmental consultants, local developers and planners were invited to facilitate workshops, and again, Malaspina students to solicit public comments.

The creativity with which the District of Ucluelet approached both planning processes, as well as the length and breadth of public deliberation were the main distinguishing features that brought this community international recognition. The town council and the district planner worked collaboratively with the students from Malaspina University-College to extend the reach to all resident groups in the community. Recognizing that some might not feel comfortable speaking at the open houses, they launched an interactive website (and subsequently created an online Wiki mechanism) allowing everyone concerned to leave their comments and feedback. Knowing that community residents often shopped at the local Co-op, they set up an information booth and staffed it with students to help answer any questions community members might have. Considering this was done by the planning staff of "one" with the help of students, we can easily come conclude this was a truly exceptional effort that ultimately brought the District of Ucluelet national and international recognition. At the time this was done, however, no one thought of prestige and awards but rather of the ways to protect their community from the unwanted consequences of tourism development.

Juggling the multitude of worldviews of community residents was indeed a challenge for Ucluelet: there were real estate agents and those considered "pro-development," there were "green" groups, and those who didn't want the community to change. There were also the "silent majority" and those too busy to take the time to attend community events and share their opinions and concerns. These concerns were of critical importance to the success of the District planning efforts—with new developments on the horizon, and the increasing numbers of visitors to the community, the District was undergoing a number of significant changes that needed to be addressed.

One might argue that tourism brought about most of the changes the community was going through. Some even pointed out it was the tourism industry that jump-started development in Ucluelet and had been sustaining the community ever since the Tauca Lea resort opened. At the same time, while tourism was perceived as a logical use of the area's natural resources and was often noted as the "core" industry, pursuing tourism development only was not an option. Ucluelet needed diversity—and for the District, it meant eco- and adventure tourism, forestry, fishing, beam cutters, metal work, and arts, among others. Abundant promises of tourism did not blind the community to the potential negative impacts—from increased real estate values, to seasonal low-paid employment, environmental degradation, and the loss of the community's social capital. The pursuit of tourism at the expense of other industries would lead the community down the path of Whistler and Tofino (both trendy and popular tourism destinations in British Columbia, with Tofino being only 26 miles away) where the consequences of poor planning and tourism development going awry were obvious to the naked eye. The District of Ucluelet watched, and learned—a lesson of the danger of becoming a "one-horse town," and a lesson of the importance of proactive and innovative planning to safeguard the community's precious natural and social capitals.

The threat of tourism development going out of control, coupled with an opportunity to collectively design a policy framework to guide potential developers through the 2003 OCP review process, provided a venue for the District of Ucluelet to take a proactive stance and reflect community vision in a policy document. Employing fresh and unconventional public engagement methods also helped the town succeed in developing a range of pioneering and innovative design and policy approaches. Those directly impacting tourism development included density bonusing (density exchanged for parkland or amenity), the provision of staff and affordable housing in conjunction with multiple family residential development, resort condominiums and hotel units, public access to the waterfront and construction of the Wild Pacific Trail, the protection of valuable ecological areas as open spaces, trails and parks, the provision of a sustainable alternative to rural sprawl housing, protecting community character by using distinctive design techniques, and the use of innovative techniques such as Smart Growth, Alternative Design Standards, riparian greenspace buffers, and others (Mazzoni, with Richards & Crowley, 2006). Ultimately, the practice of deliberative democratic planning helped this small community on the Vancouver Island safeguard its community and social capital, and exemplified fresh unconventional practices of embedding community based tourism planning into broader sustainable community planning efforts.

Discussion and implications

With more communities turning to tourism in search for diversification and innovation, tourism planners often find themselves responsible for designing and implementing complex value-based processes. While some processes remain rather simple, having to address fewer issues, others become complex as power and political dynamics change and stakes in the process rise. Understanding the intricacies of these processes has great potential to assist practicing planners in their efforts to engage broader constituencies in the processes of public decision making. As the tourism literature points out, the question is not whether to plan or not to plan, but what type of tourism planning should be done (Choy, 1991); moreover, the success of tourism plans is directly related to broad and representative resident participation in the planning and development of tourism projects (Cooke, 1982). If this is the case, both tourism and community development should carefully examine best practices of participatory community planning and decision making.

It is the examination of these practices that this article has focused on. More specifically, we examined these practices through the theoretical framework of deliberative democracy as we deeply believe it has a great potential to significantly improve existing community development and tourism planning practices. As the example of the District of Ucluelet illustrates, the philosophy of deliberative democratic planning provides communities and planners with a broad range of options for designing proactive participatory tourism planning processes. Among the most promising features of deliberative democracy that can be incorporated into tourism planning, are: (1) providing avenues for eliciting broad and representative participation in a deliberative manner; (2) ensuring an ongoing flow of information and communication between all parties involved and therefore directly supporting informed public judgment; (3) using this public judgment to design and implement administrative and policy frameworks guiding communities towards a shared vision; and (4) shifting the focus from outcomes to only recognizing and incorporating contextual and process factors to ensure meaningful citizen involvement in community based planning and decision making. At the same time, one should also remember that even though in practice the application of the principles of deliberative democracy remains an ideal to strive for, this ideal is often constrained by the issues of power, inequality of resources, and legal and policy regulations, among others (Grybovych, 2008).

The value of a deliberative democratic approach lies in its practical application. As Connor (1988) pointed out over three decades ago, although planners can no longer decide whether or not to have citizen participation, it is within their power to make it work and ensure that participation projects are not only meaningful and constructive, but also collaborative and dialogic. Experiences of the District of Ucluelet illustrate the power a genuine and deliberate dialogue holds. The example of this small remote community on the Vancouver Island not only showcases how going "above and beyond" traditional planning approaches can help capitalize on the power of community planning, but also demonstrates deliberative democracy in practice. Although we do not conclude this study with a success recipe, we nevertheless hope that it will facilitate reflection and help communities and planners consider the range of possibilities deliberative democracy provides to the future of tourism and community development.

We hope with this study will stimulate more research on deliberative democratic planning practices in tourism. Future case studies examining both successful processes and failed initiatives will greatly add to our understanding of the subject.

Notes

1. For the purposes of this paper, bottom-up resident participation in tourism planning and decision making is defined as an ongoing process of engagement and participation at the community level, supported by the policy framework at the municipal/ regional level. As one of the reviewers of this paper correctly pointed out, one might also think of this approach in terms of partnerships including a mix of bottom-up resident participation with support from above.

2. While these two approaches provide a theoretical framework for community development practices in North America, another model that deserves attention is the one of *community*

visioning/ strategic planning (*The Community Visioning and Strategic Planning Handbook*, first released in 1996, has since then been reprinted several times and is one of the *National Civic League's* most requested publications).

3. At that time, the land was owned by MacMillan Bloedel Ltd. (a company later bought by Weyerhaeuser—thus reference to "Weyerhaeuser lands").

References

Alinsky, S. (1971). *Rules for radicals. A pragmatic primer for realistic radicals.* New York, NY: Vintage Books.

America*Speaks*. (2004). *Millions of voices: A blueprint for engaging the American public in national policy-making.* Washington, DC: America*Speaks*.

Angrosino, M.V. (2005). Recontextualizing observation: Ethnography, pedagogy, and the prospects for a progressive political agenda. In N.K. Denzin & Y.S. Lincoln (Eds.), *The Sage handbook of qualitative research (3rd ed.)* (pp. 729–745). Thousand Oaks, CA: Sage Publications.

BC Stats. (2001). *Community facts: Ucluelet district municipality.* Retrieved February 15, 2008 from http://storage.ubertor.com/cl3514/content/document/2.pdf

BC Stats. (2007). *2006 Census profile: Ucluelet, DM.* Retrieved February 15, 2008 from http://www.bcstats.gov.bc.ca/data/cen06/profiles/detailed/59023019.pdf

Blackstock, K. (2005). A critical look at community based tourism. *Community Development Journal, 40*(1), 39–49.

Bridger, J.C., & Luloff, A.E. (1999). Toward an interactional approach to sustainable community development. *Journal of Rural Studies, 15*, 377–387.

Butler, R.W. (1991). Tourism, environment, and sustainable development. *Environmental Conservation, 18*(3), 201–209.

Butler, R.W., & Hall, C.M. (1998). Conclusion: The sustainability of tourism and recreation in rural areas. In R.W. Butler, C.M. Hall, & J. Jenkins (Eds.), *Tourism and recreation in rural areas* (pp. 249–258). Chichester, UK: John Wiley & Sons, Inc.

Choy, D.J.L. (1991). Tourism planning: the case for "market failure." *Tourism Management, 12*(4), 313–330.

Chrislip, D.D. (2002). *The collaborative leadership fieldbook: A guide for citizens and civic leaders.* San Francisco, CA: Jossey-Bass.

Christenson, J.A., Fendley, K., & Robinson, J.W. (1989). Community Development. In J.A. Christenson & J.W. Robinson (Eds.), *Community development in perspective* (pp. 3–25). Ames, IA: Iowa State University Press.

Connor, D.M. (1988). A new ladder of citizen participation. *National Civic Review, 77*(3), 249–257.

Cooke, K. (1982). Guidelines for socially appropriate tourism development in British Columbia. *Journal of Travel Research, 21*(1), 22–28.

Day, G. (1998). Working with the grain? Towards sustainable rural and community development. *Journal of Rural Studies, 14*(1), 89–105.

Denzin, N.K., & Lincoln, Y.S. (2005). Introduction: The discipline and practice of qualitative research. In N.K. Denzin & Y.S. Lincoln (Eds.), *The Sage handbook of qualitative research (3rd ed.)* (pp. 1–33). Thousand Oaks, CA: Sage Publications.

Dewey, J. (1925 [1981]). Experience and nature. In J.A. Boydston (Ed.), *John Dewey: The later works, 1925–1953, Volume 1* (pp. 1–326). Carbondale and Edwardsville, IL: Southern Illinois University Press.

Dewey, J. (1930 [1984]). Qualitative thought. In J.A. Boydston (Ed.), *John Dewey: the later works, Volume 5* (pp. 243–262). Carbondale, IL: Southern Illinois University Press.

Dewey, J. (1938, 1986). Logic: The theory of inquiry. In J.A. Boydston (Ed.), *John Dewey: the later works, 1925–1953, Volume 12* (pp. 1–506). Carbondale and Edwardsville, IL: Southern Illinois University Press.

Dewey, J. (1939). Creative democracy – the task before us. In *John Dewey and the promise of America. Progressive Education Booklet No.14* (p. 15). Columbus, OH: American Education Press.

District of Ucluelet. (2005). *Ucluelet community profile.* Retrieved October 12, 2007 from http://www.ucluelet.ca/communityprofile

Durant, R.F. (2001). The democratic deficit in America. *Political Science Quarterly*, *110*(1), 25–47.

Farrelly, C. (2004). *An introduction to contemporary political theory*. London, UK: Sage Publications.

Fendley, K., & Christenson, J.A. (1989). Rural reflation: An idea for community development. *Journal of the Community Development Society*, *20*(1), 103–115.

Flora, C., & Flora, J. (2008). *Rural communities: Legacy and change* (3rd ed.). Boulder, CO: Westview Press.

Forester, J. (1999). *The deliberative practitioner: Encouraging participatory planning processes*. Cambridge, MA: The MIT Press.

Freire, P. (1970). *Pedagogy of the oppressed*. New York, NY: Seabury.

Freire, P. (1985). *The politics of education*. London, UK: Macmillan.

Fuller, A.M., & Reid, D.G. (1998). Rural tourism planning: A community development approach. In S.T. Smith (Ed.), *Rural rehabilitation: a modern perspective* (pp. 260–274). Arnaudville, LA: Bow Rover Publishing.

Gallagher, D.J. (1995). In search of the rightful role of method: Reflections of conducting a qualitative dissertation. In T. Tiller, A. Sparkes, S. Kårhus, & F. Dowling Næss (Eds.), *The qualitative challenge: reflections on educational research* (pp. 17–35). Landås, Norway: Caspar Forlag.

Gannon, A. (1993). Rural tourism as a factor in rural community economic development for economies in transition. In B. Bramwell & B. Lane (Eds.), *Rural tourism and sustainable tourism development* (pp. 51–60). Clevedon: Channel View.

Gibbs, D. (1989). Towards the sustainable city. *Town Planning Review*, *65*(1), 99–109.

Godfrey, K., & Clarke, J. (2000). *The tourism development handbook: A practical approach to planning and marketing*. London, UK: Cassell.

Government of British Columbia. (1996). *Local government act*. Victoria: Queen's Printer.

Grybovych, O. (2008). *Deliberative democratic practices in tourism planning: Towards a model of participatory community tourism planning*. (Doctoral dissertation, University of Northern Iowa, 2008). ProQuest Dissertations and Theses. (UMI No. AAT 3321006).

Gunn, C.A. (1994). *Tourism planning: basics, concepts, cases* (3rd ed.). Washington, DC: Taylor & Francis.

Habermas, J. (1984). *The theory of communicative action I. Reason and the rationalization of society*. Boston, MA: Beacon Press.

Habermas, J. (1987). *The theory of communicative action II. Lifeworld and the system*. Boston, MA: Beacon Press.

Hall, C.M. (2005). Rural wine and food tourism cluster and network development. In D. Hall, I. Kirkpatrick, & M. Mitchell (Eds.), *Rural tourism and sustainable business* (pp. 149–164). New York, NY: Channel View Publications.

Hall, C.M., & Mitchell, R. (2000). Wine tourism in the Mediterranean: A tool for restructuring and development. *Thunderbird International Business Review*, *42*(4), 445–465.

Harrill, R. (2004). Residents' attitudes toward tourism development: A literature review with implications for tourism planning. *Journal of Planning Literature*, *18*(3), 251–266.

Hartz-Karp, J. (2005). A case study in deliberative democracy: Dialogue with the city. *Journal of Public Deliberation*, *1*(1), article 6.

Haywood, K.M. (1988). Responsible and responsive tourism planning in the community. *Tourism Management*, *9*, 105–118.

Hibbard, M. (1999). Devolution and community development in the US. *Community Development Journal*, *34*(1), 75–77.

Hibbard, M., & Lurie, S. (2000). Saving land but losing ground. Challenges to community planning in the era of participation. *Journal of Planning Education and Research*, *20*, 187–195.

Hutchison, P., & McGill, J. (1992). *Leisure, integration, and community* (2nd ed.). Toronto, ON: Leisurability Publications.

Hutchison, P., & Nogradi, G. (1996). The concept and nature of community development in recreation and leisure services. *Journal of Applied Recreation Research*, *21*(2), 93–130.

Innes, J.E. (1996). Planning through consensus building. A new view of the comprehensive planning ideal. *Journal of the American Planning Association*, *62*(4), 460–472.

Inskeep, E. (1991). *Tourism planning: An integrated and sustainable development approach.* New York, NY: John Wiley & Sons, Inc.

International Institute for Sustainable Development. (2000). *Appreciative inquiry and community development: from problems to strengths.* Retrieved March 10, 2009 from http://www.iisd.org/ai/

Ioannides, D. (1995). Planning for international tourism in less developed countries: Toward sustainability? *Journal of Planning Literature, 9*(3), 235–254.

Jamal, T.B., & Getz, D. (1995). Collaboration theory and community tourism planning. *Annals of Tourism Research, 22*(1), 186–204.

Jamal, T.B., & Getz, D. (1999). Community roundtables for tourism-related conflicts: The dialectics of consensus and process structures. *Journal of Sustainable Tourism, 7*(3), 290–313.

Jamal, T.B., Stein, S.M., & Harper, T.L. (2002). Beyond labels: Pragmatic planning in multistakeholder tourism-environmental conflicts. *Journal of Planning Education and Research, 22,* 164–177.

Karpowitz, C.E., & Mansbridge, J. (2005). Disagreement and consensus: The need for dynamic updating in public deliberation. *Journal of Public Deliberation, 1*(1), article 2.

Kretzmann, J.P., & McKnight, J.L. (1993). *Building communities from the inside out: A path toward finding and mobilizing a community's assets.* Evanston, IL: Institute for Policy Research.

Liu, J.C., & Var, T. (1986). Resident attitudes toward tourism impacts in Hawaii. *Annals of Tourism Research, 13,* 193–214.

Loukissas, P.J. (1983). Public participation in community tourism planning: A gaming simulation approach. *Journal of Travel Research, 22*(1), 18–23.

Lukensmeyer, C.J., & Torres, L.H. (2003, September). *Deliberation for community planning and economic development.* Discussion paper prepared for the Charrette Institute.

Madrigal, R. (1993). A tale of tourism in two cities. *Annals of Tourism Research, 20,* 336–353.

Madrigal, R. (1995). Residents' perceptions and the role of government. *Annals of Tourism Research, 22*(1), 86–102.

Marcouiller, D.W. (1997). Toward integrative tourism planning in rural America. *Journal of Planning Literature, 11*(3), 337–357.

Marcus, J., & Brennan, M.A. (2008). *IFAS community development: Empowering your community, stage 1, initiation.* Department of Family, Youth and Community Sciences, Cooperative Extension Service, Institute of Food and Agricultural Sciences, University of Florida.

Marien, C., & Pizam, A. (1997). Implementing sustainable tourism development through citizen participation in the planning process. In S. Wahab & J.J. Pigram (Eds.), *Tourism development and growth: The challenge of sustainability* (pp. 164–178). New York, NY: Routledge.

Mazzoni, F., with Richards, H., & Crawley, R. (2006). *Community Excellence Award submission: Ucluelet/ Weyerhaeuser Comprehensive Development Plan.* Retrieved August 4, 2007 from http://www.civicinfo.bc.ca/practices_innovations/ucluelet_healthy.pdf

Merriam, S.B. (1988). *Case study research in education: A qualitative approach.* San Francisco, CA: Jossey-Bass Publishers.

Murphy, P.E. (1985). *Tourism: A community approach.* New York, NY: Routledge.

Murphy, P.E., & Murphy, A.E. (2004). Planning. In P.E. Murphy & A.E. Murphy (Eds.), *Strategic management for tourism communities* (pp. 86–112). New York: Channel View Publications.

Pearce, P.L., & Moscardo, G. (1999). Tourism community analysis: Asking the right questions. In D.G. Pearce & R.W. Butler (Eds.), *Contemporary issues in tourism development* (pp. 31–51). London, UK: Routledge.

Phifer, B., with List, E.F., & Faulkner, B. (1989). An overview of community development in America. In J.A. Christenson & J.W. Robinson (Eds.), *Community development in perspective* (pp. 253–279). Ames, IA: Iowa State University Press.

Prentice, R. (1993). Community-driven tourism planning and residents' preferences. *Tourism Management, 14*(3), 218–226.

Reed, M.G. (1997). Power relations and community-based tourism planning. *Annals of Tourism Research, 24*(3), 566–591.

Reid, D.G. (2003). *Tourism, globalization and development: Responsible tourism planning.* Sterling, VA: Pluto Press.

Ritchie, J.R.B. (1993). Crafting a destination vision: Putting the concept of resident-responsive tourism into practice. *Tourism Management, 14*, 379–389.

Rothman, J. (1995). Approaches to community intervention. In J. Rothman, J.L. Erlich & J.E. Tropman with F.M. Cox (Eds.), *Strategies for community intervention (5th ed.)* (pp. 26–63). Itasca, IL: F.E. Peacock Publishers, Inc.

Sautter, E.T., & Leisen, B. (1999). Managing stakeholders: A tourism planning model. *Annals of Tourism Research, 26*(2), 312–328.

Selin, S., & Beason, K. (1991, June 9–13). *Conditions facilitating collaborative tourism planning: a qualitative perspective.* Paper presented at the Travel and Tourism Research Association twenty-second annual conference, Long Beach, CA.

Stake, R.E. (1995). *The art of case study research.* Thousand Oaks, CA: Sage Publications.

Stake, R.E. (2005). Qualitative case studies. In N.K. Denzin & Y.S. Lincoln (Eds.), *The Sage handbook of qualitative research (3rd ed.)* (pp. 443–466). Thousand Oaks, CA: Sage Publications.

Stein, D., Imel, S., & Henderson, T. (2004, October). *Creating social capital through the deliberative discussion: a case study of community dialogue.* Presented at the Midwest Research-to-Practice Conference in Adult, Continuing, and Community Education, Indiana University, Indianapolis, IN.

Stormann, W.F. (1996). Recreation's role in community development: Community recreation. *Journal of Applied Recreation Research, 21*(2), 143–164.

Timothy, D.J. (1999). Participatory planning: A view of tourism in Indonesia. *Annals of Tourism Research, 26*(2), 371–391.

Tosun, C., & Timothy, D.J. (2001). Shortcomings in planning approaches to tourism development in developing countries: The case of Turkey. *International Journal of Contemporary Hospitality Management, 13*(7), 352–359.

United Nations. (1955). *Social progress through community development.* New York, NY: United Nations Bureau of Social Affairs.

Webler, T. (1995). "Right" discourse in citizen participation: an evaluative yardstick. In O. Renn, T. Webler, & P. Wiedemann (Eds.), *Fairness and competence in citizen participation: evaluating models for environmental discourse* (pp. 35–86). Boston: Kluwer Academic Publishers.

Weeks, E.C. (2000). The practice of deliberative democracy: Results from four large-scale trials. *Public Administration Review, 60*(4), 360–372.

Weeks, E.C. (2003, Spring). Deliberative democracy. *PPPM Circle, 7*, 4.

Williams, P.W., Penrose, R.W., & Hawkes, S. (1998). Shared decision-making in tourism land use planning. *Annals of Tourism Research, 25*(4), 860–889.

World Tourism Organization, with Inskeep, E. (1994). *National and regional tourism planning: Methodologies and case studies.* New York, NY: Routledge.

Yankelovich, D. (1991). *Coming to public judgment: Making democracy work in a complex world.* Syracuse, NY: Syracuse University Press.

Yin, R.K. (1994). *Case study research: Design and methods* (2nd ed.). Thousand Oaks, CA: Sage Publications.

Engaging residents in planning for sustainable rural-nature tourism in post-communist Poland

Marianna Strzelecka and Bruce E. Wicks

Department of Recreation, Sport & Tourism, University of Illinois, Champaign-Urbana, IL, USA

This study attempts to draw attention to environmentally, socially and economically sustainable tourism development as a tool with the potential to generate social capital based on development of local ties in Poland. It uses the interactional approach to community to discuss the possibility of enhancing actors' efficacy and the building of trust among the actors influenced by participatory planning for sustainable tourism development. The interactional approach to community allows for the observation of how the realization of such inclusive planning processes can help in pursuing interactions and therefore developing local relationships. Because of interactions a community is capable of pursuing joint action toward the wellbeing of a locality. Consequently the function of such processes is not limited to pure and effective planning for development, which is its explicit and conscious purpose. The task of the paper is to expose possible latent effects occurring within the tourism development framework.

Research within the tourism discipline has for a long time concentrated on the economic aspects of the industry (e.g., Dwyer, Forsyth, & Spurr, 2006; Elkin & Roberts, 1987; King, Dwyer, & Prideaux 2007*)*, tourism influences on social processes (e.g., Crompton, 1992; Haukeland, 1984; Pearce, 1995) as well as environmental concerns (e.g., Blangy & Nielsen, 1993) each trying to document the impact tourism development has on localities, regions and national economies. However, research investigating tourism influence on local societies occurs usually when tourism is mature or in the final stages of its development and has not shown enough concern toward the social and political impact of the process of tourism planning. It has been the issue of involving local residents and other local stakeholders in decision-making that is of academic interest (Parkins & Mitchell, 2005). Not only is it important to consider the value of decentralized and inclusive decision-making for the sake of quality of decisions, but we must also realize the potential contribution of decision-making involving a wide spectrum of local stakeholders to increasing local dynamics.

Empowering stakeholders by including their voice in tourism development decision-making is a relatively new approach that became an indispensible element of the sustainable development process (Saarinen, 2006). In particular, the need for local participation and deliberation in decision-making has been stressed within the framework of "community based" or "community driven" tourism (Armitage, 2005; Saarinen, 2006; Tosun, 1998). Those who advocate stakeholders' inclusion also argue the importance of distributing power among primary users of local resources (Zanetell & Knuth, 2002; Tandom, 2008). Further they claim that balanced local power relations are critical conditions for sustainable development to happen.

Attention turned to social effects derived from a locally realized development paradigm, allows disciplines previously constrained by a one-site research perspective to evolve into more complex and comprehensive systems of knowledge contextualized in a locality. By applying different concepts this work demonstrates the potential effects that the participation of local stakeholders in planning for tourism development has on local social relationships and community cohesiveness. This study argues that even though local actors initially are more likely to become involved in a development project if they show personal interest in it and if they perceive opportunities to influence decision-making to ensure their benefits (Coleman, 1990), other, more lasting social impacts can accrue to the stakeholders. Through interaction, stakeholders are more prone to develop local relationships and shared values. They are more likely to turn their attention and later action to the general wellbeing of the locality and its prosperity. It is possible that stakeholders commit to a variety of actions that increase local dynamics and provide the opportunity to improve local connectedness (see Theodori, 2005).

This study adopts the interactional field theory significantly advanced by Wilkinson (1991) and the concept of social capital as the theoretical frameworks used to suggest a model of community field as a latent effect of an inclusive tourism planning process. An interactional perspective defines the community field as the emerging place-oriented process of interrelated actions over time carried out by actors usually, but not necessarily, working through various associations (Theodori, 2005). Therefore community is more likely to emerge from intensified interaction among local stakeholders (Wilkinson, 1991). It is postulated that participatory processes of tourism planning in Poland enhances the development of social relationships by providing spaces in which intensified interactions occur and which facilitate discovering and negotiating shared values and allow for argumentation about issues of local tourism among different stakeholders. By crossing more and more distinct social fields, development of the field of interest in tourism increases the potential for collective action and the emergence of a community.

Some actors involved in the tourism planning process also operate at the regional level and thereby link a locality to external environments by their individual vertical ties and thus increase the potential for the development of new kinds of relationships. Thereby, the social function of tourism processes cannot be perceived as limited to improving planning for specific developments—the quality of tourism decisions is only its explicit purpose. The aim of this study is to demonstrate that latent effects derived from a participatory approach to planning tourism develop-ment can have a positive impact on social dynamics in a post-communist locality. In particular, it seeks to discover how the tourism development project realized for the post-communist localities enhances the development of relationships among local stakeholders and community action. The paper introduces community field theory to tourism planning, and applies the concept of social capital to theorize about process of local interactions. Through a case study approach researchers demonstrate to what extent theory driven modifications introduced to the model of community action can be observed in tourism decision-making in post-communist Poland.

The developing argument begins with emphasis on the necessity of completing democratic consolidation processes by developing local democratic cultures in Poland and the arising need for purposeful actions to enhance the changes. We propose that a crucial element of these processes is the involvement of individuals and groups in local decision-making. Engaging them as stakeholders may happen along with local development projects such as planning for tourism. The following sections of the paper theorize how empowering local actors in tourism planning processes could result in new relationships and the emergence of the interactional community and hence in community action. The section including the case study aims to visualize those processes based on a real example.

Democratic consolidation and why sustainable tourism matters

Social and political distrust fostered by the Communist regimes are believed to have made post-communist democracies particularly prone to political instability (Putnam, 1993). For many years Poland has struggled to simultaneously build strong capitalist markets and develop democratic political systems. This is because recent governments have adopted a popular "Western" belief that economic growth relies heavily on the quality of the democratic regime. The event which significantly influenced the progress of the country's political-economic transition was the opportunity of accession to the European Union (EU). Starting on the path toward these ideological changes and the creation of the required political and economic environment permitted EU accession in 2004. Democratic consolidation, however, will complete the political transition by developing local democratic cultures founded on a "common commitment to a mode of reasoning on matters of public policy" (Habermas, 2001). Because the success of decentralized deliberative democracy implies that public participation in local decision-making will be present and discussions among citizens will be based on equality, strong local communities are essential. Hence, involvement at the local level of governance being the main component of political dynamics ensures the quality of local democratic processes (CEC, 2004d, p. 33–34). However, most citizens of rural Poland, have successively avoided engagement in any local collective action, even though participation has been voluntary (Howard, 2002). Whereas in many Western societies citizen activity in local affairs has become a central part of their social culture, in post-communist localities people are interested in their private circles and have felt little need to engage in this form of decision-making.

Pessimists may suggest that we should passively await the day when the younger generations finally replace the older mistrustful citizens still affected by years of Communist rule (Sztompka, 1999). Yet the argument that generational change would significantly affect the level of engagement in local affairs seems of doubtful usefulness, especially in reference to rural areas of Poland. It is difficult to unconditionally accept a popular belief that the new generations easily accept and assimilate proposed new local democratic practices, and thereby complete the transition toward a consolidated democratic regime (Howard, 2003). Therefore, instead of comfortably awaiting the replacement of a generation, local authorities should reach for available tools to promote democratic plannning processes and stimulate change today. This work argues that one such tool is the process of local tourism development. Perhaps tourism development does not present any greater opportunity than other forms of development but it is often less contentious than other developments and thus a good way for residents to engage in participatory planning. Recent popularization of rural tourism within Europe made it more likely that tourism development occurs as a new from of economic development in rural areas of Poland. The argument within this work rests upon the assumption that if tourism development planning occurs, then its potential effects on a local culture must be realized. Once they are realized, tourism development can serve as a point of departure to create the culture in localities for engagement in other local affairs.

Involving local stakeholders in tourism decision-making and allowing for the local exchange of arguments can inspire social change. The participatory approach to planning realized in the local context is a set of procedures in which local institutions and organizations attempt to involve diverse groups of residents and provide opportunities for them to express their needs and concerns related to issues of development, as well as making explicit their ideas about the shape and direction of the proposed developments. Engaging residents in planning constitutes a component of the social domain of sustainable development, and aims at a more equal distribution of power in local decision-making, hence contributing to the success of local democratic cultures. Perhaps one of the main advantages of sustainable tourism development programs in Poland is that they can relatively smoothly assimilate into the planning process of the EU, obligating local actors to be involved in decision-making (COM, 2001, p. 264 final).

The concept of sustainable development arose in contrast to traditional development frameworks founded primarily on economic growth principles (Pawlowski, 2008). In reality, however, the challenges that appear while putting these conceptually different development postulates into practice make it doubtful that with exiting economic priorities, sustainable development can ever absolutely reject development in which the ultimate focus is on growth, even if principles of environmental and social sustainability are gaining importance. The practice of sustainability can significantly contribute to local social development. It increases the capability of a local system to adapt while at the same time it creates opportunities (Holling, 2004). This study perceives sustainable tourism development as a generator of economic benefits, while at the same time intensifying interaction among components of the local social environment. Realizing the principles of sustainable development from the very initial stage of planning allows for parallel social and political development.

The fundamental principle of sustainable tourism requires satisfying the needs of those threatened by exclusion from the planning process (Tosun, 2001). While sustainable local planning must be concerned with the overall wellbeing of a locality, no advancement can happen without also recognizing the wellbeing of all local stakeholders (Clark, 1997; Murphy, 1983, 1988). Sustainability-focused designs also increase the likelihood of tourism becoming one of the many alternative local economic activities and therefore minimizing its negative impacts. Those who are involved in designing the sustainable futures of host communities should focus on the quality of the planning processes, and thus encourage involvement of local residents (Ryan, 2002; Tosun, 2001).

Empowering the community in decision making

The increased demand for decentralized decision-making and citizen participation has ushered in a long-term movement toward a new understanding of public administration and development (Tosun & Timothy, 2003). Inclusion of local citizens in decision-making is a key element of local empowerment (Knopp & Caldbeck, 1990; Li, 2006). Although empowerment in decision-making takes different forms and occurs at different stages of a locality's development (e.g., Keogh, 1990; Perdue, Long, & Allen, 1987) it must involve "full information available on the issues under consideration" (Lucas, 1987). For example, empowerment by mutual learning is enhanced by creating local spaces for social interaction and information sharing, as well as initiating local debates (Reid, Mair, & George, 2004; Wilkinson, 1991). However, one crucial condition is that local authorities need to be willing to learn from residents (Armitage, 2005; Austin & Eder, 2007).

The literature also demonstrates that one of the main barriers to realizing the principle of inclusion in decision-making is the non-homogenous character of many communities as (e.g. Agrawal & Gibson, 1999; Walker & Hurley, 2004). Therefore, tourism planning should not only be explicit in order to determine the developments that will follow, but must also account for different values, local experience and knowledge. The act of negotiations is likely to be an important action used to mitigate conflicts at the planning stage of tourism development (Leeuwis, 2000; Saarinen, 2006; Zanetell & Knuth, 2002). Providing physical spaces for the exchange of tourism information and negotiating local values through dialogue also creates the opportunity for community feedback that increases the quality of decisions (Hughes, 1995; Tosun & Timothy, 2003).

Although stakeholders' participation in tourism decision-making is an important concept, often the literature fails to discuss the relationship between community action, stakeholders' involvement in decisions and the democratization of local governance. This may be due to an assumption that where community actors become engaged in local and regional affairs democratic values already exist. Claiming a positive political outcome from residents' participation, such as their willingness and ability to act collectively, needs further investigation and supporting evidence. However, as the democratization of public life in post-communist localities (by empowering local stakeholders and increasing engagement in local affairs) needs to advance, research should expand our knowledge of the potential local social/political impacts of the participatory approach. Knowledge contextualized in a locality increases shared-understanding among the different disciplines, while at the same time connects these disciplines in more complex and holistic examinations of everyday life mechanisms. A method to connect the complexities of sustainable tourism development and the need for democratic planning processes is to examine the fullest range of consequences possible.

Investigating latent function

The process of tourism decision-making can have effects on a locality that are at first difficult to understand. To describe these complex effects will allow for employing the concept of "function" (see Merton, 1968). Function is referred to as an outcome, which either enhances the adaptation of a social unit or lessens its adjustment (dysfunctions) (Merton, 1968). Often however, research refers only to positive qualities when describing the effects of social processes, which may lead to potentially occurring disadvantages being overlooked. Merton (1968) for example discusses the importance of acknowledging the possibility of unintended consequences of different actions, which he names "latent functions." This study incorporates the concept of latent function (Merton, 1968) as a means of extending existing models of community action by employing the interactional approach. The paper captures emerging community action (community field) as a latent effect of ongoing tourism development activities by embracing non-tourism related components of local social life.

Studying the emergence of a community field needs to focus on the quality of the interaction among local stakeholders and thereby the fields of interests they represent, only by observing these interactions one can discover their consequences (see Wilkinson, 1970). Awareness of such possibilities helps to expand the attention beyond the inquiry about purposive effects of the performed tourism development project to other domains of the local social environment (Merton, 1968). Thus, the concept of latent function suggests that we should not confine ourselves to exclusively studying manifest effects of local tourism planning but extend our examination by recognizing the possibility of the unintentional and the often overlooked influences of the participatory approach to local tourism planning on a community. This study, in particular is interested in the latent effect of intensified local interaction occurring during tourism development planning.

Emergence of a community field from a tourism social field

An interactional approach to community states that individuals in a locality tend to interact with each other despite the fact that they may engage in external networks and other interactions outside a locality (Brown & Swanson, 2003; Wilkinson, 1991). Social interaction is a distinguishable characteristic of a community as is its empirical manifestation (Wilkinson, 1991). Research that has examined the relationship between local interaction and other changing community attributes, demonstrates that interaction is a fundamental component of community (Kaufman & Wilkinson, 1967; Wilkinson, 1991) and its wellbeing (Wilkinson, 1991). By adopting inclusive tourism planning programs, barriers to community interaction could be reduced.

The interactional approach also proposes that a community emerges from unconstrained and dynamic social fields (Wilkinson, 1991), which often shifts their focus of action. While a social field is "a process of interaction through time, with direction toward some more or less distinctive outcome" (Wilkinson, 1970), a community field turns its actions towards improving life in a locality. Looking at interaction and the dynamics of relationships over time allows us to find out about the changing attributes of the community (Wilkinson, 1970; Wilkinson, 1974; Wilkinson, 1991). Community fields may also vary over time depending on local conditions and the consequences of different stimuli (Wilkinson, 1972, 1991). The approach allows us to investigate the consequences of different stimuli on a community field.

Community actions alone serve to strengthen relationships across different social fields as they pursue general community interests. Individuals who belong to different social fields and pursue its particular interests, perceive themselves within their temporal role in relation to other "field" representatives. Although they may shape others' behavior, alternatively, they themselves are also shaped by the sequence of interaction (Mead, 1934). Even though individuals are usually more likely to pursue only beneficial interactions, unintentional and undesired encounters also shape their perceptions (Wilkinson, 1991). Hence, changing perception is an unintentional outcome (Merton, 1968) and intensifying local interactions the increases chances of a community field.

This work argues that projects engaging distinct social fields within post-communist localities must fit into actors' already existing agendas for them to turn attention to the project in the first place. Only then does the possibility exist that stakeholders will engage in other local activities to realize broader social goals. It also seems reasonable that residents of areas with limited human and economic resources, such as less urbanized and industrialized regions, would be more likely to engage in projects proposing tangible outcomes (benefits) as opposed to projects focusing exclusively on ideological goals, than the residents of areas that have already attained a higher quality of life.

The study proposes that a new social field is likely to emerge as a result of interaction occurring within a thematic framework of tourism development and operating simultaneously with other local social fields of particular local interest. The action of the newly emerged field focuses on the impact of tourism development and tourism related issues, uniting other local social fields under "tourism development." Only later can a community field distinguish itself from the tourism field. The community action that emerges as a latent effect of the tourism social field disconnects from the actions of the tourism social field to realize more general goals (as a result of generalization process). The activities of tourism stakeholders are no longer limited to realizing their interests in tourism. The processes within the community field are likely to be influenced by processes and events within the tourism social field. Because of other forces shaping community action, the dynamics of the community field mirror the tourism field dynamics only to a certain extent.

Tourism development shows potential to embrace the components of the local environment that often remain neglected in the process of decision-making. It is able to engage actors who did not become directly involved in the planning for a variety of reasons, but remain informed and sometimes passionately follow available information on the project's progress. Perhaps tourism and community research needs to turn its attention to actors who remain connected to the emerging tourism field and possibly to the community field as well, because as they remain informed and influenced by ongoing events, they may create informal spaces in which they interact. This work, however, limits discussion to actors directly involved in a tourism field. By definition social fields emerge as a result of the common interests and attitudes of its members. Such a system of interpersonal lineages is sustained through an ability to develop and maintain social capital.

Social capital within a community field

To date many researchers agree that the forces of social capital influence important political and economic phenomena (Kunioka & Woller, 1999; Putnam, 1993, 2002). The concept also illustrates the relevance of discussing of transitioning economies under the political and economic influences of the former Soviet Union (Kunioka & Woller, 1999). Assuming that interacting actors attempt to build relationships if they believe that these relationships have a positive impact on their wellbeing, social capital is perceived as a resource to which actors gain access when engaging in such relationships (Coleman, 1988). Perceiving social capital holistically as a resource for individuals, communities and regions, exposes complex community processes. This is because networks of relationships often have the potential to accelerate democratizing processes and local democratic cultures within their members. Such analysis employs the conceptual distinction between structural and attitudinal components of social capital including trust and reciprocity (Hooghe & Stole, 2003). By engaging aspects of social capital that are more related to democratic virtues, this study focuses on individuals' interaction, relationship building and trust formation.

Access to social capital arises from interaction followed by developing relationships, and high levels of social capital that can activate a community (Wall, Ferrazzi, & Schryer, 1998). For Pierre Bourdieu (1983), potential benefits perceived by individuals (for example privileged access to information) encourage them to become involved in various groups. Residents become engaged in local social fields of interests because they perceive benefits. Social capital becomes and attribute of individuals or group actors purposively engaging in beneficial interaction (Wall et al., 1998). Evaluation of the attribute, however, requires reflections contextualized in a society in which interactions occur (Sobel, 2002).

While discussing developing conditions for community action to emerge in a post-communist society one needs to look at social capital as the attribute of actors that enter into relationships with actors from a different social field (see Wilkinson, 1991). However, when looking at community field, one should perceive community social capital as an effect of the development of vertical ties in a community field operating at the local level with actors and groups operating at regional and national or even international levels. Thus the emergence of an interactional community asserts that community actors possess a certain, critical level of social capital. In other words, if participatory tourism development projects enhance development of an interactional community, the community action would be a manifestation of a certain level of social capital necessary among stakeholders to perform joint activities toward wellbeing of a locality.

Putnam (2002) indicates that actors develop social networks only when they are willing to invest their personal resources in relationships that they regard beneficial. Networks are usually considered more capable of ensuring individual benefits and actors choose them over a relationship with a single actor. Networks also facilitate the development of trust that makes the expectation of immediate benefits less important. Trust, on the other hand, further improves an individuals' willingness to cooperate and increases readiness to act collectively (Putnam, 1993; Woolcock & Natayan, 2000).

The distinct character of relationships linking actors possessing unique personal resources, differs from those between like actors (Putnam 2000) and relates to different functions of weak and strong social ties (Granovettter, 1973). Whereas weak ties improve the flow of information among actors, strong ties and the resulting bonding relationships appear less accepting of differences and thereby less valuable for local democratic culture to flourish (Hooghe & Stolle, 2003; Howard, 2002). Hence, relationships based on strong ties are less likely to facilitate community action (Howard, 2002; Wilkinson, 1991).

Given the diverse nature of tourism projects the development of weak ties is enhanced thereby fostering the acceptance of differences among the represented social fields. Also, relationships within the tourism social field are not simply static and nor is the degree of actors' involvement that may either increase or decrease. Relationships evolve, and as trust among participating actors develops, individual interests in tourism benefits may be partially replaced by a more general interest in the wellness of a place. This may be so because the perception of an individual's role in the network changes as trust develops and they identify individual wellbeing with that of the environment (Kay, 2005). Thereby, they perceive benefits accruing to the tourism field in the context of their individual interests and conditions for the community field to emerge are met.

Brehm and Rahn (1997) propose that joint action increases individual trust, and that in turn enhances trust in public institutions (Putnam, 2002). Public institutions in Poland can and should facilitate local interactions and local networks because of their trust-building potential and capability to distribute local social capital (Kay, 2005). The case study that follows demonstrates that by organizing actors within interactional spaces tourism planning projects foster the generation of local social capital (Luloff & Wilkinson, 1979), facilitate the development of local relationships and the tourism social field, and thereby create conditions for community action to emerge.

A case study of Greater Poland National Park

The project took place in post-communist Poland, where sustainable tourism development has been viewed by localities as an attractive option to improve economic diversity (Majewska, 2008). To investigate the realization of this tourism project the researchers applied methods such as active participation and the analysis of project reports (with agreement of the two organizations coordinating the project) and an examination of community interaction and actors' involvement. Frequent interaction with the projects' coordinators helped to deepen an understanding of the process and thus develop a framework to look at the potential impact the project has on participants.

Designing the planning process

The tourism project involved actors from eight administratively distinct localities surrounding the Greater Poland National Park. For many of these small areas tourism could be an alternative to traditional economic activities. Furthermore the park's managers were concerned about the increasing number of one-day visitors coming from the city and destroying protected areas. Therefore developing tourist facilities and their careful arrangement would also direct visitors to desired locations. The initiative to involve the local stakeholders (local associations, organizations, public institutions and independent individuals) in the planning process for the development of tourism and recreation facilities came from non-governmental organizations (Partners for Local Government, The Foundation in Support of Local Democracy in Poznan) after agreements with local authorities. The realization of the project proposal was co-funded by the Civic Initiatives Fund and involved the employees of the park.

The main goal of the four-month long project was to define local priorities in the development and planning for the sustainability of tourism and recreation in the communes of the "micro-region" of the Greater Poland National Park by engaging local stakeholders in the decision-making process. For example the project aimed directly at involving leaders of local associations and organizations, who then would invite residents. Organizers in cooperation with the park employees provided space for local dialogue. Interaction was pursued at two distinctive levels such as within-community (horizontal) interactions and vertical interaction with project participants usually operating at the regional level (see Allen, Korsching & Vogt 2003; Cox, 1998). Educational activities seemed an important component in the overall process of deepening local knowledge about the philosophical principles of sustainability. Finally, involved actors, endowed with additional knowledge, worked on a local tourism development plan aimed at minimizing environmental and socio-cultural impacts. This planning exercise showed that cooperation for the common purpose of tourism development emerged as an important activity for developing local ties among different social fields engaged in the tourism project.

Before the program began, however, the co-coordinating organizations (Partners for Local Government, The Foundation in Support of Local Democracy in Poznan) researched the most prominent local issues of concern. The most valuable information for further realization of the project was that the lack of communication and interaction among local governments, business owners and local residents had diminished efforts to develop recreation facilities in the past. Increased interaction and improved communication needed to occur so that solutions to expressed concerns and work toward common local goals could be reached. Also, residents regarded facilities such as bike paths and swimming pools as additional infrastructure that could be utilized by them just as extensively as by visitors. Developing tourism and recreation facilities increases local recreation opportunities, thus adding a significant quality of life component to their every-day life. Overall, many local actors expressed their interest in the possibility of increased tourism flow in the future. Tourism was mostly perceived both as an economic opportunity and as a threat to the local environment.

Actors participating in the tourism project became personally engaged in the identification of potential tourism attractions surrounding the park, and prepared a document describing local recreational opportunities. In fact, volunteer associations and local organizations (social fields) represented in the project were strongly engaged in the process of gathering tourism information. For example, a local bicycle association identified potential bicycle trails and local educators initiated an investigation by students into which recreational resources in their neighborhoods were of the greatest importance to them.

The coordinators organized meetings into topic panels about the future shape of the Park as it related to increasing the flow of visitors. Participants, who often represented diverse local social fields, exchanged visions, opinions and interests. Opening the meetings to individuals and representatives of local groups interested in shaping the future of the Park (discussions were designed so that each of the participating social fields was represented by the four topic panels) aimed at improving communication among local actors. Soon it appeared that these meetings were able to involve only a small number of ordinary residents possibly because of the difficulties in accessing the meeting place (it was accessible only by car). Therefore, the remaining need to clearly identify local recreational needs and concerns about the increasing number of visitors had not been fulfilled and led to an intensified advertising campaign to the wider general public regarding the educational "micro-regional" workshops. Micro-regional workshops provided an important space for formal interaction (debates during the meetings) and informal interaction (discussions during coffee breaks). These interactions, organized using the tourism development framework, are the fundamental conditions for the development of social relationships and the emergence of a community.

In order to increase local understanding of tourism processes, tourism experts shared their experience and their knowledge of sustainability and sustainable tourism development in a series of educational meetings directed toward local interest groups (local associations, authorities and local school teachers) participating in the project. This series of meetings was organized interchangeably with "micro-regional" workshops and topic panel groups and focused on: (1) the importance of local partnerships and collaborative decision making; (2) concepts of tourism capacity and sustainable tourism; (3) environmental protection in the EU; and (4) tourism product development and the promotion of the "Great Poland" micro-region. Information about all types of meetings was made available through local and regional magazines and newspapers publishing announcements encouraging public participation as well as short notes reporting the program achievements. Additionally, the reports were additionally released in the form of an e-newsletter. Organizers also updated the contact list after every meeting so that any newly engaged participant would receive following e-newsletters and e-announcements about upcoming events related to the project.

Maintaining the attendance lists allowed the research team to track participating individuals. The project gained the interest of 146 people indicating that planning for tourism development has the potential to gain the interest of local actors. Available data does not provide full information about how many people participating in the project were formal representatives of local groups of interest (ordinary residents) and how many people participated as independent residents, thus representing their personal interests. Therefore making any specific conclusions about ordinary residents involved in the project and their role in the tourism social field is problematic. Further the data does not provide sufficient information about people involved in the realization of the project, who did not participate in formal meetings. Additional studies of the particular problem will deepen understanding of the role of sustainable tourism development in community action.

It is believed, however, that this case study illustrates the potential of tourism development planning processes to impact the dynamics of local social life. Tourism can be a tool to enhance joint community action and accelerate the creation of shared values and interest in locality wellbeing and a tool to advance local democratic cultures by enhancing residents' participation in local affairs. Also, social capital can be injected into a locality by the project's facilitators (nongovernmental organizations) because they build links between local stakeholders' actors and participants usually operating outside the locality (for example interaction with experts and guests speakers invited to the meetings).

Conclusion

Individual actors in economically disadvantaged towns and rural areas of Poland usually remain disengaged from joint actions and any activities that require them to deal with authorities and other local stakeholders. Their disengagement and reactive social behavior links to low or diminished levels of local social capital and high levels of social distrust (Czapinski, 2007; Mihaylova, 2004). Further, the level of social capital can be associated with the intensity of social interaction within a locality.

Hence, if tourism development planning intensifies interaction among different stakeholders, it is linked to local social capital and therefore local levels of social distrust (Mihaylova, 2004). However, the research still does not provide clarification of whether enhancing the interaction and development of local relationships during the tourism project affects the actors' involvement in local affairs in the long term. This case study also does not examine whether the development of social relationships and empowerment were built beyond the tourism development planning process, and a more powerful research tool must be applied. The study does illustrate, however, that tourism planning projects should be designed in order to facilitate interactive processes through debate and connect individual and group actors with local authorities. The authors also raise the question of the potential impact of local tourism development processes on local democratic cultures in Poland. This work should be understood as an invitation to the necessary series of studies focused on similar problems over a longer time period.

Completing the consolidation of local democratic cultures in Poland is furthered by increasing engagement in local affairs (Czapinski, 2007) and implies that citizens' will to participate is necessary. Despite the intensive research dedicated to community social capital (Allen, Korsching &Vogt, 2004), there remains little understanding of how to generate social capital and how exactly it relates to community action. The authors propose that one way to enhance the development of social relationships within a locality and facilitate community action is to realize the principle of connecting local stakeholders along with the realization of tangible goals of projects organized within a tourism development framework.

Units operating at the local level, such as organizations or local governments, have access to a range of instruments to influence the direction and fashion in which they realize local development (Majewska, 2008). Therefore they have the means to empower local actors by securing their meaningful inclusion in decision-making. At the same time the units should stress the need for collaboration and need for transparent decision processes that further facilitate democratic culture. The case study illustrates that empowering local actors can occur at the planning process stage through intensified interactions. The process also allows for the generation of new values, discovering shared interests and perhaps developing additional interest in the condition of local affairs (Wilkinson, 1991). Local processes such as tourism development planning, however, usually require some level of organizational social capital in order to involve crucial local partners and facilitate the development of a relationship among them.

One important finding from the case study was the fact that decisions about participation in the planning process were often dependent upon the availability of information and also the quality of available information, from which arise the expectations about project outcomes. Increased understanding of the role of tourism in a locality would also encourage actors to engage in decision-making. In addition, social benefits from participation, such as group acceptance or the opportunity to express one's opinions shall be regarded as important motivators for actors to become involved in planning. If local governance institutions are to genuinely facilitate collaborative planning for tourism development, they must aim to improve access to information about the impacts of proposed projects. Information shapes local perception of tourism development and its influence on local dynamics.

Tourism planning projects create local spaces for interaction and develop trusting relationships. Although relationships are more likely to develop and to evolve if interaction involves shared emotions and sentiment (Sobel, 2002), the presented case study showed that motivations to interact originated in securing perceived benefits from economic development and avoiding threats to the social and natural environment. These benefits motivate actors to pursue local interactions as they develop new relationships. Coordinating organizations often share knowledge, and provide advice and guidelines to other actors, and thus allowing them to benefit from their organization's resources.

Shared values and interest in the locality's overall wellbeing emerge from the intensified interaction among actors and are facilitated by the development of trust (Putnam, 2002). This may result in collectiveness and the emergence of community action (Wilkinson, 1991) and with cooperative local authorities more positive attitudes emerge. The local government becomes a community actor that facilitates collectiveness through activities focused on community interests. Therefore tourism development projects in post-communist localities should be regarded as local opportunities to link different stakeholders together and hence they should be understood as opportunity to enhance community action.

References

Agrawal, A., & Gibson, G. (1999). Enchantment and disenchantment: The role of community in natural resource conservation. *World Development, 27*, 629–649.

Allen, J.C., Korsching, P.F., & Vogt, R. (2003). Examination of community action field theory model for locality based entrepreneurship. Paper Presented at Rural Sociological Society Meeting, Montreal, Canada.

Armitage, D.R. (2005). Community-based Narwhal management in Nunavut, Canada: Change, uncertainty, and adaptation. *Society & Natural Resources, 18*(8), 715–731.

Austin, R.L., & Eder, J.F. (2007). Environmentalism, development, and participation on Palawan Island, Philippines. *Society & Natural Resources, 20*(4), 363–371.

Blangy, S., & Nielsen, T. (1993). Ecotourism and minimum impact policy. *Annals of Tourism Research, 20*(2), 357–360.

Bourdieu, P. (1983). Forms of capital. In J.C. Richards (Ed.), *Handbook of theory and research for the sociology of education* (pp. 241–258). New York: Greenwood Press.

Brehm, J., & Rahn, W. (1997). Individual level evidence for causes and consequences of social capital. *American Journal of Political Science, 41*(3), 999–1023.

Brown, D.L., & Swanson, L. (2003). *Challenges for rural America in the 21st century*. University Park, PA: Pennsylvania State University Press.

Clark, J. (1997). A framework of approaches to sustainable tourism. *Journal of Sustainable Tourism, 5*(3), 226–234.

Coleman, J. (1988). Social capital in the creation of human capital. *American Journal of Sociology, 94*, 95–120.

Coleman, J. (1990). *Foundations of social theory*. Cambridge, MA: Harvard University Press.

Commission Communication (2001). A sustainable Europe for a better world: A European Union strategy for sustainable development (COM (2001) 264, final).

Commission of the European Communities (2004d). Building our common future (COM(2004)101, final). Office for Official Publications of the European Communities, Luxembourg.

Cox, K. (1998). Spaces of dependence, spaces of engagement and the politics of scale, or: Looking for local politics. *Political Geography, 17*(1), 1–23.

Crompton, J. (1992). Structure of vacation destination choice sets. *Annals of Tourism Research, 19*(3), 420–434.

Czapinski, J. (2007). Social capital. In J. Czapinski & T. Panek (Eds.), *Social diagnosis 2007. Objective and subjective quality of life in Poland* (pp. 166–179). Warszawa: University of Finance and Management.

Dwyer, L., Forsyth, P., & Spurr, R. (2006). Assessing the economic impacts of events: A computable general equilibrium approach. *Journal of Travel Research, 45*, 59–66.

Elkin, R.D., & Roberts, R.S. (1987). Evaluating the human resources/employment requirements and impacts of tourism developments. In B.J.R. Ritchie & C.R. Goeldner (Eds.), *Travel, tourism and hospitality research* (pp. 403–412). New York: John Wiley & Sons.

Granovetter, M.S. (1973). The strength of weak ties. *American Journal of Sociology*, *78*(6), 1360–1380.

Habermas, J. (2001). The postnational constellation and the future of democracy. In J. Habermas (Ed.), *The postnational constellation: Political essays* (pp. 58–112). Cambridge, MA: Polity Press.

Haukeland, J.V. (1984). Sociocultural impacts of tourism in Scandinavia. *Tourism Management*, *5*(3), 207–214.

Holling, C.S. (2004). From complex regions to complex worlds. *Ecology and Society*, *9*(1), 11, from http://www.ecologyandsociety.org/vol9/iss1/art11/

Hooghe, M., & Stolle, D. (2003). Introduction to generating social capital. In M. Hooghe & D. Stolle (Eds.), *Generating social capital: Civic society and institutions in comparative perspective* (pp. 1–19). New York: Palgrave Macmillan.

Howard, M.M. (2002). The weakness of postcommunist civil society. *Journal of Democracy*, *13*(1), 157–169.

Howard, M.M. (2003). *The Weakness of Civil Society in Post-Communist Europe*. Cambridge, UK: Cambridge University Press.

Hughes, G. (1995). The cultural construction of sustainable tourism. *Tourism Management*, *16*(1), 49–59.

Kaufman, H.F., & Wilkinson, K. (1967). Community structure and leadership. Bulletin No. 13, Social Science Research Center, Mississippi State University, Mississippi State, MS.

Kay, A. (2005). Social capital, the social economy and community development. *Community Development Journal Advance Access*, 1–14.

Keogh, B. (1990). Community tourism planning. *Annals of Tourism Research*, *17*, 449–465.

King, B., Dwyer, L., & Prideaux, B. (2007). An evaluation of unethical business practices in Australia's China inbound tourism market. *International Journal of Tourism Research*, *8*(2), 127–142.

Kuniokaa, T., & Woller, G.M. (1999). In (a) democracy we trust: Social and economic determinants of support for democratic procedures in central and Eastern Europe. *Journal of Socio-Economics*, *28*(5), 577–596.

Knopp, T.B., & Caldbeck, E.S. (1990). The role of participatory democracy in forest management. *Journal of Forestry*, *88*(5), 13–19.

Leeuwis, C. (2000). Reconceptualizing participation for sustainable rural development: Towards a negotiation approach. *Development and Change*, *31*(5), 931–959.

Li, W.J. (2006). Community decision-making participation in development. *Annals of Tourism Research*, *33*(1), 132–143.

Lucas, A.R. (1987). Fundamental prerequisites for citizens' participation. In B. Sadler (Ed.), *Involvement and environment* (pp. 47–57). Proceedings of the Canadian Conference on Public Participation, Edmonton: Environment Council of Alberta.

Luloff, A.E., & Wilkinson, K. (1979). Participation in the national flood insurance program: A study of community activeness. *Rural Sociology*, *44*(1), 137–152.

Majewska, J. (2008). Local government's involvement in the development of entrepreneurship in emerging tourism destination. In G. Golembski (Ed.), *Entrepreneurship and quality in tourism in light of Polish and international research* (pp. 127–146). Wydawnictwo Akademii Ekonomicznej w Poznaniu: Poznan.

Mead, G.H. (1934). *Mind, self, and society*, ed. by Ch. W. Morris. Chicago, IL: University of Chicago Press.

Merton, R.K. (1968). *Social theory and social structure*. Free Press: New York.

Mihaylova, D. (2004). Social capital in Eastern and Central Europe: A critical assessment and literature review. Policy Studies Series 2004. Center for Policy Studies, Hungary: Central European University.

Murphy, P. (1983). Tourism as a community industry. *Tourism Management*, *4*(3), 180–192.

Murphy, P. (1988). Community driven tourism planning. *Tourism Management*, *9*(2), 94–104.

Parkins, J.R., & Mitchell, R.E. (2005). Public participation as public debate: A deliberative turn in natural resource management. *Society & Natural Resources*, *18*(6), 529–540.

Pawlowski, A. (2008). How many dimensions does sustainable development have? *Sustainable Development*, *16*, 81–90.

Pearce, P.L. (1995). From culture shock and culture arrogance to culture exchange: Ideas towards sustainable socio-cultural tourism. *Journal of Sustainable Tourism*, *3*(3), 143–154.

Perdue, R.R., Long, P.T., & Allen, L. (1987). Rural residents tourism perceptions and attitudes. *Annals of Tourism Research*, *14*, 420–429.

Putnam, R.D. (1993). *Making democracy work: Civic traditions in modern Italy*. Princeton, NJ: Princeton University Press.

Putnam, R.D. (2000). *Bowling alone: The collapse and revival of American community*. New York: Simon & Schuster.

Putnam, R.D. (2002). *Democracies in flux: The evolution of social capital in contemporary society*. New York: Oxford University Press.

Ryan, C. (2002). Equity, management, power sharing and sustainability—issues of the 'new tourism'. *Tourism Management*, *23*, 17–26.

Reid, D.G., Mair, H., & George, W. (2004). Community tourism planning: A self-assessment instrument. *Annals of Tourism Research*, *31*(3), 623–639.

Saarinen, J. (2006). Traditions of sustainability in tourism studies. *Annals of Tourism Research*, *33*(4), 1121–1140.

Sobel, J. (2002). Can we trust social capital? *Journal of Economic Literature* XL, 139–154.

Sztompka, P. (1996). Looking back: The year 1989 as a cultural and civilizational break. *Communist and Post-Communist Studies*, *29*, 126–127.

Tandom, R. (2008). Participation, citizenship and democracy: Reflections on 25 years' of PRIA. *Community Development Journal*, *43*(3), 284–286.

Theodori, G.L. (2005). Community and community development in resource-based areas: Operational definitions rooted in interactional perspective. *Society and Natural Resources*, *18*, 661–669.

Tosun, C. (1998). Routs of unsustainable tourism at the local level. The case of Urgup in Turkey. *Tourism Management*, *19*(6), 595–610.

Tosun, C. (2001). Challenges of sustainable tourism development in the developing world: The case of Turkey. *Tourism Management*, *22*(3), 289–303.

Tosun, C., & Timothy, D. (2003). Arguments for community participation in tourism development. *Journal of Tourism Studies*, *14*(2), 2–11.

Walker, P.A., & Hurley, P.T. (2004). Collaboration derailed: The politics of "community-based" resource management in Nevada County. *Society & Natural Resources*, *17*(8), 735–751.

Wall, E., Ferrazzi, G., & Schryer, F. (1998). Getting the goods on social capital. *Rural Sociology*, *63*(2), 300–322.

Wilkinson, K.P. (1970). The community as a social field. *Social Forces*, *48*(3), 9–17.

Wilkinson, K.P. (1972). A field-theory perspective for community development research. *Rural Sociology*, *37*(1), 43–52.

Wilkinson, K.P. (1974). A behavioral approach to measurement and analysis of community field structure. *Rural Sociology*, *39*(2), 247–256.

Wilkinson, K.P. (1991). *The community in rural America*. New York: Greenwood Press.

Woolcock, M., & Natayan, D. (2000). Social capital: Implication for development theory, research and policy. *The World Bank Research Observer*, *15*(2), 225–4.

Zanetell, B.A., & Knuth, B.A. (2002). Knowledge partnerships: Rapid rural appraisal's role in catalyzing community-based management in Venezuela. *Society & Natural Resources*, *15*(9), 805–825.

Participatory modeling as a tool for community development planning: tourism in the Northern Forest

Lisa Chase[a], Roelof Boumans[b] and Stephanie Morse[c]

[a]University of Vermont, Extension, 11 University Way, Brattleboro, 05301 USA; [b]University of Vermont, Gund Institute for Ecological Economics, Burlington, USA; [c]Center for Neighborhood Technology, Chicago, USA

Tourism development planning is challenging for rural communities transitioning from dependence on resource extraction to a diversified economy including tourism. This research examines how participatory modeling can help communities improve their understanding of diverse perspectives and identify intrinsically linked components of tourism. Using a participatory process in six communities in the Northern Forest region of the northeastern United States, a dynamic computer model was developed illustrating complex relationships associated with recreation and tourism development. A user-friendly interface and step-by-step manual were distributed to facilitate application of the model by community planners. Evaluation of the model indicated that barriers limited widespread adoption of the model as a decision-making aid for planners. However, evaluation of the modeling process revealed positive impacts on community capacity including fostering dialogue, increasing understanding of different perspectives, and helping to build consensus.

Introduction

The rural economic landscape is changing throughout the United States as the loss of many manufacturing plants and the growth of industrial agriculture have severely limited small communities' options for economic development. Tourism has become an alternative source of growth and its related entrepreneurship opportunities are being recognized (Sinclair, 1998; Webster & Chappelle, 2001; Wilson, Fesenmaier, Fesenmaier & van Es, 2001). In the Northern Forest, a 26 million acre bioregion extending across northern New York and New England, efforts to promote recreation and tourism have received renewed attention in recent years. The inclusion of tourism and recreation in the economic mix is not new in the region; efforts to promote tourism date back well over 100 years. During that time period, tourism has been viewed as a mixed blessing and recreation and tourism development have led to mixed results (Albers, 2000). This remains the case today in the Northern Forest.

Many communities have come to rely on tourism as a way to diversify incomes in resource-dependent economies, yet tourism has a reputation for being unable to support living-wage jobs, providing only minimum wages in the service sector with few opportunities for advancement. Recreation and tourism are sometimes credited with promoting environmental conservation, and often accused of contributing to environmental degradation. Tourism creates concentrated stress on natural and man-made systems that were not designed to manage large numbers of people and heavy use (e.g., water systems, roads, garbage disposal). Many cultural attractions are supported by tourism and even created for tourists, yet tourism can diminish the small-town charm and sense of place appealing to residents and tourists alike (Krannich & Petrzelka, 2003).

Understanding the broad range of benefits and challenges—economic, social, and ecological—is essential for communities involved in recreation and tourism planning. Yet the amount of information and conflicting perspectives can be overwhelming. Identifying the intrinsically linked components of tourism is a first step in describing its potential as a development tool. Planning processes are needed that identify both the positive and negative aspects of tourism development and provide research-based tools for decision makers with regard to the type, size, scope, and potential of the development. The challenge is to bring communities together to create a shared vision that encompasses, but is not limited to, individual perspectives.

Participatory computer modeling is a methodology that involves a community in the process of collectively building a model about a particular situation that affects their lives. One of the most important aspects of modeling as a consensus building tool is the process of its development, setting a stage for stakeholders to work together, share world views and hopefully come to a common understanding of their shared systems. Computer modeling may be a powerful tool to reconcile contrasting points of view, increase shared understanding, and resolve conflicts (van den Belt, 2004).

This research examines how participatory computer modeling can contribute to tourism and recreation planning in rural communities. The paper begins with discussions of tourism development planning and participatory modeling. Next research methods are presented including the development of models and an evaluation of participatory modeling workshops. Findings related to both the modeling process and outcomes are presented. The paper concludes with implications for community development planning in the Northern Forest and beyond.

Tourism development planning and participatory modeling

Different views exist as to the best way to facilitate recreation and tourism development. Free-market economics, where individuals develop businesses and let them compete, has been critiqued as narrow in scope and often inappropriate for developing sustainable tourism opportunities that enhance the vitality of rural communities (Wilson et al., 2001). Multidisciplinary, integrated approaches to recreation and tourism planning may include elements of free-market economics but are often supplemented with community planning to promote collaborative destination development and marketing (Ashley & Roe, 1998; Jamal, Borges, & Figueiredo, 2004; Jamieson, 2001). These multidimensional strategies attempt to recognize the needs of sustainable tourism by integrating related fields including ecosystem ecology, ecological economics, and global change science (Farrell &

Twining-Ward, 2004). Collaborative approaches explicitly identify trade-offs between economic growth and costs to the environment and culture (Jamal & Getz, 1995; Keogh, 1990; Murphy, 1985; Sautter & Leisen, 1999).

Participation in planning and policy

Smith, Nell and Prystupta (1997, p. 143) define public participation as "any action taken by an interested public (individual or group) to influence a decision, plan or policy beyond that of voting in an election." In their evaluation of public participation methods, Rowe and Frewer (2000) distinguish varying levels of public involvement. Low levels of participation are typically utilized in more knowledge-based decisions and high levels of participation are more appropriate in value-based decisions (Chase, Schusler, & Decker, 2000). Evaluating the effectiveness of different participatory methods is difficult, although tools exist to help planners and managers determine appropriate participatory methods for varying contexts (Chase, Decker, & Lauber 2004; Fiorino, 1990).

While evaluating different participatory methods may be difficult and ambiguous, some argue that the need for public participation in planning and policy is clear. In discussing technical policy issues, Laird (1993, p. 341) states, "The social and economic importance of these issues create a normative requirement that they be subject to democratic scrutiny." Keogh (1990) emphasizes the importance of participation in tourism planning and decision-making, explaining that the public often perceives the negative impacts of tourism development as being greater than the positive economic gains, potentially resulting in negative feelings of the residents towards tourists and tourism. The outcomes of these studies often call for community-oriented or participatory approaches to tourism planning to provide adequate information to everyone involved.

Participatory computer modeling

Computers have long contributed to problem solving by providing decision-making support in complex systems. Dynamic model programming software allows for the quantification of components so that alternative scenarios can be simulated (Costanza & Ruth, 1998). For example, the complex system of relationships associated with tourism in a particular community can be mapped out and quantified. Then variables can be changed to examine the effects. Simulations can be created that estimate how an increase in the number of tourists will impact different businesses, traffic patterns, land prices and other variables that can be incorporated into the model as a community sees fit.

Participatory computer modeling is a "process for involving stakeholders in the conceptualization, specification, and synthesis of their knowledge and information into dynamic computer-based simulation models" (van den Belt, 2004, p. 17). Models are developed to represent a particular situation in the participants' lives, thus providing a stage for community members to come together, discuss the issue at hand, and hopefully come to a joint, deeper understanding. In this fashion, participatory modeling has been shown to serve as both a consensus-building tool and an aid in the understanding of complex systems (van den Belt, 2004).

Participatory modeling has been utilized for public involvement in a variety of natural resource and environmental management issues, but it has been applied to recreation and tourism planning only in a couple of cases. The Tourism Futures Simulator, a model developed through a joint project with Australia's Commonwealth Scientific and Industrial Research Organisation (CSIRO) and the tourism industry in Douglas Shire in North Queensland and the Cairns section of the Great Barrier Reef may be the first published example of participatory modeling of the tourism industry (Walker, Greiner, McDonald, & Lyne, 1999). Steps taken to develop this model were understanding stakeholder views, developing the concept, developing a simulation model, integrating data, building a user interface, establishing causal tracing, and developing a learning environment (Walker et al., 1999). In another case, students acted as participants and utilized participatory modeling software to develop a model representing the tourism industry in their college town. This research concluded that the participatory modeling approach may be particularly helpful in collaborative planning, destination tourism management, and as a tourism teaching tool (Jamal et al., 2004).

The fact that participatory modeling has not been used often in tourism development may be due to the complexity of the industry, but this complexity is also the reason why it may be beneficial. Farrell and Twining-Ward (2004) contend that the study of tourism is greatly lacking in its narrow, linear approach, and that capitalizing on the progresses made in multiple disciplines, such as ecosystem ecology and ecological economics, is necessary. Interactional approaches to development explicitly focus on the importance of linkages that can contribute to well-being and are often neglected in rural communities (Bridger & Alter, 2008).

However, individuals cannot be expected to take into account all of the variables associated with recreation and tourism development and come to an adequate understanding for decision-making. Costanza and Ruth (1998) explain:

> In building mental models, humans typically simplify systems in particular ways. We base most of our mental modeling on qualitative rather than quantitative relationships, we linearize the relationships among system components, disregard temporal and spatial lags, treat systems as isolated from their surroundings or limit our investigations to the system's equilibrium domain. When problems become more complex, and when quantitative relationships, nonlinearities, and time and space lags are important, we encounter limits to our ability to properly anticipate system change. In such cases our mental models need to be supplemented (p. 183).

Methods for supplementing mental models include systems thinking and systems modeling. Systems thinking involves breaking down behavior into its most basic elements or building blocks. Participatory modeling facilitates a group process of shared systems thinking within a community, allowing for the application of an interactional approach to community planning in rural areas.

This research assesses the value of participatory computer modeling for tourism and recreation planning in rural communities in the Northern Forest. The original objectives of the research were to work with six communities to develop models, compare the models in the different communities, develop a general model if sufficient commonalities existed, and create a user-friendly interface so that communities could utilize the model for decision-making. Evaluations conducted periodically assessed the value of the model to communities as well as the value of the modeling process.

Research methods

To assess the usefulness of participatory modeling for tourism development planning in rural communities, six study sites in the Northern Forest were selected using a snowball sampling method. Key representatives involved in tourism and recreation were contacted in each of the four Northern Forest states (Maine, New Hampshire, Vermont, and New York) and asked to suggest communities that would be interested in such a study and to aid researchers in making contacts. For the purposes of this research, a community was defined as any area in which local decision makers were interested in working together, regardless of scale (e.g., town, county, region, etc.) The six communities were selected based on the following criteria: population, status of tourism infrastructure, percentage of tourism revenues compared with other industries, and a community's level of interest in participating in the project. The final criterion was heavily weighted, as it was essential for voluntary participation by community members. Selected communities included: the Village of Saranac Lake, New York; the Town of Wilmington, New York; the three-county region of the Northeast Kingdom, Vermont; Franklin and Grand Isle Counties, Vermont; the Town of Colebrook, New Hampshire; and the town of Carroll, New Hampshire (Figure 1). The rural communities in the Northern Forest region represent a range among the criteria, with the exception of the required high level of interest in participating.

Key contacts were established in each community, and the researchers worked with them to identify between 10 and 20 community representatives to take part in the participatory modeling workshops. Participants included hotel and motel owners, restaurant owners, shop owners, town employees including representatives

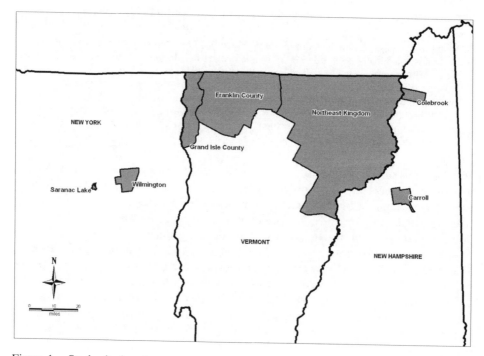

Figure 1.   Study site locations.

from law enforcement and waste management, town trustees, local planning board representatives, outdoor recreation guides, members of environmental organizations, historical society members, farmers and other large landowners, as well as representatives from the Chambers of Commerce. An effort was made to include a diverse set of stakeholders at each workshop, including elected officials, business owners, and those that represented both advocates and opponents of recreation and tourism development.

After the communities and participants were selected, a one-day workshop was held in each community between October 2004 and October 2005 (Table 1). The goal of the workshop was to develop a scoping model, or visual diagram, representing the tourism and recreation industries unique to each community. The agenda for each workshop was the same. Community members were first asked to brainstorm about any and all aspects of tourism and recreation in their community. After generating lists of components and factors in the morning, ranging from septic systems and roads to concepts such as community trust, the afternoon became focused on building a model. The modeler, using STELLA software projected on a large screen for all participants to see, worked with community participants to lay out the structure of the model by taking the components identified earlier and using the conversations to create links and ties between the variables. Participants collaboratively defined relationships and connections.

After the first round of workshops was completed, a second workshop was held in the community that expressed the most interest in continuing with the participatory modeling process: Franklin and Grand Isle Counties, Vermont in December 2005. The facilitator and modeler returned to the community with revised, more developed models. Participants discussed the changes, whether or not they felt the model reflected their community, and which components that they felt were still missing from the model. The models were then revised further and a general model was developed, which was shared with Franklin and Grand Isle Counties in Vermont at a third workshop in May 2007.

As part of the model revision process, a thorough comparison of the models was conducted to assess the levels of similarity and dissimilarity between the six site-specific iterations. This led to the construction of a general model which combined the similarities while reconciling the differences of the six models. Each site-specific model had some components that were better developed and some areas that were

Table 1. Participatory modeling workshop locations and dates.

First Workshops:	
Northeast Kingdom, VT	14 October 2004
Saranac Lake, NY	21 October 2004
Colebrook, NH	19 January 2005
Carroll, NH	17 May 2005
Wilmington, NY	7 June 2005
Franklin County, VT	25 October 2005
Second Workshops:	
Wilmington, NY	13 October 2005
Franklin County, VT	6 December 2005
Third Workshop:	
Franklin County, VT	15 May 2007

lacking. The general model essentially pulled together the best thought out pieces of each site-specific model, and then worked to fill in the gaps. The general model was developed to define relationships, leaving blank values for variables. For example, a relationship could be defined for the amount of a structure that could be built with a given investment, but the value of the investment was left undefined. This allowed for the model to be tailored to any community by inputting the appropriate data.

Because many variables needed to be defined relative to a community, and thus by community participants, a user-friendly interface was developed to aid in this step of the process. Accompanying the interface, participants were provided with a manual to walk them through each step of the process. The manual described how to navigate the model, how to input values, how to change values, how to run the model, and how to interpret the outcome charts. The manual was designed to enable the use of the model without facilitation.

At the end of each workshop, participants were asked to fill out a written evaluation regarding their reactions to the modeling process and to the model itself, assessing the usefulness of each. The evaluations for the first two workshops were similar. Participants were asked open-ended questions about the most and least valuable aspects of the workshop and the best ways to follow-up after the workshops. Participants were also asked to rate their knowledge prior to attending the workshop and once the workshop was over using a scale of 1 to 5, where 1 = no knowledge and 5 = extremely knowledgeable. Topics included systems modeling, the big picture of tourism and recreation in their community, practical ideas for improving tourism and recreation, and perspectives of other participants. Participants also were asked how likely they were to use the model on their own or with others in the future on a scale of 1 to 5, where 1 = no chance and 5 = highly probable. The evaluation form for the third workshop included similar questions to the previous evaluation forms but also additional questions about their likelihood of utilizing the model as a decision making tool and utilizing information obtained in the participatory modeling *process* to inform community decision-making. Participants also were asked whether they felt the participatory modeling *process* had been a useful method for fostering dialogue between participants, gaining new perspectives, and contributing to consensus-building. In these questions about building community capital, participants were instructed to circle the most appropriate number from 1 to 5, where 1 = strongly disagree and 5 = strongly agree. These evaluations, completed anonymously, were analyzed to assess the potential of the model and the modeling process to aid in informing decision-making processes (see Appendix for evaluation forms for the three workshops in Franklin and Grand Isle Counties, Vermont).

Results

The general model was developed with three main components contributing services to the local economy (Figure 2). These sections were identified as Cultural Outlooks, Cultural Resources, and Natural Resources, which together produce services identified by the participants including Social gatherings, Public services, Natural amenities, Summer recreation, Winter recreation, Spring recreation, Fall recreation, Housing, and Dining and lodging. The Quality of Life estimate is based on the level at which these services are available and in demand. For example, investment in Cultural Resources can increase the contribution of Homes, Rentals, Churches,

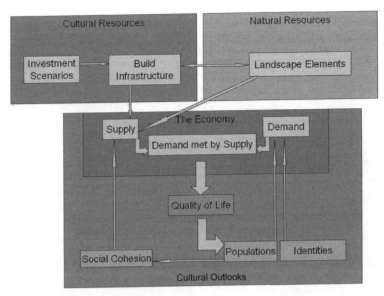

Figure 2. General model developed with three main components contributing services to the local economy.

Public info centers, Public education facilities, Public infrastructure, and Private sector businesses to the available services, while decreasing the contributions available from Natural Resources (e.g., Water, Wetlands, Grasslands, Forests, Croplands, and Mountains) (Morse, 2007).

The post-workshop evaluations asked questions about the usefulness of the participatory modeling process as well as the model itself. Three groupings of responses were considered. The first group of responses was the full set of 70 participant evaluations collected after the first round of workshops in all six communities. The second group of responses was the five evaluations collected after the second round workshop held in Franklin and Grand Isle Counties, Vermont. The last group of responses considered was the five evaluations collected after the third workshop in Franklin and Grand Isle Counties. These five participants were all present at the first workshop in Franklin and Grand Isle Counties, and three were present at the second workshop, although there is no way to isolate their particular responses. While the sample size is small and cannot be used for inferential statistics, it can be useful to assess the experience of the participants in this example.

Most valuable aspects

In the evaluation following the first round of workshops, participants were asked to comment on what they found most valuable about the workshop. Sorting of general comment types revealed eight different categories into which the open-ended comments were grouped. These categories, in order of comment frequency, are: (1) discussion and exchange of new ideas; (2) learning about STELLA and the potential for modeling; (3) discussion specific to tourism; (4) cooperation and interaction; (5) networking and meeting new people; (6) better understanding of community and its issues; (7) new information; and (8) outside input from the university (Figure 3).

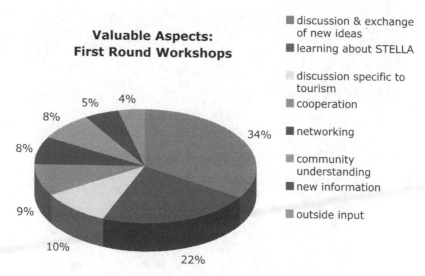

Figure 3.   Valuable aspects specified in evaluation of first round of workshops.

Discussion and exchange of new ideas was the most frequently provided comment type, making up 34% of all comments to this question. Second most frequent with 22% was the category of comments pertaining to learning about STELLA and modeling.

Participants were asked this same question regarding the most valuable aspects of the workshop after the second workshop for Franklin and Grand Isle Counties. The respondents' comments were: (1) networking and reconnecting with UVM representatives and community members; (2) further development of understanding the capabilities of a model; (3) coming to an understanding of how STELLA really applies; (4) the discussion about what went into the model and how it might be used; and (5) to see how the information we gave at the last meeting impacted the model. Categorizing revealed that 4 of the 5 comments (80%) pertained to learning about the STELLA model and the potential for modeling. The last comment valued networking and reconnecting with community members.

Similar to the question asked in the evaluations after the first and second round of workshops, in the evaluation following the third workshop in Franklin and Grand Isle Counties, participants were asked, "What did you find most valuable about the workshop today? If you participated in previous workshops, does this differ from what you found most valuable about the overall participatory modeling process? Please comment." The six comments received (one respondent provided two comments) regarding what the participants found most valuable about the third workshop were: 1) another step closer to understanding; 2) a step in the right direction; 3) group discussions about the participatory modeling process itself; 4) understanding of where other community members are coming from; 5) a vision of how the model could work; and 6) the model demonstration and how it helped to understand the complexity of the process. Categorizing revealed the most frequent comment type to be gaining a better understanding of the community and the complexity of issues with 50% of the comments falling into this group. Next was learning about the STELLA model and the potential for modeling with two of the six comments. The last comment valued the discussion of the overall modeling process.

A comparison of these responses provided after each workshop illustrate how participants' perceptions of the workshops changed over time. Participants started out by valuing coming together, meeting each other, and discussing their community. As the process progressed, the focus seemed to shift more on the model and its potential. By the end of the third workshop, participants seemed less focused on the model itself, and more interested in the overall knowledge gained through the process.

Likelihood of using the model in the future

In the evaluations given after each workshop, participants were asked: "How likely are you to use the STELLA model (on your own or with others) in the future? Circle the most appropriate number from 1 to 5, where 1 = no chance and 5 = highly probable." In the first round of workshop evaluations, the mode response was 3 (Figure 4). The average, however, was slightly higher at 3.19, perhaps indicating a slightly more positive response. One interesting note regarding the responses obtained to this question is that 10 out of 70 participants indicated a "highly probable" likelihood of using the STELLA model in the future, while only two participants indicated a "no chance" likelihood of using the model.

To develop a better basis for comparison between the first, second and third workshops, it was useful to isolate the 12 participants from the first round of workshops that were specifically in the Franklin and Grand Isle Counties workshop (Figure 5). Considering these participants, the mode response to the question regarding using the STELLA model in the future was 3. The average in this case though, was a bit higher at 3.75. In this group's responses no participants indicated a value less than 3 and 25% responded with a "highly probable" likelihood of using the STELLA model in the future. After the second workshop, the mode response was 4 and the mean was 4.2. Again, no respondent indicated a value less than 3, and

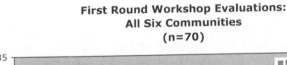

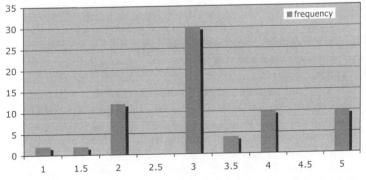

Figure 4. Likelihood of using STELLA model in the future specified in the first round of workshops.

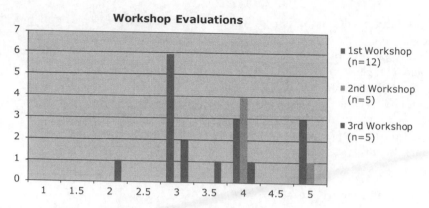

Figure 5. Likelihood of using STELLA model in the future for first, second, and third workshops in Franklin and Grand Isle Counties, Vermont.

after this workshop, one respondent indicated a "highly probable" likelihood of using the STELLA model in the future.

After the third workshop in Franklin and Grand Isle County, this same question was evaluated again to analyze a potential change in participants' perceived likelihood of using the STELLA model. The mode response dropped back down to a value of 3 and the average dropped to 3.1. This time, one participant indicated a value less than 3 regarding the likelihood of using the model in the future. Another interesting observation of these results is that not one participant responded with a value of 5. These results are potentially indicative of the difficulty encountered when attempting to utilize the model. This was the first time participants were actually asked to run the model themselves. Perhaps initial optimism regarding the model was slightly diminished due to the difficulty encountered. Where the model started out as the primary focus, this faded as participants delved deeper into discussions. The model seemed to shift from being the main goal to being seen as facilitating the goal of developing a better understanding of the issues discussed.

Overall process

In the evaluation given after the third workshop in Fanklin and Grand Isle Counties, participants were also asked a series of questions considering the participatory modeling *process* as a whole. Regarding fostering dialogue between participants, the mean value reported was 4.4, with three respondents indicating a value of 4, and two respondents answering 5. A mean value of 4 was obtained regarding gaining new perspectives, with three participants choosing a value of 4, one participant indicating a value of 3 and one a value of 5. Pertaining to consensus-building, a mean value of 3.8 was obtained from four respondents indicating a value of 4 and one indicating a value of 3. Participants were also asked, "How likely are you to utilize information obtained in the participatory modeling *process* to inform community decision-making? Circle the most appropriate number from 1 to 5, where 1 = no chance and 5 = highly probable." For this question, a mean value of 3.5 was obtained with responses varying from 2 to 4.5. Of all of the responses to all four questions (20 responses in total) pertaining to the value or usefulness of the participatory modeling *process*, only one response fell below a value of 3, and only three values of 3 were reported. The mode response of 4 here indicates that participants' impressions of the participatory modeling *process* were generally positive and that they see this as a useful method for fostering dialogue, gaining new perspectives, and consensus-building.

Conclusions

Participants' evaluation responses indicated a generally positive response regarding intentions to use the STELLA model in the future, however observations from the third workshop revealed barriers to application. In the third workshop in Franklin and Grand Isle Counties, participants attempted to utilize the model without the help of a facilitator to assess its usefulness as a tool in and of itself. Participants had difficulty understanding the variables and determining how to assign values for them, and they frequently asked questions of the facilitator and modeler. Participants realized that confidence in the output obtained from the STELLA model was greatly dependent on the level of confidence in the values they were inputting, which was oftentimes very low. While participants may want to utilize the STELLA model as a decision making tool, this would require more work on the model in terms of data collection and calibration, as well as more assistance in facilitating the use of it. This is not an unrealistic goal, and with continued community interest and further research and modeling time, the STELLA model holds potential as a decision making tool. However the time investment and lack of data inputs are barriers that need to be addressed.

The participatory modeling process, however, seems to have had more immediate positive results. The form of the model suggests that participants developed a deeper understanding of the linkages of recreation and tourism with rural community development. What started out as a brainstorming activity to generate all aspects and components of recreation and tourism became a discussion of quality of life in all six workshops. During the discussions, participants had difficulty isolating recreation and tourism components; these issues pervaded all aspects of their lives. This idea was reflected in the shape of the model, which became centered around quality of life, with the economy and tourism and recreation industries being one part of a much bigger picture. Enabling community members to come to this realization jointly illustrated the power of a participatory process as a method for understanding the interactional effects of recreation and tourism.

Not only did the participants develop a deeper understanding of the impacts of recreation and tourism development, but the environment in which they did this seemed to enhance community vitality. As recognized by respondents in the evaluations, participants saw the process as a useful method for fostering dialogue, gaining new perspectives, and building consensus. These findings in Franklin and Grand Isle Counties, Vermont are likely relevant elsewhere in the Northern Forest and may extend to other rural communities throughout the US.

References

Albers, J. (2000). *Hands on the land: A history of the Vermont landscape*. Cambridge, MA: The MIT Press.

Ashley, C., & Roe, D. (1998). Enhancing community involvement in wildlife tourism: Issues and challenges. *Wildlife and Development Series No. 11*. London: International Institute for Environment and Development.

Bridger, J.C., & Alter, T.R. (2008). An interactional approach to place-based rural development. *Community Development: Journal of the Community Development Society*, *39*(1), 99–111.

Chase, L.C., Decker, D.J., & Lauber, T.B. (2004). Public participation in wildlife management: What do stakeholders want? *Society and Natural Resources*, *17*(7), 629–639.

Chase, L.C., Schusler, T.M., & Decker, D.J. (2000). Innovations in stakeholder involvement: What's the next step? *Wildlife Society Bulletin*, *28*(1), 208–217.

Costanza, R., & Ruth, M. (1998). Using dynamic modeling to scope environmental problems and build consensus. *Environmental Management*, *22*(2), 183–195.

Farrell, B.H., & Twining-Ward, L. (2004). Reconceptualizing tourism. *Annals of Tourism Research*, *31*(2), 274–295.

Fiorino, D.J. (1990). Citizen participation and environmental risk: A survey of institutional mechanisms. *Science, Technology, & Human Values*, *15*(2), 226–243.

Jamal, T., Borges, M., & Figueiredo, R. (2004). Systems-based modeling for participatory tourism planning and destination management. *Tourism Analysis*, *9*, 77–89.

Jamal, T.B., & Getz, D. (1995). Collaboration theory and community tourism planning. *Annals of Tourism Research*, *22*(1), 186–204.

Jamieson, W. (Ed.). (2001). *Community tourism destination management: Principles and practices*. Pathumthani, Thailand: Saengsawang World Press Co.

Keogh, B. (1990). Public participation in community tourism planning. *Annals of Tourism Research*, *17*, 449–465.

Krannich, R.S., & Petrzelka, P. (2003). Tourism and natural amenity development. In D.L. Brown & L.E. Swanson (Eds.), *Challenges for rural America in the twenty-first century* (pp. 190–199). University Park, PA: Pennsylvania State University Press.

Laird, F.N. (1993). Participatory analysis, democracy, and technological decision making. *Science, Technology, & Human Values*, *18*(3), 341–361.

Morse, S. (2007). *Participatory modeling of recreation and tourism*. Unpublished master's thesis, University of Vermont, Burlington.

Murphy, P.E. (1985). *Tourism: A community approach*. London: Methuen.

Rowe, G., & Frewer, L.J. (2000). Public participation methods: A framework for evaluation. *Science, Technology & Human Values*, *25*(1), 3–29.

Sautter, E., & Leisen, B. (1999). Managing stakeholders: A tourism planning model. *Annals of Tourism Research*, *26*(2), 312–328.

Sinclair, M.T. (1998). Tourism and economic development: A survey. *The Journal of Development Studies*, *34*(5), 1–51.

Smith, L.G., Nell, C.Y., & Prystupta, M.V. (1997). The converging dynamics of interest representation in resources management. *Environmental Management*, *21*(2), 139–146.

van den Belt, M. (2004). *Mediated modeling: A system dynamics approach to environmental consensus building*. Washington: Island Press.

Walker, P.A., Greiner, R., McDonald, D., & Lyne, V. (1999). The tourism futures simulator: A systems thinking approach. *Environmental Modelling & Software*, *14*, 59–67.

Webster, H.H., & Chappelle, D.E. (2001). Tourism and forest products: Twin resource sectors for effective community development in the Lake States. *Journal of the Community Development Society*, *32*(1), 88–105.

Wilson, S., Fesenmaier, D.R., Fesenmeir, J., & van Es, J.C. (2001). Factors for success in rural tourism development. *Journal of Travel Research*, *40*, 132–138.

Golden geese or white elephants? The paradoxes of world heritage sites and community-based tourism development in Agra, India

Surajit Chakravarty[a] and Clara Irazábal[b]

[a]Department of Urban Planning, ALHOSN University, Abu Dhabi, UAE; [b]Graduate School of Architecture, Planning, and Preservation, Columbia University, New York, USA

This study examines the relationship between World Heritage Sites (WHSs) and local community development in Agra, India. We investigate two interrelated themes: the role of planning in developing the tourism potential of the Taj Mahal and other WHSs in Agra, and the impact of the WHS framework on the development of the city. We analyze the weaknesses of the institutions and agencies responsible for Agra's inability to convert the development potential created by its three WHSs into significant economic, community and infrastructure improvements. The Agra case reveals a set of developmental paradoxes, whereby the restructuring of the tourist industry induced by the designation of WHSs does not lead to proportionate advances in local community development. Several factors were found to be systemic problems, but some recent schemes are worth supporting and expanding. The paradoxes and potential of economic, tourism, and community development in Agra echo those of other developing localities which host WHSs around the world. Following an assessment of problems and challenges, a set of recommendations is directed toward the development of pro-poor, community-based heritage tourism with the aim of informing integrated planning for the community and for heritage and tourism resources in the future.

Introduction

This study examines the relationship between World Heritage Sites (WHSs) and local community development where these sites are located, particularly in the context of small cities in the developing world. Our case study is the city of Agra in India, where three WHSs, including the renowned Taj Mahal, are located in close proximity to each other. We investigate two interrelated themes: the role of planning in developing the tourism potential of the Taj Mahal and the other WHSs, and the impact of WHS-related policies in the development of the city of Agra. This inquiry stems from the observation that the city of Agra has not converted the development potential created by the presence of three World Heritage designated sites into significant economic, community and infrastructure improvements. In its *Final Report on 20 Years Perspective Plan of Uttar Pradesh*, the state where Agra is located, the Department of Tourism, Government of India notes that "Agra has very poor civic conditions with dirty roads, lanes and drains" (2002, p. 3). Further, in profiling of the city, the National Institute of Urban Affairs (NIUA) reports that:

> Agra is growing rapidly and lacks the infrastructure to cope with its rapidly increasing population... Agra faces a remarkable number of challenges in water, sewerage, municipal finance and administration. The municipal solid waste system, for example, is unable to cope with some 650 tons of garbage generated daily, more than a third of which lies uncollected in the streets. (NIUA, 2001)

The Agra case study reveals a set of developmental paradoxes whereby a city is unable to convert World Heritage designation into proportionate advances in local community development in a context where it is sorely needed. It is therefore legitimate to ask whether, in the context of developing cities, WHSs are "golden geese" or "white elephants"—i.e. are they catalysts for community development or added burdens on local infrastructure and budgets?

Several institutional and planning variables were found to be systemic problems in the quest for socio-economic development in Agra, including dearth of funds, the overlapping and indistinct agendas of various agencies, a lack of cross-sectoral coordination, conflicting interests and motives of stakeholders, and the lack of a pro-poor, community-based heritage tourism vision. Our recommendations include change in the organizational structure of tourism management, spatial innovation, and increased community involvement.

Effects of World Heritage designation on community-based tourism development

2010 marked the 40th anniversary of the signing of the United Nations Educational Social and Cultural Organization (UNESCO) World Heritage Convention, which launched the concept of "world heritage" and began the process of listing sites deemed to possess "outstanding universal value." WHSs are some of the most recognized locations around the world. They are irreplaceable, usually government-owned, have iconic status related to national identity, and are significant contributors to the tourism industry. In addition, conservation and tourism development in and around significant heritage sites often involves a large number of stakeholders. Issues such as WHS designation, interpretation, marketing, visitor management, and revenue generation are often complex and controversial. The responsibility of managing them appropriately and ensuring that resources are not damaged by visitors, conflicts of interest, or environmental conditions is therefore vital.

Cultural heritage planning and management is a global phenomenon governed by a series of internationally recognized codes and charters (including the Venice Charter, 1994, and the UNESCO World Heritage Convention, 1970). These transnational agreements systematically advocate that responsible parties "maintain the cultural values of cultural heritage assets for the enjoyment of present and future generations" (McKercher & du Cros, 2002, p. 43). The purpose of this is to conserve a representative sample of cultural heritage worldwide, and to interpret its intrinsic value for widening public appreciation. This is done for both tangible (physical evidence of culture, e.g., the built environment) and intangible (continuing cultural practices, knowledge, and living experiences) heritage on varying scales and with varying complexity (Bowen, 2004; McKercher & du Cros, 2002).

But clearly this agenda is not having the intended results or benefits in Agra, where three sites have been designated WHSs: existing conditions there, with respect to infrastructure provision, the quality of the tourist experience, and the financial benefits being drawn from heritage sites, are far behind and woefully disproportionate to the city's—and its sites'—potential. This presents a fundamental developmental paradox, whereby valuable cultural resources such as WHSs can become burdens in two compounded ways: on the one hand, by exerting costs in terms of restoration, maintenance, and policing expenses associated with the preservation and management of the monuments and the impact that tourists have on quality of life, in terms of use of services and infrastructure; and on the other, by exacerbating inequalities among the city's residents, and among city residents and people at other scalar points (state, nation, and globe), depending on the inequitable distribution of opportunities, costs, and benefits of tourism development associated with the WHSs.

Notes on methodology

We are in agreement with Shanks (2009) that in tourism studies, "[t]he industry's elasticity means that quantitative projections are less helpful in understanding what politics is, and for identifying prospective winners and losers, than are qualitative sketches outlining how power relationships are elided in different spheres." Schyvens (2007, p. 132) also suggests that "rather than focusing too much on tourism's 'impacts' we need detailed studies of systems, processes, places and interactions between people, in order to understand how culture and power influence the actions of tourism stakeholders." Thus, our analytical framework includes exploring the motives, powers, and interrelationships of the various stakeholders; a critical examination of plans and policy outputs; interviews with key informants in government, para-statal, and NGO sectors; and on-site reconnaissance, photographic surveys, and informal interviews.

Research material was collected using a variety of methods, including a review of theoretical literature related to heritage tourism planning and management as well as official charts, mandates, proposed and accepted plans, and regulations pertinent to the case study. For additional information we conducted semi-structured interviews with representatives of various relevant agencies, including the Agra Development Authority (the principal planning agency), the Archaeological Survey of India (in charge of managing heritage sites), the Center for Urban and Regional Excellence (an NGO working on community-based projects in Agra), the Indo-USAID Financial Institutions Reform and Expansion Project (agency supporting governance reforms and community-based solutions), and the National Institute for Urban Affairs (a para-statal organization advocating municipal reforms). These interviews were carried out between May 2008 and August 2009. Finally, our own observations regarding land use, urban design, and transportation in the study area, as well as informal interviews of site residents and visitors, complement the other findings.

The management and planning of heritage tourism in Agra

(i) Agra and its world heritage sites

Located on the banks of the river Yamuna, Agra city lies within Agra District (the equivalent unit to "county" or "borough" in the US context), which falls within the

State of Uttar Pradesh (UP). The city is 202 kilometers from India's capital, New Delhi, and 378 kilometers from Lucknow, Uttar Pradesh's capital. The city was founded by Sikandar Lodhi to be the capital of the Lodhi dynasty. Sikandar Lodhi's son Ibrahim was defeated by Babur in 1526, and the Mughal dynasty was established in India. It was Babur's great-great-grandson Shah Jahan who built the Taj Mahal between 1632 and 1653.

The city is famous as the site of one of the most sought-after tourist experiences in the world – the Taj Mahal, but also includes two other important sites: Agra Fort and Fatehpur Sikri. The Fort was constructed under the Emperor Akbar (grandson of Babur) in 1565. "This bastionned fortress, with walls of red sandstone rising above a mat, encompasses within its enclosure walls of 2.5 kilometers, the imperial city of the Mogul rulers" (UNESCO, 1983). Both the Taj Mahal and the Agra Fort were inscribed as UNESCO World Heritage sites in 1983. There is yet another WHS in the Agra District, Fatehpur Sikri, only 40 kilometers from Agra City. Fatehpur Sikri was built as a large palace and city by Akbar in 1571, and was used as the capital until it was abandoned in favor of Agra Fort in 1585. It was instated as a UNESCO World Heritage site in 1986.

The iconic position and marketing of the Taj Mahal as India's "brand ambassador" (Khosla, 2009, recorded interview) and "the ultimate symbol of love" cannot be overstated. The Taj is the centerpiece of the "Incredible India" campaign launched recently by the Ministry of Tourism, where it is described as "the most photographed monument in the world." A 2001 study by the Agra Development Authority reported that the monument attracted 2.25 million visitors annually, of whom about 11% were foreigners. According to the Ministry of Tourism, by 2005 that number rose to 2.48 million, 24% of whom were foreigners.

The Taj Mahal is globally recognized and appreciated as a symbol of India. Most foreign dignitaries visit the monument, with the press sending pictures around the world. In the early 1980s, reports of damage to the white marble surface of the monument from air pollution drew concern from diverse groups (including research organizations, private corporations, and the UN), showing both a sense of respect and of ownership of the monument beyond national boundaries. This resulted in prompt action from the responsible agencies to institute pollution control measures in the vicinity of the structure and appropriate restoration funds to polish the marble surfaces. Since it is so much in the public eye and part of the branding of the country itself, a well-managed Taj would presents an image of efficient governance. On the other hand, mismanagement suggests weak institutions and a lack of accountability.

The Taj's potential for attracting tourists has not, however, been translated into significant tourist spending that benefits community development. One reason is the lack of integration with other tourist sites in the city. Although Agra was an important center in India's first (ultimately unsuccessful) struggle against British rule in 1857, the city's history is inadequately highlighted in the tourist experience. There is also a lack of promotion of its other two World Heritage sites. Information regarding these sites appears in most tourist guidebooks, but the Taj so overshadows everything else in Agra that few people even know the name of the city before they begin to make their travel plans. This translates to the Taj being perceived as the only important site to be seen there, even though Agra is also home to Itmad'ud Daulah, Akbar's tomb, Ram Bagh, Jama Masjid, Chini ka rauza, Mariam's tomb, and Guru ka tal, among other sites. Although these places are not all designated as World Heritage Sites, they have great historic and cultural significance in India.

Another problem is that although the Taj Mahal draws tourists from around the world, it only holds them for a couple of hours. Once it has been admired from all angles, and digital cameras have been filled up, tourists move on. Some will visit the other two World Heritage sites. For most, Agra will still remain a city that can be "covered" in one day. It is common for tourists not to stay overnight in Agra, preferring instead to make a day trip from Delhi, or to stay just one night in order to have a "thorough" experience.

Edensor's (1998) authoritative work on the tourist experience of the Taj Mahal is a rich source of information about the local tourist industry gathered from stakeholder groups on both the demand and supply sides. Edensor reports voices of business owners, tour guides, and the local unemployed, among many others. Studying these narratives uncovers the monument's many meanings. Some of the main themes to emerge are the significance of the Taj in popular consciousness; foreign tourists' disappointment with the quality of the experience beyond the structure itself; and the sheer complexity of the management of the site, considering the diversity of government agencies, political motives, and social needs. Edensor's critique is supported by our fieldwork; however, he offers little in terms of ideas about what to do about it. We get commentary on various issues (e.g., the theming of tourism), but not a critical examination of the issues themselves.

(ii)   Agencies with planning and management roles

In order for a site to be designated as a WHS, proponents—usually a combination of environmental or cultural preservationist groups and local and national govern-ments—need to comply with a series of requirements that document the site and its importance, and also offer specific proposals and commitments to plan and manage it. This process of "getting an act together" for the purpose of achieving a favorable evaluation on the part of the UNESCO Committee can result in a positive boost for planning, management, and development of the site and its surroundings. For instance, a condition of designation as a World Cultural Heritage Site is the adoption of a zoning plan and legal framework for protection and management. Such a zoning plan focuses on promoting sustainable development of heritage resources in harmony with the natural and social fabric of the site. It attempts to achieve a balance between protection of heritage sites, planned development of tourism, and urban or rural development. The pertinent government is expected to establish agencies to manage the site and regulate development (Wager, 1995).

Harrison and Hitchcock's (2005) study of WHS management from around the world points out an underlying tension between global strategies for attaching meaning to heritage and managing it, and local particularities represented by the needs and expectations of communities at given places and times. According to Gregory Ashworth, there are "inherent logical contradictions, intrinsic inconsis-tencies, unsatisfactory procedural compromises, and unresolved policy dilemmas that surround the idea and practice of world heritage" (Ashworth, 2006, p. 274; Drost, 1996; Harrison & Hitchcock, 2005). This may be because in many localities there is a "gap between ideal conservation management and the reality of urban development trends and tourism activities" (Shetawy, 2009, p. 1).

Although both tourism and world heritage designation have been studied at length, there is relatively less research on WHSs in the context of cities in developing countries. Nuryanyti (1996) describes how cities in developing countries often have to deal with the challenge of having a WHS "in the middle of living communities" (p. 256), often with large and dense populations, more pressure on infrastructure, and the tendency for development of any kind to be treated as a sectarian political project. They face the added challenges of limited funding resources and inadequate institutional capabilities (p. 257). Under these conditions, substantive and sustainable community development often takes a back seat to personal agendas, and participation becomes knee-jerk rather than constructive and proactive. Thus, achieving sustainable and equitable community-based tourism development (CBTD) in developing countries faces serious challenges related to tourism management and power dynamics (Ryan, 2002). These challenges and some basic actions to tackle them were clearly stated by Brohman (1996, p. 48):

> The Third World [sic] tourism industry has grown rapidly, but has also encountered many problems ... including: excessive foreign dependency, the creation of separate enclaves, the reinforcement of socioeconomic and spatial inequalities, environmental destruction, and rising cultural alienation. To avoid such problems, institutional mechanisms need to be created to encourage active state and community participation in tourism planning.

Thus it is important to examine the functioning of local agencies responsible for WHS management in Agra. Planning and development of the WHSs and tourism there fall under the jurisdiction of various government agencies at various scales. In this section we analyze the relationships and plans of these various agencies and highlight some of their weaknesses. We also discuss the role of another agency, the Taj Expressway Authority.

Archaeological Survey of India (ASI)

The Archaeological Survey of India works under the Ministry of Culture in India's central government. ASI's mandate includes archaeological research, preservation of protected monuments and areas of national importance, maintenance of site museums, and overall regulation of legislations related to antiquities and art treasures (ASI, 2008). ASI handles the management of historic structures and the immediate enclosures around them: the upkeep and maintenance of all aspects of the area inside the entry gates, including cleanliness, protection from environmental damage, and architectural restoration. Recent restoration work at the Taj Mahal has included filling-in missing inlay work, mudpack treatment for restoring marble luster, structural work, and the renovation of broken pedestrian paths. As a representative of ASI told us in an interview, the agency has no direct collaboration with other agencies involved beyond giving comments to ensure conformance with aesthetic guidelines.

ASI is also the agency that proposes sites to the United Nations for qualification as WHSs. It is responsible for liaising with the UN and ensuring that the proposed sites meet the parameters and guidelines associated with World Heritage designation. Assigning these tasks to ASI shows that the national government wants to keep this process within its own purview. The central government does not, however, attach a similar level of importance to the management of the urban contexts within which the structures are located. This shows that while the cultural significance of the WHSs is understood, their potential as income-generators and community development instruments has not been given proper attention at the national level.

Other national actors

In the case of the Taj Mahal, the Indian Administrative Service (IAS) has formed the Taj Monitoring Committee, which is a working group that brings together officers from the various districts around Agra. The Supreme Court also has its own focus group working solely on the Taj Mahal, scrutinizing every proposed development that may affect it. These agencies work primarily to preserve the Taj from the prospect of damage due to hasty or unplanned development.

Uttar Pradesh Tourism

At almost 200 million inhabitants, Uttar Pradesh (UP) is the most populous state of India; it is also home to many sites of religious and architectural significance. Tourism in India is fairly decentralized; state governments have the mandate to develop tourism programs and infrastructure in their jurisdictions. UP Tourism's planning is largely non-spatial. The department makes programs, issues licenses (to hotels, tour operators, guides, etc.), and does publicity work. The department also does some construction work, limited to properties operated by it, such as guest houses, parks, etc. UP Tourism has no influence on the planning and development of Agra city. Indeed, spatial planning and community development in Agra is not viewed as intrinsically related to the planning and development of tourism.

Agra Nagar Nigam (Agra Municipal Corporation)

The Municipal Corporation is responsible for various functions at the city level. These are mostly related to urban infrastructure and services (street lighting, road maintenance and cleaning, water supply, waste collection, etc.). The Municipal Corporation has no construction or urban planning role, and its involvement in planning for tourism is minimal. Even so, road cleaning and maintenance, a responsibility of the Municipal Corporation, is one of the main problems around the WHSs. Roads leading up to the monuments are in poor repair and have minimal traffic management. In Agra, where image and marketability are paramount and resources are few, an innovative approach to managing access to heritage monuments is necessary.

Agra Development Authority (ADA)

The Authority was established in 1975 to handle housing and carry out the planned development of the city. Its scope of work includes the preparation of the Agra Master Plan, approving building and site plans, controlling and regulating development according to land use plans, road construction, drainage, and construction and maintenance of parks and recreation facilities. This profile of activities makes ADA the primary agency responsible for the physical development of the city, including the area around the heritage sites.

The ADA Master Plan for 2021, approved in 2001, lists 45 sites in and around Agra protected by ASI. As indicated, three of these are WHSs. The plan has a special section on tourism, which proposes a Taj Heritage Zone. Provisions include the relocation of industrial units from inside to outside the zone; a ban on construction within 500 meters of the Taj grounds and 100 meters of other monuments; and a height limit of 3.75 meters (that is, one floor only) within 100–300 meters of protected monuments. A Mughal-style façade is required on all proposed buildings in the zone. The plan also includes land reclamation from the Yamuna River behind the Taj Mahal for creating a park and a dam downstream from the Taj to allow high water levels to be maintained year round near the monument, thereby encouraging boating and views from the water. Sewage disposal in the river will be diverted to a downstream location to keep the river water clean in the tourist area. Finally, pedestrian paths and street improvements will create better access to the monuments. The new zone has in fact been created, and some improvements are underway.

The Master Plan is generally well thought-out and helpful (except for the river reclamation and sewage disposal plans, which need a more thorough environmental approach). However, it reflects the constraints of resources, political will, and popular opinion. In addition, to some extent it displays the classic flaws of rationalist planning—lack of public involvement and a top-down approach with very little flexibility. And it has a limited physical-planning approach and spatial scale (relative to the actual area it is likely to influence). Tourism planning is limited to a small area around the Taj Mahal, most of which comprises parks, river, and the existing old city. There is no proposal, for example, to spatially integrate multiple major landmarks and monuments, or to institute year-round programming, or to incorporate parts of the old city. The limitations of the plan are partially the result of a technocratic and bureaucratic planning system that has made every agency responsible for isolated functions with no incentives to cooperate or innovate.

Taj Expressway Authority (TEA)

This large-scale project was abandoned due to sectarian politicking. The Taj Expressway Plan, which proposed the connection of Agra and Delhi by a new expressway, would have cut the driving time from 5 to 3 hours. TEA, which was created to plan development along the corridor (an 8-lane highway), proposed Special Development Zones (SDZs) along the expressway corridor to be developed using private capital. Core activities proposed for SDZs included information technology, bio-tech and other industries, recreation, and entertainment retail, although 15% of the land was reserved for residential use. The thinking behind the plan was that tourists who were staying in Agra for a very short time, could be enticed to stay longer if the area had entertainment-retail complexes—under the apparent presumption that the areas three WHSs were not enough.

Summary: lack of efficient institutional structure and clear mandate

Planning for a city in Agra's position must involve job creation and training, private sector incentives for development, and transportation and urban design improvements as its core elements. However, as the breakdown of responsibilities above demonstrates, the presence of too many agencies and stakeholders with overlapping goals and approaches makes such an integrated effort challenging.

In India, city development is the responsibilities of local authorities. This policy works fine in large cities such as Delhi and Mumbai, which have greater technical capacity and financial resources. But in a relatively less-endowed context like Agra's, local authorities usually have deficient technical, financial, and/or managerial capacity. Municipal authorities and development corporations, the two local bodies responsible for urban infrastructure and development, can barely maintain day-to-day operations within their limited budgets.

At present, there is no single authority or coalition that is responsible for creating and executing a comprehensive vision for realizing the full potential of the Taj Mahal and the other WHSs. Tensions between global institutions, national image-making projects, and local planning needs are embedded in planning processes, and each set of agents operates with independent agendas and little regard for the others. Mr. Chetan Vaidya (2008), Director of the National Institute of Urban Affairs (NIUA), explained the situation in an interview: "the national government does economic planning with little regard for the spatial aspects, and at the local level spatial planning ignores economic aspects."

In addition, political success or failure at the city level has only a small, usually insignificant effect of the outcome of national elections. The state government, on the other hand, could make political gains by pursuing local community development, but lacks the vision for change. The municipality has no organizational, technical, or financial capacity to make big plans. The present arrangement of agencies and their lack of cross-sectoral coordination are, in part, responsible for the community development potential of the WHSs not being fully realized.

Aside from the multitude of Indian agencies already discussed, UNESCO is also a powerful stakeholder, as the maintenance of World Heritage designation is contingent upon its approval of plans in and around the sites. But like local and state agencies, UNESCO World Heritage Committee historically has restricted its purview to its direct mandate: preservation of the monuments and the environmental issues that may threaten them, with scant, if any, attention granted to community development issues. Likewise, the ASI, a powerful lobby, is interested in no more than its jurisdiction—which is the monuments and the parks and facilities inside their walled compounds. Meanwhile, the array of stakeholders involved has limited direct engagement in development plans.

Assessment of tourism development in Agra

Lack of holistic planning

There is a need to plan a more comprehensive heritage tourist experience tapping into the multifaceted assets of Agra. Cultural heritage tourism worldwide has gone from a small niche market to be "firmly established as a mainstream, mass tourism activity" (McKercher & du Cros, 2002, p. 135), and so should be leveraged for maximum benefit. Cultural heritage planning and management ought to incorporate tourism into plans both for providing for tourists and the locals, and for protecting heritage assets (McKercher & du Cros, 2002). Yet, as Bowen (2004, p. 409) suggests,

> While tourism professionals assess cultural assets for their profit potential, cultural heritage professionals judge the same assets for their intrinsic value. Sustainable cultural tourism can only occur when the two sides form a true partnership based on understanding and appreciation of each other's merits.

Relationships between heritage tourism and local people involve more than jobs and wages. They include questions of land ownership and property rights, competition between the old and the new, changing lifestyles, questions such as what to preserve for whom/what purpose, and the interaction between tourists and host communities whose different socio-cultural structures and expectations can lead to misunder-standings and conflicts (Nuryanti, 1996).

In this framework, community development opportunities abound: locals can be trained and employed for the creation, maintenance, and improvement of the tourist infrastructure and services; ADA could design and execute a plan to create an integrated multi-destination circuit along major well-maintained thoroughfares; tourists should be encouraged to get the full experience of the destination by touring all its small sites; options for consumption, entertainment, and even worship could be offered; and the promotion of some sections of the neighborhoods around the Taj as living cultural quarters could be considered. A religious/spiritual center/museum could be created to complement and interpret the state's tourism offerings, which include many spiritual destinations. The objective of these interventions would be to tie together the region's major heritage tourism attractions with its everyday cultural offerings.

Lack of basic infrastructure and funds

Due mostly to a chronic lack of funds, Agra's poor level of physical infrastructure makes it hard to sell as a destination city. The streets are congested and broken, the traffic is chaotic, traffic lights do not work, public transport is only basic, and hotels and other tourist infrastructure and services are minimal. Social infrastructure to improve health, education, and tourism-oriented job training are also lacking. It falls to the government at the city and state levels to rectify these problems through investments, incentives, and regulations.

Stunted private involvement

Heritage tourist development as a planning strategy requires the organization of land use so as to strategically take advantage of the proximity of monuments. This land is best suited for parks, promenades, museums, pedestrian-only shopping multi-purpose streets, etc. Some of these uses require private sector investment. The government, however, must zone for and encourage such development through tax breaks, subsidies, public-private partnerships, and small entrepreneurial opportu-nities such as microfinance and industry incubators.

Currently, there is surprisingly little innovation in Agra. To some extent the responsibility lies with the government's lack of planning for private sector opportunities. For example, when the Taj Expressway Plan finally attempted to attract investment, its plan did not fit the profile of strengths and weaknesses of Agra. Authorities should have realized that visitors could not be enticed to stay in Agra in order to do something they could easily do in Delhi, such as shopping at malls. The Expressway was, however, an attempt to try something new at a regional scale, an idea that should be revisited.

The way forward: rethinking governance, community and space

Ashley and Roe (2001, p. viii) have proposed pro-poor tourism (PPT) strategies, which "aim to increase the net benefits for the poor from tourism, and ensure that tourism growth contributes to poverty reduction. PPT strategies aim to unlock opportunities for the poor—whether for economic gain, other livelihood benefits, or participation in decision-making" (see also Harrison & Schipani, 2007; Kakwani & Pernia, 2000).

Responsibility for cultural heritage management has gradually been transferred from the non-profit public sector to the for-profit, private sector. Although this has created new challenges, it has also opened new models of cultural heritage management and the tourism industry, a continuum "from full partnership cooperation, through parallel existence and blissful ignorance, to full and open conflict." The result of each side continuing to ignore, misunderstand, or fight the other is "the suboptimal delivery of cultural tourism products and then continued unsustainable development of this sector" (Bowen, 2004; McKercher & du Cros, 2002, p. 23). In addition to striking a fruitful balance between public, for profit and also the NGO sectors, planning for a cultural heritage asset to be used as a tourist product, including assessing its "robusticity/ability to cope with visitors" (McKercher & du Cros, 2002, p. 172), must include consideration of the legislative/political context, neighboring assets and regional tourism activity, the socio-historical setting, cultural and economic needs of the host community, physical setting, and accessibility.

The recommendations in this study specifically address the problems of capacity and organizational setup, with a particular view towards equity and encouragement of diversity in both the processes and outcomes of planning. Through these proposals we hope to show one way to instill elements of "formality" within the planning and governance process, which we understand to be includes accountability, inclusive planning, and advocacy for, and production of, pro-poor, community-based heritage tourism development.

In order to coordinate functions performed by various agencies at various scales—conserving WHS monuments, the development of tourism in the (nested) jurisdictions within which these monuments are located, and planning for the land and community of Agra—a reorientation is necessary. Instead of planning for structures or sites of heritage value, agencies should plan for socio-spatial units (that is, *communities within places*) where heritage is a major resource. We propose a method of merging these three functions into a single planning and management system focusing on governance, spatial innovation, and community involvement. This can have the additional benefits of engaging investors (from major to minor) and community stakeholders in the planning process, and ensuring that long-term funding is accurately estimated and guaranteed.

I. Governance: reorganization of tourism development

73rd and 74th Constitutional Amendment Acts

The 73rd and 74th Constitutional Amendments Acts of 1992 gave urban and rural local governments in India the opportunity to address their financial situation with new powers of taxation. Where used effectively, these powers have allowed local governments to build financial capacity through municipal tools like infrastructure bonds and also to tap into private capital through partnerships. We suggest that, as a first step, Agra Municipal Corporation taps into the opportunities afforded by these Constitutional Amendments to reorganize its financial systems in keeping with international municipal standards, which increasingly are becoming the norm in India. This is particularly important given the national and global significance of

Agra, and will benefit the local government's institutional capacity for raising funds and executing public works projects.

Jawaharlal Nehru Urban Renewal Mission (JNNURM)

The JNNURM program was created for the purpose of funding infrastructure projects and encouraging management reform in urban areas in anticipation of their contributing 65% of the GDP by 2011 (Ministry of Urban Development and Ministry of Urban Employment and Poverty Alleviation, 2006, p. 3). More than US $20 billion will be disbursed by 2012—$10 billion from the central government and matching grants from state-level or local level authorities (Infrastructure Leasing and Financial Services, 2006a). Agra is one of the cities identified, but JNNURM resources have not been pursued actively by the local authorities.

In 2006, Agra Nagar Nigam (Agra Municipal Corporation, 2006) created a "City Development Plan" with the help of Dutch consultants Allianz Securities Limited, seeking funds for various infrastructure works. Some of these included preservation of heritage buildings and improving streets. According to a newspaper report from March 2008, 16 projects (for water supply, solid waste management and sewage disposal) had been approved in the state of Uttar Pradesh at the time, but work had not begun on any one of them (Indian Express, 2008). According to Mr. Chetan Vaidya, Director of the National Institute of Urban Affairs (NIUA) and a consultant in the establishment of the JNNURM program, it is the lack of implementation of 23 mandatory reforms prescribed under the JNNURM program as well as the 74th and 75th Amendments that are keeping Agra behind other comparable World Heritage-holding sites in India (Khosla, 2009).

Establishment of a central government authority

We suggest the creation of an overarching governing authority directly under the Central government's Ministry of Tourism. This agency would be responsible for planning and developing the zones described below, along with assuring funding and execution of projects in coordination with community and private sector stakeholders.

In India, there is precedent for such an institutional arrangement. The Delhi Metro Rail Corporation (DMRC), which has successfully implemented an extensive mass transit system in the capital, was established as a Special Purpose Vehicle (SPV). This arrangement was so successful that it is now being replicated in Chennai, Mumbai, and elsewhere. DMRC is also consulting on Jakarta's mass transit project, while students from MBA programs as far away as the USA are making it a case study for efficient management. The core idea of the SPV is that it is an entity formed exclusively for the implementation of a single large-scale infrastructure project. In the case of DMRC, the SPV was formed by the central government and the Delhi state government. Funding sources were clearly earmarked at the beginning of the project, and thus risk was minimized. With an SPV, the new company can deal financially and receive its own credit rating independent of the ups and downs of the "parent" companies. The SPV was also given special powers of planning and execution that overrode the jurisdiction of the Delhi Development Authority and the Municipal Corporations of both Delhi and New Delhi. We propose that tourism in Agra and cities with similar conditions be developed under a similar direct intervention by the central and state governments.

II. *Spatial innovation: community-based tourism promotion zoning*

Global resources, such as WHSs, sitting in the middle of an unreasonably undeveloped urban context, project an image of inefficiency and institutional failure. The character and community in the quarters around Taj Mahal are part of the experience of the structure. Cultural programming, including seasonal concerts and festivals, could enhance the experience of Agra for tourists. Hence, we propose a network of permanent and impermanent destinations and programming around the theme of the city's cultural heritage surroundings its monuments.

These would be part of a system of Community-Based Tourism-Promotion Zones (CBTPZ, or CTZ for short, at the neighborhood scale) with the WHSs as their focus. The proposed Central Authority, acting directly under the national government, would implement selective capital investments, land use, zoning, building and design regulations, and economic incentives to execute the vision. The proposed zones would allow special land uses, such as mixed-use areas and redevelopment where appropriate. At the outset this idea appears to be akin to that of a Special Economic Zone (SEZ). It is important to note, however, that unlike these, the proposed Community-Based Tourism Promotion Zones are intended for intense community-based commercial use (with emphasis on pro-poor interventions, including light industry). Our proposal draws on and improves on the Taj Expressway idea of creating mixed-use development to in order to draw tourists to Agra and keep them there longer, while at the same time expanding job opportunities for locals. There is precedent for this idea in India: with funding from the JNNURM project, Jaipur's Municipal Corporation is developing a project at Jal Mahal combining conservation of the monument with sustainable tourism and recreational opportunities, including rooftop cafés, boating, tourist cottages and clubs, heritage resorts, villages, a craft market, a floating restaurant, and light and sound shows (Infrastructure Leasing and Financial Services, 2006b).

The first of these CTZ could be sited in the dense part of the city immediately surrounding the Taj, which is already mixed-use, and where people have been living for over 200 years. Visits to this area, known as Taj Ganj, could be integrated with the experience of the Taj Mahal, and visitors could learn about the everyday life of residents alongside their WHS experience. Some of the structures in these areas are interesting historical attractions; a few houses in this district have already been turned into hotels and budget hostels. Other tourist-oriented uses (e.g., restaurants, mini-museums, and craft workshops) could follow. The government could provide incentives for infrastructural and façade improvements, secure tenure, and enhanced training opportunities. A large number of signs in many foreign languages already abound on shop fronts there—Hebrew and Korean are particularly popular. A targeted tourist marketing campaign, including language training for local tourism workers, could further expand such incipient tourist markets. Agra could then go on to invest in other old streets and neighborhoods, such as Sadar Bazar, Raja Mandi, and Fuhara, in order to offer tourists the chance to enjoy not only the WHSs, but also their context—the city and community that is their home.

Greater focus on tourist products is also advisable. Multiple case studies have revealed that "specific soft elements of the urban tourism product are the ones that matter most in determining the attractiveness of a city for international visitors, and yet they are often overlooked by city planners" (Russoa & van der Borg, 2002, p. 631). These include quality, accessibility, and image projection—overall, a sense of "visitor-friendliness," which serves "to assess whether investments in culture and hospitality genuinely respond to the impulses coming from the market" (ibid., p. 631). Cultural heritage assets can be bundled around a theme, creating heritage precincts and tours, organizing festivals, or building heritage centers (Bowen, 2004; McKercher & du Cros, 2002). All of those arrangements address a need to provide an explanation, a message or story about a heritage asset, through an experience in which tourists feel engaged, and which matches goals of sustainability and equity.

The idea of a spiritual/religious center and museum/park could create a worthy addition to Agra's attractions. The center could be where the relationships among the monuments could be explained and where tourists' appetite for further heritage interpretation could be whetted. Faith and spirituality are also one of the important motivations for tourist visits in India and Uttar Pradesh. An inter-faith religious center could become a centerpiece for showcasing the state's and country's traditions of faith and spirituality, telling a comprehensive story of the evolution of religions in India, with emphasis on the UP region. Such an establishment could offer a spiritual, pluralistic experience not partial to any single faith. It could be complemented by the inclusion of visitor accommodations in the vicinity (including guest rooms in residences within the community), if multi-day seminars, workshops, and retreats are offered.

III. Community involvement

Already, a large number of people derive their income and subsistence directly or indirectly from industries related to the WHSs in Agra. This includes traditional industries such as leather, marble inlaying, carpets, and jewelry, which are heavily dependent on tourists for their sales. Further, a common occupation for Agra's youth is guiding tours. The government issues licenses for guides (but these are easily manufactured illegally too). Other businesses, such as motels, transportation, restaurants and similar services also depend on the tourist economy. The businesses and residents of Taj Ganj should be part of the planning process from the start. In addition, there are also other (relatively smaller and low-income) communities ripe for holistic integration in the tourism industry. Civil society groups have been working with these communities—for example, the Tourism Guild of Agra, a conglomeration of major players in the tourism industry who have organized themselves as an interest group, and the Center for Urban and Regional Excellence (CURE), an NGO involved with creating opportunities for the poor in the tourism sector.

One of the best examples of local initiatives to benefit the community is the Crosscutting Agra Project (CAP), initiated by the Center for Urban and Regional Excellence (CURE) in 2005, and assisted by the private sector (particularly the Tourism Guild of Agra) and USAID's Indo-US Financial Institutions Reform and Expansion Project (Indo-US FIRE-D project). This urban innovation is aimed at "leveraging Agra's lesser-known heritage sites for improving sanitation and livelihood in low-income communities" (Indo-US FIRE-D Project, 2007, p.1). The project area was close to the Taj Mahal, other heritage sites, and the low-income community of Kucchpura. A one-kilometer loop identified as a "Heritage Walk," linked several low-income communities (about 2,000 households) with "lesser-known monuments" and architectural features. Micro-enterprises were set up for women, and some young men from the communities were trained to help tourists on the Heritage Walk. The communities were also mobilized to undertake waste disposal schemes, and community and individual toilets were constructed. Ms. Renu Khosla, the Director of CURE, underlined the need to plan for and utilize all heritage sites in Agra, and not only the WHSs (Khosla, 2009).

We support the CAP idea and recommend that the Authority under the Central government work on these kinds of community-based partnerships, with specific attention to Promotion Zones. Through this framework we expect that the lesser-known monuments and intangible assets of Agra, such as its folk tales and traditions and the history associated with the city, as well as expressions of contemporary local culture in clothing, cuisine, craftsmanship, dance, and everyday life in the bazaars and on the banks of the river Yamuna, can be brought into tourists' experience of Agra and leveraged for the benefit of the local community members, with particular attention to the poorest among them.

IV. Revisiting UNESCO's role

We offer three suggestions regarding UNESCO's potential impact on cities that are host to World Heritage Sites. In the context of developing countries with limited resources, what responsibility could be taken by UNESCO in ensuring that WHS monuments benefit the communities in which they are located? In relatively small cities, especially those of such paramount importance as Agra, UNESCO could contribute more than the WHS designation. Firstly, the procedures for World Heritage designation and the monitoring of WHSs could be more forceful in demanding and evaluating explicit plans, benchmarks, time-frames, and financial commitments for the promotion of pro-poor, community-based heritage tourism development around WHSs.

The second contribution that UNESCO could make is assisting in raising funds from other sources and channeling financial resources towards the development of WHS-hosting *cities*. This is not simply a demand for more funds, but rather for recognition of the need to support host cities, not just the heritage properties. In the case of Agra, a UNESCO report shows two UN contributions: $17,865 to address pollution issues and $20,788 to be shared between the site of Konarak temples and Taj Mahal for "technical cooperation" (UNESCO, 2002). Additionally, according to a UNESCO report, a French private enterprise committed $236,735 for a three-year research project on conservation of the Taj. Another UNESCO report shows "extra-budgetary funds mobilized by the UNESCO Division of Cultural Heritage from 1998–2003 total[ing] $158,200 for research and conservation training." The benefactor in this case is named as Foundation Rhône-Poulenc. We suggest that UNESCO, in collaboration and coordination with UNDP and UN-Habitat, also assist in developing plans to assist in for tourism-related projects and in managing the urban context of the WHSs. Agra needs these plans and funds to break the cycle of inadequate infrastructure development leading to poor performance in the tourism sector, which in turn would serve UNESCO's stated goals.

Thirdly, UNESCO could provide institutional support in terms of capacity-building. We suggest a deeper commitment in organizing (or encouraging and demanding) training workshops for local professionals, getting urban planning and business schools involved in the process. In general UNESCO should enlarge its focus from designation of World Heritage Sites to helping heritage communities develop thoroughly sustainable preservation and development practices—which again would serve its stated goals.

Discussion

There is no doubt that Agra's three WHSs distinguish it as a city of world significance. However, existing conditions with respect to infrastructure provision, the quality of the tourist experience, and community benefits being drawn from heritage sites are woefully disproportionate to their potential. The Agra case reveals a developmental paradox, whereby advances new opportunities in the tourist industry created by World Heritage designation do not lead to proportionate advances in local community development, and can actually exacerbate local developmental challenges and socio-spatial inequalities.

Problems in the tourism sector reflect deep institutional weaknesses that affect other aspects of development too. "Heritage tourism raises more than planning and management issues for developing countries; they are fundamentally the problems of development" (Nuryanti, 1996, p. 249). In the context of this study, Ananya Roy's (2009) criticisms of planning in India are particularly relevant. According to Roy, the problems of urban governance in India originate from the "idiom" of informality. Roy argues that this informality is embedded within planning practices and institutionalized through the writing (open-ended and susceptible to misuse) and selective implementation of plans, which creates an "axis of inequality" in Indian cities. Further, Roy criticizes the State itself as an "informalized entity" (p. 81). Roy's analysis of the lack of order in the planning process is pertinent to this discussion. What we see in Agra is a similar phenomenon, where many "arbitrary and fickle practices" can be held responsible for failures of planning. We have discussed many of these in foregoing sections of this paper.

What Roy critiques as "informality" is in our opinion a restatement of the problems of unequal power relations in processes of planning and development. As such, these problems are present in all planning cultures to some extent. What we have found in Agra in terms of the looseness of institutional roles and successive uncoordinated planning exercises may be understood in terms of informality; yet Roy's critique leaves little room for planners and communities to move forward. We believe that "informality" of this kind can be addressed within the planning process. Partially overcoming the shortcomings that this informality produces is possible by changing governance and planning practices (Irazábal, 2005).

The problem (certainly in the case of Agra, and in urban India in general) lies in political manipulation (leading to flawed visioning), lack of capacity of local agencies, and an unclear mandate fragmented among numerous agencies. Drawing on successful ideas (e.g., SPVs for infrastructure development, community-based projects etc.) we have tried to show that, given the presence of political will and community support, informality in governance restructuring can give way to focused action.

Following Irazábal (2009), the emancipatory promise of planning—in Agra or elsewhere—can be realized to the extent that opportunities for the creation and nurturing of network power, liberating knowledge, empowering subjectivities, and spaces of solidarity are expanded. In Agra, the promotion of pro-poor, community-based heritage tourism development would be critically instrumental in redressing the current developmental paradox. The specific recommendations offered here can assist in setting a basic platform for the unleashing of the impressive community-development potential and emancipatory promise of planning laying dormant around Agra's WHSs and other assets.

We have not included in the scope of this paper strategies to combat corruption, party politics (including strained center-state relations when different political parties are in power), or resistance by the central government towards decentralization and devolution. It is critical, however, that these issues are addressed through fair political accountability, power-devolution, and profit-sharing arrangements. Our proposal, nonetheless, does provide the outline for a change in governance structure in conjunction with spatial planning and community participation, so that heritage sites and the city where they are located may benefit each other.

The paradoxes and potential of economic, tourism, and community development in Agra echo in other developing localities with World Heritage sites around the world (Irazábal, 2009b; Irazábal & Morán, 2008). Rooted in an assessment of the problems and challenges of each locality, the lessons of pro-poor, community-based heritage tourism development can offer the hope of turning white elephants into golden geese.

References

Agra Municipal Corporation. (2006). *Agra City Development Plan*. Agra: AMC

Ashley, C., & Roe, D. (2001). Making tourism work for the poor: Strategies and challenges in Southern Africa. *Development Southern Africa, 19*, 61–82.

Ashworth, G. (2006). Book Review (The Politics of World Heritage: Negotiating Tourism and Conservation, Edited by David Harrison and Michael Hitchcock. Channel View Publications, 2005). *Annals of Tourism Research, Vol. 33*, No. 1, pp. 273–275, 2006.

ASI. (2011). *Activities*. Retrieved March 20, 2008, from http://asi.nic.in/asi_aboutus_activities.asp

Bowen, Heather. Book Review (Cultural tourism: the partnership between tourism and cultural heritage management. Bob McKercher and Hilary du Cross; The Haworth Hospitality Press, Binghamton, New York, 2002) *Tourism Management 25* (2004) 409–416.

Brohman, J. (1996). New directions in tourism for third world development. *Annals of Tourism Research, 23*(1), 48–70.

Department of Tourism, Government of India. (2002). *Final report on 20 years perspective plans for Uttar Pradesh, November, 2002*. Prepared by A.F. Ferguson and Co. Delhi. Retrieved March 20, 2008, from http://tourism.gov.in/pplan/up.pdf

Drost, A. (1996). Research notes: Developing sustainable tourism for world heritage sites. *Annals of Tourism Research, 23*(2), 479–492.

Edensor, T. (1998). *Tourists at the Taj: Performance and meaning at a symbolic site*. Routledge: London.

Hall, C.M. (Ed.) (2007). *Pro-poor tourism – who benefits? Perspectives on tourism and poverty reduction*. Current Themes in Tourism. Clevedon: Channel View Publications.

Harrison, D., & Hitchcock, M. (2005). (Eds.) *Politics of world heritage: Negotiating tourism and conservation*. Channel View Publications: Clevedon.

Harrison, D., & Schipani, S. (2007). Lao tourism and poverty alleviation: Commounity-based tourism and the private sector. In C.M. Hall (Ed.), *Pro-poor tourism – who benefits? Perspectives on tourism and poverty reduction*, Current Themes in Tourism (84–117). Clevedon: Channel View Publications.

Indian Express. (2008). *Lack of coordination continues to haunt JNNURM in the state*. Retrieved March 20, 2008, from http://www.expressindia.com/latest-news/lack-of-coordination-continues-to-haunt-jnnurm-in-the-state/285067/

Indo-US Financial Institutions Reform and Expansion Project (2007). *Project Note no. 37: Leveraging Agra's Lesser-known Heritage Sites for Improving Sanitation and Livelihood in Low-income Communities Crosscutting Agra Project (CAP), Uttar Pradesh, India*. New Delhi: Indo-US FIRE(D).

Infrastructure Leasing and Financial Services (2006a). IL&FS IDC Services offered for JNNURM and UIDSSMT Schemes. Accessed on November 14, 2009 from http://www.ilfsindia.com/downloads/bus_concept/JNNURM.pdf

Infrastructure Leasing and Financial Services (2006b). Projects: Jal Mahal, Jaipur. Accessed on November 14, 2009 from http://www.ilfsindia.com/projects1.asp?Category=1&Project=8&subLink=16

Irazábal, C. (2005). *City making and urban governance in the Americas: Curitiba and Portland*. Aldershot: Ashgate.

Irazábal, C. (2009a). Realizing planning's emancipatory promise: Learning from regime theory to strengthen communicative action. *Planning Theory, 8*(2), 115–139.

Irazábal, C. (2009b). (Un)Planning Costa Rican coastal development: Tourism and the Nature-City Paradox in Jacó. Paper presented at the Association of Collegiate Schools of Planning Conference, "Reinvesting in America: The New Metropolitan Planning Agenda", October 1–4, Crystal City, Virginia.

Irazábal, C., & Morán, O. (2008). Planning implications of tourism development: The Mexican Pacific Riviera. Paper presented at the Joint Association of European Schools of Planning (AESOP) and Association of Collegiate Schools of Planning (ACSP) Conference, July 6–11, Chicago.

Kakwani, N., & Pernia, E.M. (2000). What is pro-poor growth? *Asian Development Review, 18*(1), 1–16.

Khosla, R. (2009). Personal Interview, 2 January.

Leask, A., & Fyall, A. (Eds.). (2006). *Managing world heritage sites*. Oxford: Butterworth-Heinemann.

McKercher, B., & du Cross, H. (2002). *Cultural tourism: The partnership between tourism and cultural heritage management*. Binghampton, New York: The Haworth Hospitality Press.

Ministry of Urban Development and Ministry of Urban Employment and Poverty Alleviation. (2006). *Jawaharlal Nehru National Urban Renewal Mission: Overview*. Retrieved 20 March, 2008, from http://jnnurm.nic.in/nurmudweb/toolkit/Overview.pdf

NIUA. (2001). *City profile, Agra*. Retrieved March 20, 2008, from http://www.niua.org/city_des.asp?title=Agra

Nuryanti, W. (1996). Heritage and postmodern tourism. *Annals of Tourism Research, 23*(2), 249–260.

Roy, A. (2009). Why India cannot plan its cities: Informality, insurgence and the idiom of urbanization. *Planning Theory, 8*(1), 76–87.

Russoa, A.P., & van der Borg, J. (2002). Planning considerations for cultural tourism: A case study of four European cities. *Tourism Management, 23*, 631–637.

Ryan, C. (2002). Equity, management, power sharing and sustainability issues of the 'new tourism. *Tourism Management, 23*, 17–26.

Schyvens, R. Exploring the tourism-poverty nexus. In C.M. Hall (Ed.), *Pro-poor tourism – who benefits? Perspectives on tourism and poverty reduction*. Current Themes in Tourism (127–141). Clevedon: Channel View Publications.

Shanks, C. (2009). The global compact: The conservative politics of international tourism. *Futures, 41*(6), 360–366.

Shetawy, A.A.A., & El Khateeb, S.M. (2009). The pyramids plateau: A dream searching for survival. *Tourism Management, 30*(6), 819–827.

UNESCO (2002). *State of conservation of the World Heritage Properties in the Asia-Pacific Region*. Retrieved January 10, 2009, from http://whc.unesco.org/archive/periodic reporting/apa/cycle01/section2/252-summary.pdf

Vaidya, C. (2008). Personal interview, 31 December.

Wager, J. (1995). Developing strategy for the Angkor World Heritage Site. *Tourism Management, 16*(7), 515–523.

Wager, J. Developing a strategy for the Angkor World Heritage Site. *Tourism Management, 16*(7), 515–523.

Index

Page numbers in *Italics* represent tables.
Page numbers in **Bold** represent figures.